RETURN

RETURN

> > > > **Nationalizing Transnational Mobility in Asia**

Xiang Biao, Brenda S. A. Yeoh, and Mika Toyota, eds.

Duke University Press   Durham and London   2013

© 2013 Duke University Press
All rights reserved
Printed in the United States of America on acid-free paper ∞
Cover by Heather Hensley. Interior by Courtney Leigh Baker.
Typeset in Minion Pro by Tseng Information Systems, Inc.

Library of Congress Cataloging-in-Publication Data
Return : nationalizing transnational mobility in Asia /
Xiang Biao, Brenda S. A. Yeoh, and Mika Toyota, editors.
pages cm
Includes bibliographical references and index.
ISBN 978-0-8223-5516-8 (cloth : alk. paper)
ISBN 978-0-8223-5531-1 (pbk. : alk. paper)
1. Return migration—Asia. 2. Asia—Emigration and
immigration. I. Xiang, Biao. II. Yeoh, Brenda S. A.
III. Toyota, Mika.
JV8490.R48 2013
325.5—dc23
2013018964

CONTENTS

ACKNOWLEDGMENTS

This book is the fruit of five years of collaboration that started with the Conference on Return Migration in Asia held at the Asia Research Institute, National University of Singapore, in the summer of 2008. We thank ARI for funding the conference and providing additional support throughout these years. Most of the chapters before our readers are in their fourth or fifth versions. The project would be impossible without all the contributors' enthusiasm and generosity. Vani S., Lin Weiqiang, and Saharah Abubakar offered valuable comments at the editorial stage. We also thank Ivan Small, Sallie Yea, and Priscilla Koh for their important inputs and support.

Return and the Reordering
of Transnational Mobility in Asia

▲ XIANG BIAO ▼

When the Washington-based Migration Policy Institute asked a number of leading migration experts in the world what surprised them most in 2006, Howard Duncan, the executive head of the high-profile International Metropolis Project, identified the return migration of professionals to Asia as the most striking. "Although return migration is a common phenomenon, the number of returnees, especially to Hong Kong, is significantly higher than one would expect," he commented.[1] The significance of the large-scale return migration from the West to Hong Kong should be understood in the context of the historical return of Hong Kong to the People's Republic of China (PRC). Between 1984, when the Chinese and British governments signed the handover agreement, and the handover in 1997, more than half a million left Hong Kong due to their apprehension about the handover (Ritter 2007). By 2005, however, a third of those who had migrated to Canada—the single largest destination country—returned, primarily attracted by the intact or even enhanced prosperity of the former colony.[2] At least 120,000 returned in 1999 alone.[3] The return of Hong Kong to the PRC and the subsequent return of Hong Kongers can be seen as powerful manifestations of a new global geopolitical order. This order is defined by the rise—or the "return" or "redux"—of Asia.[4] Indeed, the return of West-based professionals and entrepreneurs to Asia, especially to China and India, is perceived as a "return to the future"—in the rush ahead of global business and technology curves. Return is a project driven by enterprise rather than by nostalgia.[5]

The reverse flows of professionals constitute only a small part of return migrations in Asia. Much larger numbers of "irregular" migrants have been forced to return to their country of citizenship, often from one Asian country to another. This became particularly evident after the financial crisis in 1997. From June 1997, when the crisis broke out, to January 1998, Malaysia sent back more than 10,000 Bangladeshi and Pakistani workers, South Korea expelled between 150,000 and 300,000 migrants, and Thailand repatriated 6,000 Burmese (Varona 1998). Initially an emergency measure, forced return was soon turned into a routine. Malaysia deported tens, or even hundreds, of thousands of migrants in each of the half dozen crackdowns since the end of the 1990s. Japan expelled an average of 54,000 migrants a year in the 1990s and early 2000s.[6] The scope and density of forced return in Asia are striking when compared to other parts of the world: in the 2000s Australia removed and deported about 10,000 a year, the United Kingdom more than 60,000, and the United States nearly 400,000 in 2011 (compared to just over 30,000 in 1990 and less than 200,000 in 2000).[7] Indeed, the Malaysian Home Affairs Minister Azmi Khalid called the Ops Tegas (Operation Tough) campaign in March 2005, which expelled 600,000 to 800,000 irregular migrants,[8] "one of the biggest transmigration programs in the world" (Holst 2009).

Of an even greater scale are compulsory returns of legal labor migrants. The overwhelming majority of the fifteen million workers who migrate from one Asian country to another are on strictly temporary terms and have to return home once their contracts are due (P. Martin 2008). Migrant-receiving countries across the region commonly adopt a "no return, no entry" policy. That is, they determine the number of new arrivals from a particular country according to the returns to that country. This can mean that about three million migrants are returning to various Asian countries from the Gulf alone every year. Apart from professionals and labor migrants, the return of refugees and victims of human trafficking are also major policy concerns in the region.

These diverse return flows are related to each other in that they are encouraged, facilitated, and often enforced by states. They are all part of an overarching mode of governance that emerged in Asia in the 1990s. This mode of governance seeks to regulate mobility through mobility. The states regulate mobility not by blocking but by facilitating movements. Return migrations not only intensify individual migrants' level of mobility when the migrants move back and forth but also put more people on the move as new recruitments are constantly needed to replace the returned.[9] But return is a mobility of such a kind that it tames mobility.[10] Constant in-and-out circulations order movements and fit movements into the framework of nation-states. Return thus nationalizes transnational mobility.

Following Georg Simmel's celebration of the "miracle of road" for its "freezing movement in a solid structure" (Simmel 1997, 171), we may liken return programs to roundabouts. Roundabouts do not directly control the movement of each vehicle, but they channel the traffic into certain patterns that can be monitored and regulated from a distance. The movements on the ground do acquire their own momentum, and drivers do break rules from time to time; but the movements are shaped into flows that are governable to nation-states. "Nation-state" here stands for particular operational frameworks and organizational principles, not for closed territorial containers. Nationalization is a way of ordering transnational mobility instead of a means of territorial fixing. In contrast to the common proposition that transnational migrations challenge state sovereignty (e.g., Sassen 1996, 67–74) and defy national policies (e.g., Castles 2004), transnational circulation in Asia serves as a (national) method of migration regulation.

While we follow Lynellyn Long and Ellen Oxfeld's call for developing an "ethnography of return migration" that pays full attention to the diversity, complexity, and instability of return as human experiences (2004, 1–15), this book treats return primarily as a policy subject, as an idea, and as a strategic moment when the intersection between nation-states and transnational mobility is particularly visible.[11] For this book, return is not a type of migration—a migration behavior with distinct attributes and patterns like "student migration" or "marriage migration." Empirically, return is essentially ambiguous. The Philippine government, for instance, stages state ceremonies before Christmas every year in the Manila airport to welcome the returnees, but at the same time the government encourages the migrants to go overseas again after the holiday season. We would be missing the point by fixating on whether the return should be seen as real return; what matters is the fact that both the government and the migrants invest an enormous amount of energy in making the journey a kind of return.[12] We ask: why is such fictive return regarded as necessary, appealing, and productive? Why are returnees sometimes treated very differently from one another, and yet are sometimes lumped together under the rubric of "return"? And what does this tell us about the general socioeconomic developments in Asia and beyond? The heterogeneity of the experiences of return and the ambiguity of its meaning should not be seen as difficulties in studying return; they can be turned into sources of theoretical innovation.

Asia as a Method for Global Studies

"Europe is hard to get in but easy to stay on; Asian countries are easy to get in but hard to stay on." This was what a would-be migrant in northeast China told me when he compared different options. Asian countries are hard to "stay on" because the migrants have to return.[13] It is far from accidental that various kinds of return migration in Asia have intensified. This reflects particular articulations between state interventions and the free market, and between national regulation and transnational flows in the region. Most Asian countries strive to globalize their economies, but at the same time the countries jealously guard their national sovereignty and state power. The combination of strong and often authoritarian states with free-market economies was a crucial condition of the East Asian economic miracle of the 1970s and 1980s (Evans 1995). The postdevelopmental states that emerged in the 1990s are even more entrepreneurial and market oriented, but they remain uncompromisingly nationalistic (Ong 2000, 2004). The so-called ASEAN (Association of Southeast Asian Nations) way of regionalization is driven by the twin objectives of pursuing region-wide economic integration and safeguarding member states' political autonomy and sovereignty. The ASEAN nations encourage international migration, and precisely for this purpose they make it an explicit rule that each member must consider others' concerns on sovereignty when determining its own policies.[14] Thus there is no surprise that return migration is commonly encouraged and effectively enforced in the region. Conversely, return migration offers a productive lens to examine how territory-bound sovereignty and flexible transnational mobility can work together instead of exclude each other. As such, examination of return migration helps shed light on the "return" of Asia.

The intensification of return migration is not uniquely Asian. On the contrary, experiences in Asia are analytically important precisely because they cast in relief some general developments across the world. The return of trafficking victims and refugees has been a common concern in Europe and other parts of the world. In terms of labor mobility, the EU has promoted "circular migration" between Europe and non-EU countries since the late 2000s. Return is a defining feature or even a precondition of migration (see Castles 2006; Commission of European Communities 2007; Martin, Abella, and Kuptsch 2006). The British Parliament member Frank Field advocated a migration scenario of "one man in, one man out," very similar to how labor migration is managed in Asia (2008). The Nobel laureate economist Paul Krugman dubbed the proposal for permanent guestworker programs in the United States "the road to Dubai" (2006).

Just as we take return as a conceptual lens, we take Asia as a method for global studies. In his seminal work, "China as Method," Yuzo Mizoguchi (1989) urged us to reverse the conventional approach in China studies that took the "world" as the method (reference point) to measure China as the subject. Since there is no such thing as a truly global standard, the "world" often means particular European experiences in practice. In contrast, the "China as method" approach examines specific historical developments in China as part of the global history, and thereby rethinks the world as the subject matter from the perspective of Chinese experiences. In this framework, China and the world become dynamic, interentangled processes instead of static entities in isolation. What Yuzo argued for is obviously not specific to China studies. Chen Kuan-Hsing recently extended the proposition into an advocacy for "Asia as method." The approach of "Asia as method" encourages scholars in Asian countries to take each other as reference points, and by doing so develop a scholarship that is free from Western colonialism and imperialism, and that is both locally rooted and generalizable (Chen 2010). *Return: Nationalizing Transnational Mobility in Asia* takes Asia as a method in both senses as articulated by Yuzo and Chen. Firstly, our subject matter is global conditions, and it is the last agenda of ours to claim Asian uniqueness or exceptionalism. Secondly, we approach the global by juxtaposing a range of Asian cases and examining interactions between Asian countries. We discern the various logics, rationalities, and strategies practiced here as part of a global experimentation. An edited volume provides an ideal form for pursuing such a research strategy.

Taking Asia as a method certainly does not assume that the rest of the world is becoming like Asia or that societies worldwide are adopting "Asian methods" of development. Asia as a method is an analytical strategy. By developing new perspectives based on experiences in Asia, we hope to discern problematics in the world that are otherwise less obvious or dismissed as aberrations. Modern social research is to a great extent a product of the practice of using Europe as *the* method. The mainstream scholarship on international migration, for instance, has long been overshadowed by the European experiences about refugees, especially the Holocaust, and this explains why certain concerns and concepts (e.g., individual rights and formal citizenship) are prioritized while others are marginalized (e.g., collective orders). It will not take us very far to simply critique this scholarship for being biased; we may instead appreciate its value as well as limiting it more by explicating its relation to the specific historical context. Rather than jettisoning established theories for being Eurocentrism, it may be more productive to develop multipolar, decentered ways of knowledge production. Asia as a method aims at exactly that. We take Asia as a method not because Asia is special or superior, but because it enables an extrication of migration research from Western concerns and at the same time provides a solid ground for developing substantive theories.

Asia is a method instead of a case of global studies because the relation of Asia to the world is not that of a part to the whole. Asia is actively interacting with the world rather than simply reflecting it. More important, Asia for us is not only a physical place to be studied but it also provides a critical epistemological position from where we study the world. As such, geographical coverage per se is of secondary importance in selecting cases. Our chapters instead aim to cover different kinds of return regulated by different political systems at different times.

The book starts with three chapters on the historical role of return migration in nation building in Asia. They are followed by five chapters on return migration in the current globalization era. Before turning to the specific cases, it is necessary to have an overview of returnees' historical relations to nation-states and global orders, and particularly how post–Cold War Asian states form differentiated, partial, selective, unstable, and conditional relations with returnees. The practice of differentiation is accompanied by a tendency of coalescence. That is, states seek interstate agreements and international consensus in order to enforce returns, and the all-embracing, naturalizing notion of "return" in public discourse ascribes particular universalistic meanings to diverse return flows. It is through the dialectic between differentiation and coalescence that an overarching sociopolitical order is constituted from increasingly diverse transnational mobilities.

The Returnee and the Nation

Return has been a norm rather than an exception in human migration.[15] Ernest Ravenstein's (1885) "laws of migration" stipulated that every migration stream is accompanied by a counter flow, and the migration-system theory of the 1970s identified return as an integral part of all migration systems (Mabogunje 1970; see also Nijkamp and Voskuilen 1996). It was historically commonplace that migrants moved back and forth before the erection of national borders.[16] It was precisely when return became more difficult that the figure of the returnee acquired new symbolic and political significance. Contemporary returns are no longer a so-called natural demographic phenomenon that can be predicted by laws. They are inextricably tied to the politics of nation-states. The word *return* itself has now become a vocabulary of the nation: migrants seldom return to their place of birth (Upadhya, this volume),[17] and what the word *return* actually means is the movement from overseas to any part of one's *nation* of origin. As Wang Gungwu (1981) has established so clearly, overseas Chinese had been either unmarked or thought of as traitors until the Qing court in the late nineteenth century officially named them *huaqiao* (Chinese sojourners)— temporary migrants who waited to return. The overseas Chinese acquired this name not because they suddenly became inclined to return but because the Qing government now perceived China as a nation instead of a civilizational empire potentially covering the entire world, and the government therefore felt compelled to define its relation with its overseas population in explicit terms as a way of defining its relation to the world. The nationalization of the notion of return can thus be seen as a discursive strategy with which the state laid claim to the mobile subjects.

Returnees of the modern times in Asia can be notionally divided into four generations, though the empirical boundaries between them are always blurred. Each group has distinct relations to the nation-states involved. The first generation refers to the large number of circular migrants, primarily traders and laborers, who had, for a long time and particularly from the mid-nineteenth century, been undertaking regular return trips before nation-states broke down transnational mobility and connections in the mid-twentieth century.[18] The second generation is represented by such iconic figures as Mahatma Gandhi, José Rizal, Jawaharlal Nehru, and Lee Kuan Yew, who returned to become founding fathers of their nations in the early twentieth century. Their returns were regarded as so important that in 2003 the Indian government designated January 9, the date when Gandhi returned from South Africa after a twenty-year sojourn (in 1914), as Pravasi Bharatiya Divas (Overseas Indians' Day), a day celebrated with great fanfare. This generation of returnees did not invent nationalism; they were pioneering nationalists in Asia because they were most familiar with Western imperialism and were directly exposed to political contestations in various parts of the world, which made them particularly capable of dealing with colonial powers and transforming protonations into the form of the modern state. The nation-building project was a global response to global colonialism and a result of global dialogue and learning (Anderson 1991, 4; Chatterjee 1986). Prasenjit Duara says, "Nations are constructed in a global space premised upon institutional and discursive circulations" (2009, 6). In this process the second generation of returnees served as global mediators by disseminating and modifying the general idea of nation, as well as by bringing their particular nation-building projects into the global public imagination through their consciously declared return.

The third generation returned between the 1950s and 1990s. Their returns were either pulled by the new nation or pushed by heightened ethnic conflicts during the process of nation building in countries of residence (see Sasaki, this volume; Wang, this volume), or both.[19] These returnees were no longer global mediators; they typically cut off overseas connections after return. The return of the fourth generation after the Cold War is different still. Return in the context of escalating globalization once again became part of back-and-forth movements instead of the definite end of a journey (Upadhya, this volume).

History seems to have come full circle: the first and the last generations appear to have similar experiences of return. But, while the first generation moved back and forth over long distance because of the nonexistence of nation-states, the fourth group does so because many nation-states in Asia have developed sophisticated mechanisms for engaging with transnational movements. Contemporary returnees simultaneously attach themselves to the nation and participate in global circulations. Their national attachment often serves as a basis for their participation in globalization, and conversely their global positions are leverages in their interactions with national institutions. If the second generation of returnees nationalized their home societies, and the returnees of the third generation were themselves nationalized by becoming full-fledged citizens residing inside of the hardened national border, members of the latest generation remain transnational subjects but have their mobility nationalized in the sense of how their mobility is regulated and how their mobility acquires social meaning.

Chapters 1, 2, and 3 in the book provide broad historical overviews of how returnees of different generations establish relations with nations amid wars, revolutions, ethnic conflicts, and ideological battles. Koji Sasaki's chapter traces the little-known debates about return—whether one should return and how—among Japanese migrants in Brazil throughout the twentieth century, and how transnational flows are domesticated by national concerns. The migrants, most of whom left Japan at the end of nineteenth century and the early twentieth, yearned to return in the first half of the twentieth century. But at that time Japan was preoccupied with imperialistic expansion and the emigrants' return was discouraged. When the Japanese government reached out and opened special channels for the migrants and their descendants (Nikkeijin) to migrate to Japan to work in the 1990s, permanent return lost its sentimental purchase among the migrants because their lives were deeply nationalized. The Nikkeijin ended up as quasi-returnees in Japan who enjoy more benefits than other foreigners but cannot claim citizenship. This quasi-returnee status reconciles the Japanese public's desire for ethnic homogeneity, the economic need for cheap labor, and the state's tight control over migration. In the wake of the 2008 financial crisis, the Japanese government offered to pay the Nikkeijin for returning to Brazil on the condition of not rereturning to Japan as unskilled workers for three years. Many did return to Brazil.

Mariko Asano Tamanoi's chapter focuses on a special group of returnees—the former soldiers of the Japanese Imperial Army who returned from the battlefields well after the end of the Second World War. By highlighting the awkwardness of the return, the chapter sheds new light on Japan's transformation from a militarist empire to a nation and that transformation's implications for Japan and Asia today. The soldiers' return in the 1950s was awkward because their presence reminded the public of Japan's atrocities overseas in which many ordinary Japanese people were implicated. The return disrupted the dominant narrative that the Japanese nation was a victim of a handful of rightist elites and upset the effort to forget the complicity. A few soldiers who returned in the 1970s triggered little awkwardness in comparison on the part of the Japanese public, and the returnees became celebrities instead. By that time the memory of the war had faded away; the nation was fascinated by the soldiers' experiences of hiding in jungles for nearly three decades as a biological miracle. It was

FIGURE I.1. "Need assistance to return?" A postcard from the International Organization for (IOM) Migration targeting irregular Chinese migrants in Europe. The postcard promises that the IOM will assist with travel documents, itineraries, and reintegration to the home society. Assisted return has become one of the most important activities of the IOM since the 1990s.

however awkward for the soldiers to be treated as biological miracles. Although they were enthusiastically embraced by the nation, the soldiers felt out of place as such questions as why they had to go to war in the first place and why their fellow soldiers had to die were pushed aside. Underlying this awkwardness of the delayed returns is Japan's unsettled relation to its past, which remains a source of tensions in Asia today.

Wang Cangbai's chapter examines even more dramatic experiences of return, specifically on how Indonesian Chinese returnees were nationalized into Mao's China (1949 to 1979). The returnees, many of whom were fleeing the anti-Chinese sentiment in postcolonial Indonesia, were initially warmly welcomed by the PRC as fellow Chinese. But they were soon subject to harsh policies aimed at reforming them from "classed others" into part of the proletarian People when the basis for the definition of citizenry shifted from ethnic identity to class position. The state invented the special category of *guiqiao* (returned sojourners) and devised a series of institutions and policies in order to accommodate, monitor, and assimilate the returnees. The policies ranged from setting up special preparation schools for returned students, establishing isolated overseas Chinese farms for returned families, honoring the few who fit the party's line, and imposing close surveillance on the majority of others. Since the end of the Cultural

Revolution, however, the state not only permits but also encourages transnational connections, both old and new. The new approach is primarily rationalized by the notions of modernization and globalization, while the emphasis on ethnic allegiance and socialist rhetoric remains salient. As a result, the relation between returnees and nation-states becomes much more complex.

The Victim, the Ambiguous, and the Desirable

As Wang's chapter demonstrates, whether one was a returnee or not was deeply consequential for one's life in Mao's China. The fact of being a returnee, regardless of what kind and how one returned, invited harassment and even humiliation during the Cultural Revolution. In the post–Cold War era, what matters more is what kind of returnee one is. This is true not only in China but across the region as well. The heterogeneity of returnees should not be taken as a given fact; returnees are made different by various policies and discourses. The differentiation is not meant to reflect returnees' varying experiences; it rather results from states' multiple, and sometimes contradictory, objectives. For instance, states simultaneously seek economic growth (Upadhya, this volume), national security (Cowan, this volume), identity allegiance (Lu and Shin, this volume), and political legitimacy (for which rights protection for victims is increasingly important; Lindquist, this volume). These objectives are often at odds with one another in practice. Differentiation enables nation-states to form partial and selective relations with returnees and fit them into multiple state agendas.

According to how they are treated by state policies and how they are presented in public media, returnees can be grouped into three categories: the "victims" (refugees and especially victims of human trafficking), the "desirable" (primarily the highly skilled and investors), and the "ambiguous" (unskilled or irregular migrants who are economically needed but socially undesirable). Nation-states form differentiated relations with each of the three figures.

Refugees were the first target group of state initiated return programs after the end of the Cold War. Because refugee issues during the Cold War were deeply politicized and were attributed to Communist authoritarian regimes, the decisive victory of capitalist liberal democracy was supposed to reduce the number of refugees dramatically. The UN refugee agency UNHCR identified voluntary repatriation as the optimal durable solution for refugee problems and designated the 1990s as the "decade of repatriation" (Koser and Black 1999). In Asia, the return of the five million refugees from Pakistan and Iran to Afghanistan between 2002 and 2009 was "the single largest return program" in the history of UNHCR.[20] If the provision of protection for refugees during the Cold War was based on apparently universalistic, but deeply politicized, humanitarianism, the return of refugees was predicated on the belief that the nation-state, now supposedly free of ideological struggles, was the natural and neutral institution that every person should belong to. The world was beginning to be imagined as a depoliticized "national order of things" (Malkki 1995b).

The depoliticized perception about the world order also underpins the return of victims of human trafficking. The four Rs—rescue, return, rehabilitation, and reintegration—are recommended by international organizations as well as national governments as the optimal solution to human trafficking (Lindquist, this volume). Return is perceived as such a desired outcome that international organization staff are sometimes reluctant to identify a person as a victim who may not have a place to return to, because where there is no point of return, there is no solution.[21]

Although the return of refugees and victims is supposed to help restore a sense of normalcy, the returnees' experiences on the ground can be traumatic. Sylvia R. Cowan's chapter focuses on the relation between the normalizing intention of return policies and traumatizing experiences of return. Some former Cambodian refugees and their children were deported from the United States for committing minor crimes, even after they had served their full prison terms. The repatriation was implemented based on bilateral agreements in a time when negotiation was preferred to military intervention to deal with international affairs, and was thus meant to maintain law and order by peaceful means.[22] But on the ground the repatriations were violently disruptive for the deportees and their families. They were typically repatriated suddenly, without warning, and many grew up in the United States and had no knowledge of their home country. The forced return was also historically related to U.S. military interventions in postcolonial Indochina and the refugees' consequent displacement within the American host society that turned them into gang members. The succession from one type of displacement to another as experienced by the refugees illustrates the changing global order in the latter half of the twentieth century.

The second group of returnees—primarily unskilled labor migrants whose position is ambiguous for the states—is quickly growing in size. My own chapter describes how compulsory return is central to the control of unskilled labor mobility in East Asia. Compulsory return effectively renders the relations between migrants and the host state nothing more than a labor contract. A number of countries identify pregnant women and sick migrants as primary subjects of repatriation precisely because these "problematic" bodies bear the danger of developing social relations beyond economic contracts with the host nation. Return is enforced through intricate collaborations between states, employers, recruiters, and other institutions across countries. Such connections between the multiple actors constitute an institutional basis for enforced return and making order from migration.

The third group of returnees, the highly skilled and the capital rich, embodies even more complex logics of order making. The return of the highly skilled is supposed to bring the nation into the global circuit of flexible capital accumulation and knowledge production, as evidenced by the rise of the so-called brain-circulation paradigm in the policy thinking of the 1990s (Global Commission of International Migration 2005). But global economic integration is always mediated by specific social institutions and political ideologies. Carol Upadhya's chapter on returning technopreneurs in Bangalore, India, suggests that the elite returnees are not only bringing back capital, know-how, and international connections but also generating "neonationalism." Neonationalism bases national pride on the nation's position in the global market instead of independence and self-sufficiency, defines national belonging in cultural terms, and considers economic redistribution and political participation less important. In contrast to the nationalism that led India's independence movement, neonationalism is outward looking, culturalist, and often elitist.

Finally, Melody Chia-Wen Lu and Shin Hyunjoon, whose study is based on returning Korean Chinese from China to South Korea, make a strong case that it is policy differentiation, rather than experiential difference, that matters. The Korean Chinese were in the 1980s regarded as representatives of the global Korean diaspora, and victims who were forced to leave the Korean peninsula by historical injustices such as Japanese colonialization. As such their return visits were welcomed and encouraged as a means to redress these past injustices. The position of the Korean Chinese, however, became much more ambiguous in the late 1990s when South Korea attempted to formalize its relations to Korean diasporas as part of its state-led globalizing agenda. Korean Chinese were privileged compared to other foreigners due to ethnic connections, but they were treated less favorably compared to the more-recent emigrants to the West. The government changed this policy due to protests from the Korean Chinese in South Korea in 2004 and replaced nation of residence with one's education level and occupation as the central criteria for differentiating the return migrants. In practice the Korean Chinese are still required to submit more documents to prove their education levels than their counterparts returning from developed countries. Thus, the returnees are differentiated, and the criteria and methods of differentiation also vary from time to time.

The case of the Korean Chinese shows that nation-states remain the defining framework that organizes transnational mobility. The concerns about ethnic identity and economic competitiveness are supposed to enhance the national position of South Korea. The South Korean vision of globalization is equally about opening up the nation to the world as it is about nationalizing connections, knowledge, labor, and capital among the dispersed Korean diaspora. And in order to maximize the benefit of return to the South Korean nation, potential returnees were differentiated according to their current nation of residence, especially the nation's position in the global hierarchy. One of the reasons for the 2004 policy change that favored the Korean Chinese was the rise of China. The apparent ethno-nationalist stance has not undermined the relationship between migrants to the sending or receiving nations, as defined in civic terms. This international dimension of nationalization leads to the tendency of coalescence, which is an equally important aspect as differentiation in governing mobility through return.

Nationalizing and Naturalizing

What is remarkable about the governmental differentiation of returnees in Asia is that migrant-receiving and -sending states are increasingly in agreement with each other on how the returnees are to be differentiated. The highly skilled are desirable for the country that they return to partly because they are desirable in the country of residence. Unskilled or irregular migrants are unattractive to both the receiving and the sending countries; nevertheless the countries agree that return is a migrant's right that cannot be denied and an obligation that cannot be easily waived. Compulsory return has been a basis for intergovernmental agreements on labor migration in East Asia since the end of the 1970s (Xiang, this volume). As for victims of human trafficking, it is now an obligation for legitimate sovereignties to repatriate the victims and to admit the returned.[23] Sending states are willing to collaborate with receiving states because this enables them to establish closer relations with their overseas citizens and to tap into outmigration for national development. Receiving states also share some authority in regulating immigration with the sending states, for instance, by delegating power to government and private agencies in the sending countries for selecting and screening would-be migrants (see Xiang, this volume). This is because, given that immigration control is being tightened across the world, "the labor-sending state is perhaps the institution most able to effectively resolve the contradictory forces of labor demand and immigration restriction" (Rodriguez 2010, xxiii). Malaysia and Indonesia have developed relatively effective transnational operational systems to enforce return (Lindquist, this volume). Instead of resisting the pressure from Malaysia to receive deportees, Indonesia as the country of origin in fact has used this momentum to tighten its regulations of outmigration.

Such interstate institutional coalescence means that return programs enable nation-states to enhance their sovereign power transnationally and mutually. Both the sending and receiving states become more powerful in relation to migrants. As such, the central tension in international migration is no longer the one between migrants and the receiving society or that between the sending and receiving states, but is rather the one between migrants and alliances of states. An unskilled migrant worker violates regulations of *both* the sending and receiving countries if he or she fails to return as required, which can be punishable by both countries. In contrast, a highly skilled or a successful entrepreneur can make himself or herself more valuable to the multiple countries by moving back and forth between them. It is important to note that such institutional coalescence between states is largely an intra-Asia phenomenon. The repatriation of migrants from Europe and North America to many Asian countries remains cumbersome and is subject to ad hoc bilateral negotiations due to the lack of general consensus.

There is also an ideational coalescence regarding return migration. The fact that the notion of "return" is used to refer to migration journeys of vastly different natures should not be seen as a problem of misnomer. It instead indicates the construction of a hegemonic framework, a good common sense, that gives migration particular meanings. As Johan Lindquist's chapter suggests, the return discourses deployed by governments, NGOs, and public media on different types of migrants echo each other and collectively naturalize return and home. Since everyone is supposed to love home and is protected at home, return is assumed to be unproblematic for all migrants. What's wrong with asking someone to go back to where he or she "really" belongs?

The sense of naturalness lends return policies strong legitimacy. The Chinese word for destiny, *guisu*, literally means the "lodge to return to" (see also Wang, this volume, on the meaning of *gui*). The official Japanese term for foreigners taking up Japanese citizenship is *kika* (return and convert).[24] The word *return* establishes the directionality of mobility—directionality in ethical terms instead of only in the physical sense. To return is to reach one's destiny.

Apart from the naturalizing and normalizing effects, return can be energizing. The anthropologist Charles Stafford (2001) was puzzled by the Chinese custom of sending off and then receiving deities annually.[25] Why don't the Chinese make the gods permanent residents in their houses? This is because, as Stafford argued, alternating departing and returning is crucial to establishing, maintaining, and renewing social relationships. Departure and return make us feel sad and joyful and urge us to reflect on the past and yearn for the future, thus bringing constant dynamics to relationships. In a world where imagined communities reach far beyond the national border (see Appadurai 1996), returnees from overseas are probably more capable than the supposedly quintessential, deep-rooted peasants or tribal populations of energizing nationalism. If the Tomb of the Unknown Soldier is one of most arresting emblems of nationalism, as Benedict Anderson (1991, 50–51) pointed out so aptly, in the time of globalization, the returnee is a powerful embodiment of nationalism. If the Tomb of the Unknown Soldier combines the senses of the sacred and the profane that are essential to modern nationalism, the returnee reconciles territoriality and extraterritoriality, which is crucial for neonationalism in the globalizing age.

The naturalizing effect of return is of course nothing natural in itself. Our chapters show that such effect is historically specific. The natural appearance of return is constituted by particular international agreements, and by the participation of NGOs, public media, business associations, and private agencies that specialize in recruitment and transport. It is these institutional arrangements that underpin the dialectics between differentiation and coalescence, between the national and the transnational, and thereby contribute to the ordering of mobility without hindering it.

What does the nationalization of transnational mobility mean for migrants' political agency? On the one hand, migrants face tremendous obstacles in challenging the system of tightly interrelated nation-states. State-facilitated returns curtail the political agency of transnational connections. Michael Hardt and Antonio Negri's envisaging of the multitude might be too optimistic (2000, 2004). On the other hand, the naturalization of return renders to migrants the appropriate hegemonic discourse to "speak back" to nation-states to demand justice and dignity. As Lu and Shin's chapter shows, the Korean Chinese drew on the state ethno-nationalist discourse to claim return as their right, which must be met with equitable, nondiscriminatory policies. The nationalization of migration may also lead to a nationalization of migrant politics; that is, migrants use nation-states as the central scale in organizing their actions, take national discourses as the main target of critique as well as the main resource for articulating their demand, and identify changing national policies as their primary objective. For instance, the contestation of the meaning of "return" among the former Japanese soldiers and Nikkeijin engendered critical reflections of the hegemonic perceptions about the Japanese nation and its role in the war. For both the highly skilled Indian professionals who circulate freely and voluntarily on the global scale and the forced Cambodian returnees, working with national and local organizations seems to be the most realistic strategy for making changes in their own lives and beyond. But just as the nationalization of mobility does not imply spatial fixing, the nationalization of migrant politics is certainly not territorially closed. The U.S.-originated NGOs play active roles in Cambodia in assisting the returnees, and the Indian returnees' engagement with the local public is to a great extent shaped by their position in the global market. The Chinese migrant workers in Japan, as my chapter demonstrates, contested restrictive regulations of the Japanese and Chinese states by refusing to return to China. Their refusal was meant to ensure that they would be able to seek justice through the Japanese national legal system and government, and at the same time create international pressure on the Chinese government to redress problems on the sending side. The transnational dimension of nationalization will to a great extent condition both how mobility is regulated and how migrant politics evolve in the future.

Notes

1. Migration Information Source, "Migration Experts Size up 2006," December 2006, www.migrationinformation.org, accessed October 10, 2009.

2. The exact number of returnees to Hong Kong is difficult to establish. According

to a survey by Hong Kong Baptist University in 2002, 3 percent of Hong Kong residents chose the category of "returnee" as their cultural identity (Hong Kong Transition Project 2002, 13).

3. This is believed to be discounted due to "substantial under-reporting . . . [o]wing to the rather sensitive nature of the subject" (Census and Statistics Department of HKSAR 2000, 48; see also Ley and Kobayashi 2005, 116).

4. For a representative text of the increasingly popular discourse of the "return" of Asia, see Mahbubani 2008. The notion "Asia redux" was proposed by Prasenjit Duara (2010). While "return" calls attention to Asia's resumption of its position as a global hegemony, "redux" emphasizes the reactivated connections between different parts of Asia that were weakened due to their subjugation to colonial powers and the Cold War divide.

5. *People's Daily*, China's flagship state media, reported that 186,200 Chinese students had returned home throughout 2011, an increase of more than 38 percent compared to 135,000 over 2010. *People's Daily* (English), "818,400 overseas students return to China," March 16, 2012, http://thepienews.com/news/number-of-returning -chinese-students-up-38/, last accessed February 8, 2013.

6. Ministry of Justice, Japan, *Booklet on Immigration*, Tokyo, 2005, 10.

7. For Australia, see the Department of Immigration and Citizenship Annual Reports for the 2000s, available on http://www.immi.gov.au/about/reports/annual/, last accessed February 8, 2013. For the UK, see UK Home Office, "Control of Immigration: Statistics, United Kingdom 2008," 68, August 2009, http://rds.homeoffice.gov.uk/rds /pdfs09/hosb1409.pdf. For the United States, see U.S. Department of Homeland Security, *2011 Yearbook of Immigration Statistics*, 2011, 102, http://www.dhs.gov/files/statis tics/publications/yearbook.shtm.

8. The campaign mobilized up to 500,000 officials and volunteers, and sent 600,000 to 800,000 migrants home, including 400,000 who left voluntarily for fear of harsh punishment and 200,000 to 400,000 who were deported. See "Give Ops Tegas a Chance," 2005. See also Chin 2008.

9. Martin Ruhs and Philip Martin (2008) have argued that constraints on migrants' settlements and access to citizenship in the destination country, reinforced through compulsory return, will increase the number of migrants. Conversely, countries that provide more rights to migrants will have to admit fewer migrants.

10. When the Japanese government finally started admitting foreign labor after twenty years of debates, it swiftly introduced a "departure order system" in 2004 as an integral part of the general regulation of mobility (Ministry of Justice, Japan, *Booklet on Immigration*, Tokyo, 2005). Globally, return has also become a crucial method of regulating mobility. The International Organization for Migration (IOM) is almost an organization solely for return migration: as much as 70 percent of its budget is allocated to return programs, particularly the Assisted Voluntary Return Program; in 2005 it managed more than one hundred return projects globally and assisted in the return of 3.61 million migrants since the mid-1990s (International Organization for Migration 2006, 409). The German government paid IOM USD 10 million in 2002 alone for repatriating unwanted migrants (International Organization for Migration 2002, 5).

11. Michel-Rolph Trouillot sees forced return as the moment when mobility encounters the state most directly and even violently (2001, 125).

12. Rhacel Salazar Parrenas (2001) documents how return became a major theme of Filipino migrants' literature in Hong Kong, and the preparation for return dominated the life of Filipino entertainers in Japan beginning with their arrival.

13. Li Minghuan (2001) has detailed how EU immigration policies induced the perception among Chinese migrants that once one got to Europe, one could always stay. See also Skrentny et al. 2007 for a similar comparison between Asia and Europe.

14. Association of Southeast Asian Nations, "ASEAN Declaration on the Protection and Promotion of the Rights of Migrant Workers," http://www.aseansec.org/19264 .htm, accessed April 14, 2012. Graziano Battistella and Maruja M. B. Asis (2003, 10) conclude that the ASEAN "regional approach [to migration management] remains at the consultative level, with minimal impact on policy process and decision-making in the individual countries."

15. The three ports of Xiamen, Shantou, and Hong Kong in south China, for example, recorded 14.7 million departures between 1869 and 1939, and 11.6 million returns between 1873 and 1939. See Sugihara 2005. On the other side of the world, one-fourth to one-third of transatlantic migrants returned from North America to Europe between 1870 and 1940, amounting to ten million (King 2000, 29). For a careful research on the high level of return migration from the United States to Europe at the turn of the twentieth century, see Wyman 1996. For a recent review of return as a historical phenomenon, see Ley and Kobayashi 2005, 112.

16. For a revealing case study of how Indian seafarers had moved back and forth without the intention of settling in the UK for a long period of time, see Balachandran 2012.

17. Other studies that established this phenomenon include Unger 1986; de Haas 2006; Labrianidis and Kazazi 2006.

18. A recent major publication on this topic is Tagliacozzo and Chang 2011.

19. For the case of the return of scientists to India in the 1950s, see Krishna and Khadria 1997, 353–58.

20. Integrated Regional Information Networks (IRIN), "Limited Scope to Absorb More Refugees," March 15, 2009, http://www.irinnews.org/Report/83474/AFGHANI STAN-Limited-scope-to-absorb-more-refugees, last accessed February 8, 2013.

21. The return of victims as a means of protection is in practice closely related to the return of irregular migrants as a punishment. Diana Wong (2005, 69) traces the current global "rumor of trafficking" to the concern about irregular migration in Europe following the fall of the Berlin Wall. In Asia, the "Bangkok Declaration on Irregular Migration," signed by nineteen governments in Pacific Asia in 1999, made a clear link between irregular migration and human trafficking. "Timely return of those without right to enter and remain is an important strategy to reduce the attractiveness of trafficking." (Article 13 of the Declaration, http://www.iom.int/jahia/webdav/site /myjahiasite/shared/shared/mainsite/policy_and_research/rcp/APC/BANGKOK _DECLARATION.pdf, accessed May 23, 2013). Commenting on the high-profile Ops Tegas campaign, the then deputy prime minister of Malaysia, Datuk Seri Najib Razak,

warned that no category of irregular migrants would be spared, including those with documents issued by UNHCR (*Star* 2005). Forced return is now regarded as an effective means to reduce irregular migration and unsuccessful asylum seekers worldwide (see Ghosh 1998; Koser 2000, 69–70; Lakzco 2000).

22. A number of researchers have elaborated on how deportation is related to the Constitution of the United States as an immigrant nation and to social control. See de Genova 2002; Ngai 2004; Peutz 2006.

23. Since the late 1990s, multilateral governmental agreements, such as the Coordinated Mekong Ministerial Initiative against Trafficking (COMMIT), have created the infrastructure as well as pressure for national governments to enforce the return of victims of human trafficking.

24. The high-profile Abu Dhabi Dialogue on Temporary Contractual Labor for Cooperation between Countries of Origin and Destination in Asia, attended by ministers from twenty countries in 2008, endorsed the so-called life-cycle approach in managing labor mobility. This approach suggests that migration has a natural life cycle that consists of four stages: recruitment, employment abroad, preparation for return, and reintegration. See P. Martin 2009, 60–61. Return is presented to be "natural" and inevitable with this discourse of "life cycle."

25. One of the most important Chinese festivals (which is also celebrated in Vietnam) is the sending off of the Kitchen God (Zaoshen or Zaojun) to Heaven on the twenty-third day of the twelfth lunar month, and then welcoming his return four days later.

▶ ▶ ▶ ▶ ▶ ▶ ▶ ▶ ▶ ▶ ▶ ▶ **CHAPTER ONE**

To Return or Not to Return

*The Changing Meaning of Mobility among
Japanese Brazilians, 1908–2010*

KOJI SASAKI

In 1938, Shungoro Wako, an officer of the Japanese Imin Takushoku Gaisha (Company for Emigration and Colonization) in Brazil, made this remark in the introduction to his collection of statistical and historical data on Japanese migrants in a rural region in São Paulo:

> If someone asks me to choose between return and permanent settlement, I, with all my sincerity, would never hesitate to answer, "I ardently desire to return." . . . [However,] I will work very hard until I am buried in this country [Brazil]. I will cherish the visions of my dear homeland [Japan] and will pray for its prosperity until the last moment of my life. Nonetheless, I will dedicate my body and soul to raise my children as outstanding Brazilians. (1938, 3, 11)

His painful inner struggle may look puzzling to today's readers. What compelled him to suppress the burning desire to return? How should we reconcile his deep attachment to Japan and the determination to raise offspring as Brazilians? It is evident from his writing that his dilemma did not arise from his calculation of conflicting personal interests, but was rather deeply ideological and even morally charged. Indeed, to return or not to return was a question of utmost importance among the Japanese community in Brazil during a good part of the twentieth century. Never a straightforward question, whether or not to return aroused considerable agony and confusion. The intention to return was driven not only by economic considerations but also by migrants' emotional perceptions of their relations to the larger global political order, particularly the rise and fall of the Japanese empire and the consolidation of the Japanese and Brazilian nation-states.

This chapter examines the changing perception of return among the Japanese in Brazil from the beginning of the twentieth century to the early part of the twenty-first century. It follows the analytical strategy of regarding "return" as an idea, or, more precisely, as an imaginary that defines the directionality of one's physical movement, gives particular meanings to mobility, and shapes the mobile subjects' self-positioning in the world (Xiang, introduction, this volume). By taking mobility as a medium through which the migrant intentionally acts on the external world, this chapter teases out how the meaning of return changes with the rise and fall of the Japanese empire over three time periods. These narratives span the first half of the century, the establishment of a new world order centered on nation-states since the 1950s, and the reemergence of transnational networks with intensified globalization after the 1980s.

While the meaning of return has been contested and never stable, a particularly sharp historical turning point took place in the 1950s. In the first half of the twentieth century, the migrants' return was discouraged because Japan was preoccupied with its imperialistic expansion project; furthermore, return was unlikely due to economic and transport constraints. Nevertheless, return remained a major concern among the migrants during that period and it was in fact an important topic of heated debate among them whether they should return and under what conditions. This continued to be the case for a short while even after the Second World War ended in 1945. In the second half of the century, however, return gradually lost its ideological and sentimental connotation as the migrants had succeeded in establishing a respected minority status in Brazilian society. As a result, when tens of thousands of descendants of former Japanese emigrants (Nikkeijin) headed to their ancestors' homeland in the 1980s and 1990s, they hardly viewed their experience as a return. Rather, the cultural and linguistic differences caused an immense sense of alienation on the part of these migrants. The Japanese government, on the other hand, exploited the ambiguity of their status by creating a special legal migration channel for these descendants on the basis of their blood relations with Japanese citizens. This channel, exclusive to the Nikkeijin, allowed them to live and work in Japan relatively freely, although it was less liberal in allowing, let alone encouraging or supporting, the Nikkeijin's permanent settlement. Under this system of quasi-return, the preference for ethnic homogeneity and the need for cheap labor in a time of increasing globalization were also reconciled. In this sense, the history of return is a history fraught with changing logics of what it means to be a mobile subject. Specifically for the Japanese Brazilians, their subjectivity shifted continually from self-styled imperial subjects to national citizens (of Brazil) and to transitional labor.

The Desire to Return as a "Disease"

The Japanese emigration to the Americas began as part of a state-initiated program designed to counter the twin problems of overpopulation and rural poverty during the Meiji period (1868–1912) (see Gaimu-sho 1941). In the late nineteenth century, the government sent groups of Japanese to Hawaii and North America. With the rise of the anti-Japanese movement in the United States in the early twentieth century, however, the Japanese government and numerous "emigration companies" (private enterprises that specialized in recruiting and sending Japanese citizens abroad for fees) looked to South America for alternative destinations. Meanwhile, Brazil was looking for a solution to the labor-shortage problem that it faced on its coffee plantations following the abolition of slavery in 1888 and the Italian government's prohibition of emigration to Brazil in 1902 (Lesser 1999, 85). These events resulted in massive migration from Japan to Brazil. After the first Japanese migration to São Paulo in 1908, initiated by the private Imperial Colonization Company, more than 183,000 Japanese had headed to Brazil until 1941 (Gaimu-sho 1941, 179–80).

The migrants largely perceived their emigration to Brazil as an alternative to the rural-urban seasonal migration (*dekasegi*), which was commonly practiced by Japanese farmers in the Meiji period. The farmer-migrants undertook work in the Brazilian coffee fields for a number of years, and they expected to return to Japan after that. "Kokyo ni nishiki wo kazaru" (to return to the homeland dressed in brocade), as the Japanese saying goes, was the ultimate goal of migration. This mentality was further reinforced by the fact that the reality of working in the Brazilian coffee plantations was far from what was originally promised in the advertisements of the emigration companies. In addition to the extremely harsh working conditions that were carried forward from the slavery system, the poor harvest in the first years and low wages fell greatly short of the migrants' expectations. The Japanese migrants were eager to return to Japan as early as possible, and they were largely indifferent to improving their long-term life prospects in Brazil.

Such an attitude was however criticized in the 1920s by the educated members of the migrant community, especially editors of immigrant newspapers, leaders of immigration organizations, and Japanese diplomats. During the 1920s and 1930s, immigrant newspapers took it as their primary duty to analyze the life of the Japanese in Brazil and to critique their behaviors. Usually featured on the front page, opinion editorials often sought to pinpoint the problem with the wider Japanese migrant community and even provided detailed guidelines on what constituted desirable attitudes and behaviors. In this sense, the newspapers were not mere disseminators of information but a means of moral guidance. The editorials of such newspapers as *Burajiru Jiho* (Brazilian news, 1917–41) and *Nippak Shimbun* (Nippak journal, 1916–41) were particularly influential among the migrants. Despite their diverse social origins and political orientations, the editors agreed that the migrants should abandon their "sojourner mentality" (*dekasegi konjo*) and instead uphold the "determination for permanent settlement" (*eijuu ketsui*). For instance, an editorial published in *Nippak Shimbun* in 1924 bitterly bemoaned the fact that the migrants lacked the determination to stay: "Because the Japanese immigrants are not liberated from the temporary, sojourner disposition, we have not succeeded as much as we could have. . . . Most of the newly arriving immigrants have repeated the same mistakes, without being able to establish a firm basis. Indeed, this temporary, sojourner disposition is the fundamental disease that inhibits the development of the Japanese immigrants" (*Nippak Shimbun* 1924; my translation).

This criticism of the desire for return can be attributed to the perception that some migrants' inclination for short-term economic success was detrimental to their own agricultural development in Brazil because agricultural development required long-term investments. However, the educated migrants' desire to assimilate into the Brazilian society and opposition to return reflected their consciousness about Japan's rise as an international power. To many migrants, Japan's rising status required its subjects to demonstrate to the world respectful cultural dispositions. The anti-Japanese movements in North America, which excluded Japanese immigrants as racially and culturally inferior, made the migrants even more eager to prove that they were capable of assimilating into the host society. For example, in 1921 Toshiro Fujita, the Japanese consul in São Paulo, advised Japanese migrants in Brazil to follow Brazilian cultural norms. He insisted that every one of them "should respect the manners and customs of this country and make efforts in assimilating our clothes, foods, housings and even the everyday behaviors into those of the people in Brazil" (Fujita 1921; my translation). Remarkably, this call for assimilation even led to an official recommendation of naturalization, that is, acquiring a Brazilian citizenship. For instance, *Burajiru Jiho*, which was run by the quasi-governmental Kaigai Kogyo Kabushiki Gaisha (Overseas Development Company), supported the naturalization of Japanese subjects in Brazil throughout the 1920s (*Burajiru Jiho* 1920b; my translation). The newspaper stressed that the migrants should see themselves as pioneers in the mission of Japan's overseas development, declaring that "there is no reason why being a Japanese requires living and dying in Japan" (*Burajiru Jiho* 1920a; my translation).

These views, stemming from agricultural and diplomatic reasoning, were solidified in the late 1920s with the emerging cosmopolitanism of the Taisho (1912–26) and the early Showa (1926–89) periods. In the 1920s, a number of Japanese local "overseas associations"—not-for-profit organizations set up by prefectural governments throughout Japan between the 1910s and 1930s aimed at promoting overseas emigration and development through education, research, and recruitment—acquired lands in the rural São Paulo regions to build new plantations to facilitate long-term settlement of the Japanese migrants. Some of the settlers in these plantations were members of a newly formed middle class in Japan, who sought to use the migration and colonial developments as an opportunity to carry out social experiments that were typically informed by cosmopolitan utopian visions (Gaimu-sho 1953, 45). Yoshiyuki Kato, a leader of Burajiru Takushoku Kumiai (Cooperativa de Colonização do Brasil; Society for Colonizers in Brazil), for instance, launched a movement in 1934 aimed at introducing Western-style collective farming and puritan moral values in the new settlements (Handa 1987, 454). With the motto of "loving the soil, settling permanently" (*aido eijuu*), the movement represented settlement as an expression of progressive thinking, contrary to the conservative desire to return.

Imagined Remigration to New Territories of the Empire

The 1930s witnessed a decisive shift in the political landscape in Japan and in Brazil. After the Manchuria Incident in 1931, when Japan forcefully annexed a large part of northeast China, the ultranationalist military took full control of the Japanese government. The Japanese public was convinced as well that Japan's imperialist expansion in Asia was justifiable and even benevolent. While politico-theoretical concepts such as the Greater East Asia Co-Prosperity Sphere, the Southern Expansion Doctrine (*Nanshinron*), and *Hakko ichiu* (the whole world under one roof) were mostly focused on the new imperialist order in Asia, the immigrant intellectuals in Brazil actively sought to interpret these theories in order to redefine their positions (Handa 1966, 114). The earlier dichotomies of to return or not to return, and of being Japanese or being a new Brazilian, were replaced by more complicated and varied concerns such as whether they should return to new Asian territories occupied by the Japanese empire.

This reorientation toward the expanding Japan instead of toward the host society of Brazil was reinforced in the late 1930s as Brazil's nation-building efforts led to tougher restrictions on the immigrants' lives. When Getúlio Vargas took over the presidency of Brazil in 1937, his Estado Novo (New State) regime implemented a series of policies aimed at national unification and imposed severe constraints on foreigners' activities. Education and publications in the Japanese language, along with other languages, such as German and Italian, were strictly prohibited (see Comissão de Elaboração da História dos 80 Anos da Imigração Japonesa no Brasil 1992, 160). Moreover, Japan's attack on Pearl Harbor in 1941 led to the cancellation of diplomatic relations between Japan and Brazil. This in turn resulted in the general repatriation of Japanese diplomats via the Swedish wartime civilian exchange ship and left the Japanese migrants in a state of great anxiety over fear of being abandoned and losing contact with the homeland government. During these years, many were arrested for speaking Japanese in public. It was in this climate of great insecurity that Shungoro Wako made the remark about his painful decision to stay in Brazil, which I quoted in the beginning of this chapter. Despite Wako's determination to stay, a survey in a rural São Paulo region that he conducted in 1938 showed that as many as 85 percent of the migrants there hoped to return to Japan (Wako 1938, 1). Despite such a rise in the desire for return, however, very few migrants could afford the costly trip to Japan (see figure 1.1).

FIGURE 1.1. A celebration for the repatriation of a shop owner (the third man in the front from the right) to Japan. Bastos, São Paulo, in 1935. (Courtesy of Museu Histórico da Imigração Japonesa no Brasil)

This anxiety about the new political situation of Brazil, the resumed desire for return, and the development of Japanese imperialism collectively resulted in a new conception of return. Rokuro Koyama, the editor of *Seisyu Shimpo* (News of São Paulo, 1921–41), one of the leading Japanese newspapers in Brazil, argued that the Japanese in Brazil should remigrate to the Southeast Asia region that recently came under control of the Japanese empire.[1] According to Koyama, before Japan's expansion to the Chinese continent, the Japanese were forced to engage in what he called a "hybrid migration" (*konko ijuu*), wherein emigrants had to adopt the culture of the destination country. The new geopolitical condition, he argued, allowed for an "ethnically pure migration" (*minzoku-teki jun ijuu*), in which the migrants were no longer required to assimilate and would thus remain "pure" Japanese.[2] He insisted that the assimilative policy of Brazil was inconsonant with the latter migration and that the Japanese people should now engage in nonassimilative migrations within the power zone of the Japanese empire. *Seisyu Shimpo* published a series of editorials in 1941 that advocated a "glorious retreat" (*kouei aru taikyaku*) from Latin America to Asia "under the Japanese flag" (Kawabata 1941; my translation).

Although some contending voices saw a retreat to the homeland as something that would undermine Japan's expansion in the world (Kishimoto 1947, 169),[3] this imperialist concept of return acquired strong currency in the migrant community. Ordinary migrants, whose life in Brazil saw few signs of improvement but whose desire to return had been criticized and suppressed by immigrant intellectuals, embraced this new notion enthusiastically. Kiyoshi Ando, the editor of a literary journal in the late 1930s in São Paulo, recalled that "this feverish desire was so influential that the majority of the people expected to remigrate to the Greater East Asia Co-Prosperity Sphere even after Japan's unconditional surrender" (1949, 311; my translation). Curiously, the migrants' eagerness for imperial return or remigration was hardly appreciated by their homeland government, and the desire for migration from one colony to another was largely unrealized. The imagined collective return from Brazil to Japan's Asian empire was the migrants' cautious but desperate response to the dramatically changing political conditions, reflecting their predicament of being caught up between cosmopolitan ideals, imperialist ideology, and emotional pining for home.

The Cult of Return

After its defeat in the Second World War in 1945, Japan changed its role as an imperialist empire with expanding territory to that of a small nation-state. The empire suddenly ceased to exist when it lost former colonies, such as Korea, Taiwan, Manchuria, and many islands in the north and the south of the Japanese mainland. The glorious imperial ideologies evaporated overnight. This radical change required another corresponding revision of the subjectivities of its citizens, both in Japan and overseas. With regard to the Japanese community in Brazil, however, this process was slow and was marked by a series of reactionary incidents. Communication broke down during the war, and it took a few years for the migrants in rural plantations to be fully informed about the outcome of the war. Many Japanese migrants in Brazil still believed that Japan had won, or was winning, even after August 1945. The "convictionists" (*vitoristas* or *shinnen-ha*), who believed in Japan's victory and persistently rejected the news of Japan's defeat, gained great popularity. When the "recognitionists" (*esclarecidos* or *ninshiki-ha*) organized campaigns to inform the community about Japan's

FIGURE 1.2. A street demonstration organized by the Sakura Volunteer Army in Praça da Sé, São Paulo, on February 3, 1955, demanding that the Japanese government repatriate them. The banners read "Ethnic Return" and "Complete Repatriation of 400,000 Compatriots." (Courtesy of the Museum of the Japanese Immigration in Brazil, São Paulo)

defeat, militant members of the Shindo Renmei (League of the Ways of the Emperor's Subjects), the central organization of the convictionist group, organized terrorist attacks and killed many recognitionist leaders (Miyao 2003, 70–72).

It was against this background that various rumors about return emerged in São Paulo in the early 1950s. In order to exploit ordinary migrants' lingering desire to return, rumors were spread among the migrants that the victorious Japanese government would soon come to rescue them from Brazil. Numerous tricksters swindled the migrants out of large amounts of money by persuading them to sell off their properties in a rush to be ready for "repatriation ships" that would arrive anytime to send them back to Japan (*São Paulo Shimbun-sha* 1960, 3–9).

In the midst of this turmoil and confusion, the Sakura-gumi Teishintai

(Sakura Volunteer Army) was formed as a cult of return in 1953. Although the agenda of the group was fundamentally driven by a desperate desire to return to Japan, the members presented their proposals as critical engagement with global political developments. The leaders urged the Japanese migrants to join the U.S.-led UN forces in the Korean War, but at the same time to "fight alongside communists to liberate Taiwan." The leaders advocated "forced repatriation of all Japanese immigrants in Brazil" (*São Paulo Shimbun-sha* 1960, 10–11; *Paulista Shimbun-sha* 1977, 37). They organized street demonstrations and even a collective hunger strike to pressure the Japanese embassy to repatriate them, only to be scorned by the general public due to the group's deeply controversial agendas and eccentric behaviors (figure 1.2). In 1955, frustrated members attacked the Japanese consulate in São Paulo and injured several officials (*O Estado de S. Paulo* 1955).

The Japanese migrants' desire to return finally faded away by the mid-1950s as they learned that their war-torn homeland could no longer welcome them. The new wave of migrants from Japan in the 1950s reinforced this perception. The new wave took place as part of a government program to counter an overpopulation problem after the war. The national population increased by ten million in eight years from 1948 to 1956, which was partly due to the baby boom of the late 1940s, but more directly resulted from the surge of six million returnees (*hikiage-sha*) from former Japanese colonies that consisted of soldiers and civilians (see Tamanoi, this volume).[4] The government swiftly rebuilt the emigration apparatus, including the nation-wide recruitment network, training centers for emigrants, a special loan agency, and an advisory committee in the cabinet. After the government resumed its overseas emigration program in 1953, about 51,000 people were sent to Brazil by 1975 (Kokusai Kyoryoku Jigyo-dan 1987, 36–39).

The postwar emigration policy was characterized by its general discouragement of return. As the emigration program primarily aimed to reduce the size of the population, the state obligated the applicants to avow that they would permanently live in their destination countries (Wakatsuki and Suzuki 1975, 110–13). For example, a 1955 agricultural youth-emigration program required all applicants to fill out a detailed questionnaire, in which they had to declare that they were physically fit and mentally determined to live in Brazil for the rest of their lives.[5] While relentlessly emphasizing the glorious image of overseas emigration through a wide range of political instruments—such as official publications that were entirely devoted to the promotion of emigration and that promulgated the popular motto of "*kaigai yuhi*" (bravely fly overseas)—the government did not put in place any substantial policies or organizations to address the migrants' possible need to return to Japan. For this reason, the postwar immigrants to Brazil rarely saw themselves as temporary workers but understood their relocation from Japan to Brazil as a one-way journey.

On the other hand, the Japanese immigrants and the descendants in Brazil rapidly assimilated into the Brazilian society. Various institutions were built to reorganize the former overseas imperial subjects into a community with a distinct history and political demands. At the same time, memory of the state emigration program largely disappeared from the everyday concerns of the Japanese people as the standard of living rose dramatically after the war, and the public image of the Japanese migrants in Brazil greatly improved in the 1950s and 1960s as the group's leaders succeeded in reconstructing its image as an important contributor to Brazil's modernization project.

In this context, some Japanese politicians began to see the overseas Japanese emigrants in a new light. During the late 1950s and through the 1960s, hundreds of Japanese politicians and business leaders in Japan organized conventions to celebrate the achievements of the Japanese emigrants and their descendants abroad. The Kaigai Nikkeijin Taikai (Convention of the Overseas Japanese and Their Descendants), convened by proemigration politicians, gave rise to a renewed popular interest in the emigrants (Kaigai Nikkeijin Renraku Kyokai 1960, 11). Once despised as an abandoned people (*kimin*), the migrants were now portrayed as pioneers in foreign lands, whose struggles and moral strength won praise and respect in their host countries. The convention was also one of the first occasions in which the term *Nikkeijin*—the Japanese emigrants overseas and their descendants—was used in public. Such reevaluations of the emigrants' achievement were welcomed by the Japanese community in Brazil, and sympathetic politicians and business leaders in Japan provided rare channels for the migrants to engage with Japan. In 1964, the leaders of the Japanese immigrant community held the 1º Congresso Latino-Americano de Colônias Japonesas (First Congress of the Nikkeijin in Latin America), gathering the representatives from the Japanese immigrants and their descendants in South America. Representatives at this meeting raised various concerns with regard to the Japanese government's responsibility to the overseas community and, above all, demanded the extension of political rights, including the right to vote, to the Nikkeijin (*São Paulo Shimbun-sha* 1966, 57). In this way, Nikkeijin emerged as a new subject in both Japanese domestic politics and international relations.

The Return of the Nikkeijin?

Postwar economic development and advancement in long-distance transport and communication created new conditions for international mobility. The Brazilian economic crisis in the 1980s and 1990s had meant that many Brazilian citizens were compelled to go abroad to look for work. The high inflation, which was at 110.2 percent in 1980, 224.4 percent in 1985, and 1,764.9 percent in 1989 ("Índice Geral de Preços" [General Index of Prices] by Fundação Getúlio Vargas, cited in Mori 1995, 495), and the stagnant development of the lost decade (*década perdida*) in the 1980s continued to devastate the Brazilian economy in the 1990s. As a result, many Brazilians chose to work abroad and remained in the United States, Europe, and other Latin American countries. By the end of the 1990s, as many as 1.8 million Brazilian citizens resided abroad (Instituto Brasileiro de Geografia e Estatística 2003, 18), and the number rose to 4 million in 2008 (Ministério do Trabalho e Emprego 2003, 9).

Meanwhile, Japan suffered from the shortage of unskilled labor, which caused many small- and mid-scale companies to go bankrupt (Chusho Kigyo-cho 1987). In response to the dire economic situation in Brazil and the labor shortage in the Japanese manufacturing industry, some of the prewar first-generation Japanese immigrants and the second-generation descendants in Brazil started visiting Japan and working in factories in the mid-1980s. Some of them engaged in employment without proper documentation. In a bid to counter the growing numbers of illegal foreign workers in the country, the Japanese Ministry of Justice implemented a reformed Shutsu Nyu-Koku Oyobi Nanmin Ninteihou (Immigration Control and Refugee Recognition Act) in June 1990. The amendment included the Nikkeijin up to the third generation and their spouses in a list of foreign populations who were eligible for "long-term-resident" status and a visa.[6] The visa, granted by the Japanese minister of justice largely for humanitarian reasons, was also given to other foreign nationals such as non-Japanese children closely related to Japanese citizens and Asian refugees desiring to reside with their families in Japan. With few regulations as to the economic activities of the visa holders, it was in a sense an exceptional category in the Japanese immigration policy, which typically restricted foreigners from engaging in unskilled labor. The inclusion of Nikkeijin in this list was consistent with the earlier guideline set by the government's Kaigai Ijuu Shingikai (Council for Overseas Emigration) in 1979, which obliged the Japanese government to be responsible for the welfare of the second- and third-generation overseas descendants.[7]

The minor amendment in visa regulations, however, led to an unexpected growth of migrant workers from Brazil. Residents of Brazilian nationality in Japan, which numbered only about 2,000 in 1985, increased to about 148,000 in 1992, and to 316,000 in 2007 (Homu-sho Nyuukoku Kanrikyoku 2008) — over 20 percent of the total Nikkeijin population (1.4 million) in Brazil (Centro de Estudos Nipo-Brasileiros 2002). The great majority of residents were from the states of São Paulo and Paraná and lived in Japanese provincial industrial cities such as Toyota in Aichi Prefecture, Hamamatsu in Shizuoka, and Ota and Oizumi in Gunma. Many were recruited through the transnational networks between travel agencies (*agências*) in Brazil and temporary work agencies (*empreiteiras*) in Japan (see Higuchi 2005). In addition to introducing jobs, they also offered comprehensive packages that included housing, translation services, and daily commuting transport. But since the Nikkeijin visa did not tie the residents to particular employers, many were constantly in search of better jobs and often disappeared from their workplaces and officially registered addresses. Even the local governments, responsible for the services provided to the foreign citizens, frequently lost sight of the migrants and their children.

As some researchers have suggested,[8] one may argue that there is a certain element of return in this movement in the sense that the migration started because of their ancestral connections. With the long-term-resident visa, Nikkeijin up to the third generation and their spouses could engage in any occupation of their choice without the state's approval. In order to apply for the visa as a Nikkeijin, one must submit formal evidence to prove his or her blood connections to Japan. Essential evidence included copies of a family register issued in Japan or, in the case of the third generation, proof of grandparents' identity and parents' birth certificates and marriage certificates.

These new waves of reverse migration were some of the most important developments for the Japanese community in Brazil. Newspapers of the migrant community featured every detail of the phenomenon and debated its impacts on the development of the community. Community leaders established such groups as Centro de Informação e Apoio ao Trabalhador no Exterior (Center of Information and Support for the Workers Abroad), Instituto de Solidariedade Educacional e Cultural (Institute of Educational and Cultural Solidarity), and Comissão de Estudos Relacionados aos Dekassegui (Dekassegui Research Committee). The leaders urged both the Japanese and Brazilian governments to address the needs of the migrants. While the notion of "return" was rarely evoked explicitly, the migrants' ancestral connections to Japan provided the grounds on which such demands were made.

Yet it can be misleading to label the migrants as returnees. In addition to the term's deviation from the definition of "return migration" by the International Organization for Migration (International Organization for Migration 2004, 10), the great majority of the migrants did not consider their journey to be *return*. The term did not reflect their actual experiences. In fact, among those who migrated to Japan in the 1990s, only a handful were literal returnees—those who were born and had lived part of their lives in Japan before migrating to Brazil.[9] Instead, the majority of Nikkeijin migrants to Japan were second- and third-generation descendants, for whom Japan was merely their ancestors' homeland. Despite their physical resemblance to other Japanese nationals, the Portuguese-speaking Latin American migrants experienced immense linguistic and cultural barriers in Japan. Furthermore, they moved back and forth between Japan and Brazil regularly, facilitated by travel agencies whose transnational operations straddled Brazil and the temporary work agencies in Japan. This pattern of migration is referred to as *dekassegui*, Japanese for "migrate to work," as if to liken the pattern to their ancestors' practice of temporary work in Brazil. For many Nikkeijin migrants, work in Japan was merely a temporary alternative to their economic lives in Brazil. In other words, their transnational migration was a consequence of a purely rational choice, which had little to do with the ethnic preference demonstrated by the new visa category.

The term *return* was absent in the Japanese government's formal documents. From the very beginning, Japanese government officials had been reluctant to promote dekassegui migration from Latin American countries or to provide assistance to those who had already migrated to Japan. By distancing itself from the notion of "return," the Japanese government could use its diaspora community in Latin America as a reserve of labor power with minimal political complications, welfare provisions, or moral responsibility. In this sense, the Brazilian migrants, who obtained a relatively privileged visa status due to their blood connection to Japan, nevertheless remained vulnerable to changes in the economic and political structures that demanded their labor and therefore presence.

The vulnerability of the Nikkeijin's quasi-return status became particularly evident in the wake of the global financial crisis in 2008–9. In late 2008, in a bid to counter the general loss of sales due to the global financial crisis, the top Japanese manufacturers reduced their production, causing large-scale redundancies in the capacity of related suppliers. Most of the Brazilian migrants were working on temporary contracts brokered by temporary work agencies, so they were the first to lose their jobs. This further damaged the very basis of the migrants' lives in Japan, because they were dependent on these transnational agencies for detailed and comprehensive support, including collective housing, language assistance, and transportation. When the migrants lost their jobs, some became homeless and had to return to Brazil. Around 86,000 Brazilians left Japan between 2007 and 2010, amounting to 27 percent of the registered Brazilian population in precrisis 2007.[10]

In response to the crisis, the Japanese Ministry of Health, Labor, and Welfare launched a program with the name Nikkeijin Rishokusha no Tame no Kikoku Shien Jigyo (Support for the Return of Unemployed Nikkeijin) between April 2009 and March 2010. The program provided a subsidy of 100,000–300,000 yen (about USD 900–2,700) to Nikkeijin who wanted to return to their countries of origin. The government initially announced that it would only provide support on the condition that the person would not reenter the country under the same type of visa, but later added that the person may reenter the country after three years. Between 2009 and 2010, about twenty thousand Japanese Brazilians applied for the program and received the grant to fly back to Brazil.[11] The program was to some extent designed to reduce the welfare costs incurred by Nikkeijin workers by cutting off their ties to Japan. In this sense, the ambiguity of the quasi-returnee status provided the state with extra room for maneuver, and quasi-return was eventually replaced by one-way "real" return.

Discussion

When Wako expressed his passionate determination to settle in Brazil, and when Koyama meticulously theorized his vision of remigration to Japanese Southeast Asia, "return or not to return" was a matter of vital importance. Return was seen as a direct expression of their subjectivity to the larger political project of the Japanese empire. During Japan's imperial expansion, Japanese migrants in Brazil acutely followed the developments in their homeland and regarded themselves as subjects of the emerging Japanese empire. The question of return was thus deeply politicized and moralized. The postwar development of the cult of return in the case of Sakura-gumi Teishintai and the Japanese government's nonreturn policy of emigration further illustrated how politically and ideologically sensitive the issue of return can be.

In contrast, at the beginning of the twenty-first century, it seems, concerns about empire, nation, and collective political identity were all gone. The transnational migration of the Brazilian Nikkeijin was opened up by the state's introduction of a legal status, but its fundamental driving force was the flexibility of the transnational labor-supply system. When the migrants engaged in factory work, they heavily depended on the packaged lifestyle provided by the transnational temporary-work agencies. Unlike in the earlier regimes of migration, intense moral and political reasoning no longer seemed to define the meaning of the migrants' mobility. Instead, personal experiences such as working conditions, lifestyle, and local relations came to define people's perceptions of migration. The question of whether or not to return was largely a matter of economic reasoning with regard to the constantly changing condition of work. This does not imply that the state no longer played a role in these transnational mobilities. Not only did the Japanese government introduce a privileged legal channel for the Nikkeijin primarily because of their ethnicity and their ancestral connection to Japan but it was also careful to maintain a distance from them. This ambiguity was an effective source of control that allowed the government to regulate the flow of migration and citizenship. It is precisely through such selective and partial relations that the Japanese state in the new millennium accommodates an increasingly transnational form of mobility into its notions of sovereignty, citizenship, and nationhood.

Notes

The complexity of the directionality of transnational migration and its perceptions by differently positioned actors renders it difficult to describe the subjects of this chapter in a single term. For example, the Japanese citizens who left for Brazil in the beginning of the twentieth century were perceived as emigrants by the Japanese government but immigrants by the Brazilian public. When their descendants moved to Japan in the late twentieth century, they were immigrants from the Japanese point of view but emigrants from the Brazilian point of view. In order to avoid confusion, I will, wherever possible, use the generic term *migrant* to refer to the subjects of this chapter. However, I am also aware that the neutral term (i.e., *migrant*) may also give an impression of a mobile subject compared to the other variations (i.e., *immigrant* and *emigrant*) and is not quite suitable to describe those who lived in the host country for decades. In fact, the terms *immigrant* and *emigrant*, deliberately used by the subjects themselves or by the government, take on specific political effects by implicating where the subjects should ultimately belong. For this reason, I will also use the term *immigrant* and *emigrant* where it is more appropriate.

1. Takashi Maeyama (1982) analyzes Koyama's advocacy of remigration as part of the "revitalization movement" of the Japanese immigrants in Brazil.

2. Koyama published a series of editorials in July 1941 under the pseudonym of Kosonju. See Kosonju 1941a, 1941b, 1941c; my translations.

3. Koichi Kishimoto, an educator and the founder of Gyosho Gakuen (Gyosho School System) in São Paulo closely analyzed the migrants' opinions on the issue of remigration. Although he was attentive to the rise of his homeland, he argued that the Japanese immigrants should nonetheless stay in Brazil.

4. In 1956 the first white paper of the Ministry of Health and Welfare expressed its grave concern for the consequences of the rapidly increasing population: "The postwar development of the national economy was certainly remarkable. However, the growth of our population and the transformation of its structure have decelerated this development. It has impeded the improvement of the national living standard and distorted the lives of our people caused by the rapid modernization." See Kosei-sho Daijin Kambo Kikakushitsu (1956, 1; my translation).

5. From a brochure on the 1955 Cotia Sangyo Kumiai Tandoku Seinen Koyo Imin (Cotia Agricultural Cooperative's Youth Employment Emigration) (Cotia Sangyo Kumiai 1956).

6. The long-term-resident status is granted to "those who are authorized to reside in Japan with a period of stay designated by the minister of justice in consideration of special circumstances." Shutsu Nyu-Koku Kanri Oyobi Nanmin Ninteiho, Beppyo Dai 2 (Immigration Control and Refugee Recognition Act, Annexed Table 2).

7. "Kongo no kaigai iju to iju seisaku no arikata" [The guideline for overseas Emigration and Migration Policy] was proposed by the Council for Overseas Emigration on January 31, 1979.

8. See Yamanaka 1996; Tsuda 2003. Takeyuki Tsuda uses the concept of "ethnic return migration" to describe the migration of descendants to their ancestors' homeland.

9. In fact, these first-generation immigrants held Japanese citizenship and were absent from the immigration statistics published by the Japanese Ministry of Justice. It is commonly said among the Japanese community in Brazil that most of them definitely went back to Brazil—their original destination—by the late 1990s.

10. Homu-sho Nyukoku Kanrikyoku (Immigration Bureau, Ministry of Justice), "Minato-betsu nyuukoku gaikokujin no kokuseki" [Nationalities of the foreigners

who entered by port] and "Minato-betsu shukkoku gaikokujin no kokuseki" [Nationalities of the foreigners who departed by port], http://www.moj.go.jp/housei/tou kei/toukei_ichiran_nyukan.html (accessed February 11, 2012).

11. Kosei Rodo-sho, Ministry of Health, Labor, and Welfare), "Nikkeijin Kikoku-shien Jigyo no jisshi Kekka" [The report of the Nikkeijin Repatriation Aid Program], http://www.mhlw.go.jp/bunya/koyou/gaikokujin15/kikoku_shien.html (accessed November 4, 2010).

Soldier's Home

War, Migration, and Delayed Return in Postwar Japan

MARIKO ASANO TAMANOI

The protagonist of Ernest Hemingway's short story "Soldier's Home" (published in 1925) is a Methodist college student in Kansas, Harold Krebs, who "enlisted in the Marines in 1917 and did not return to the United States until the second division returned from the Rhine in the summer of 1919" (1996, 69). By the time of his delayed return, after "the greeting of heroes was over," his town "had heard too many atrocity stories to be thrilled by actualities," so "to be listened to at all he had to lie, and after he had done this twice he, too, had a reaction against the war and against talking about it" (69). Indeed, people in his town "seemed to think it was rather ridiculous for Krebs to be getting back so late, years after the war was over" (69). Although Harold is a hero to his sisters and parents, who had waited for his return for many years, their attitudes toward him soon begin to change (70). The story thus ends when Harold is urged by his parents to get "a definite aim in life," to which he is unable to amass energy to respond (75).

The passage of time, whether short or long, seems to do many things to the minds of people. The stories recounted by the victorious soldiers who returned immediately after the victory in the First World War created a sense of national pride in their town. Yet the more atrocious stories that Harold had to make up "to be listened to at all" after his delayed return spawned "a reaction against the war and against talking about it," not only among his town's people but in his own mind as well (75). The passage of time, then, seems to relate in complex manners to ideas and practices of "return."

The protagonists who appear in *my* story are the defeated soldiers of the Japanese Imperial Army, who had been left behind in Japan's once vast empire and made returns many months, years, or decades after Japan's unconditional surrender to the Allied Forces at the end of the Second World War.[1] The reasons for their delayed returns vary. Some were kept as prisoners of war (POWS) or war criminals for longer than they had expected in the United States, the Soviet Union, and the People's Republic of China (after 1949). Others, unsure of Japan's defeat, continued to fight against "the enemy." Some participated in the Chinese Civil War between the Nationalists and the Communists or in the anticolonial independent movements in India, the Philippines, and Indonesia. Others decided to make their living in the places where they heard the news of Japan's capitulation and married local women and postponed their return home. These ex-servicemen thus returned at various points between 1945 and 1974. I examine the changing relationship among these returning solders, the Japanese public, and the Japanese state and ask how and why they returned, how postwar Japan accepted them, and what this manner of acceptance caused in the minds of returning soldiers. I also ask what kind of political and cultural logics (that might have changed over time) were working behind Japan's struggle with the last military conflict, or more specifically, the violence committed by the defeated soldiers, for the very purpose of reconstructing the nation. Time is an important component here to understand these political and cultural logics. The meaning of *patriotism*, along with the meaning of *nationalism*, changed over the divide of 1945, and has further changed since then, long before scholars began discussing the connection between patriotism and globalization (see Anderson 1994; Appadurai 1993).[2]

I HOPE THAT THIS chapter will find a place in migration studies, for the legal machinery to address the issues of *displaced person, forced migration,* or *refugees,* the terms that contemporary scholars of migration routinely use, came about at the times of two world wars. Yet scholars of migration seem to have neglected one particular aspect of migration that always accompanies a war, the migration of soldiers: soldiers move, often extensively, from one country to another, and from one battlefield to another. Furthermore, while the study of soldiers' migration may be part of the so-called war history, the subject does not always belong to the past for the simple reason that soldiers' migration never ends with the war's end. While some hope to return home after they are disarmed, others stay where they gave up combat and choose to move to other destinations years or even decades after the end of war. In this respect, their returns may teach us many lessons not only about war but also about peace.

Closing the War and Forgetting It in Postwar Japan

Sengo is the Japanese term that literally means "after a war." It is a generic term that points to the era after any warfare. Japan fought many wars from the onset of the Meiji era (1868–1912), so its modern history has had several sengo. In contemporary Japan, then, "sengo" means after the end of the Second World War, which has been remembered among the Japanese by such names as the Greater East Asia War (Dai-tōa sensō), Pacific War (Taiheiyō sensō), Asia-Pacific War (Ajia-Taiheyô sensô), or Fifteen-Year War (Jūgonen sensō).[3] Although the Japanese government declared the end of this sengo in 1956, the term is still in use by the very government that declared its end as well as the media and people, not only to remember the last war in which Japan fought but also to gauge the nation's progress (or deterioration for some) since August 15, 1945. My story should thus properly begin on this day.

At noon on August 15, 1945, through a radio broadcast, the emperor announced to his subjects Japan's unconditional surrender to the Allied Powers. Most, but not all, soldiers of the Japanese military, for whom the emperor had been the supreme commander-in-chief, immediately laid down their arms. Two weeks later, the victor, the U.S.-led Occupation Forces, landed in Japan to occupy the country. Yet in this radio broadcast, the emperor, speaking "in a manner that divorced him from any personal responsibility" for his country's many years of aggression (Dower 1979, 35), proceeded to "offer himself as the embodiment of the nation's *suffering*, its ultimate victim, transforming the sacrifices of his people into his own agony with a classical turn of phrase . . . 'my vital organs are torn asunder'" (36, emphasis added). Indeed, the country of Japan, in which more than sixty cities were flattened due to U.S. bombing, was in ruins.

Approximately 1.74 million armed men were killed. An incalculable number of civilians, perhaps more than 2 million in Japan proper alone, died. In addition, about 6.5 million Japanese, of whom 3.5 million were soldiers, were left overseas after Japan's capitulation, and their fates were unclear at the time of Japan's defeat. Whether in Japan proper or overseas, those who had survived the war's ordeal were suffering from hunger, malnutrition, epidemic diseases, and the loss of loved ones. Many survivors of the atomic bombs, war orphans, war widows, and disabled veterans became abandoned and homeless (see Dower 1986, 293–301, 1999, chapter 1). Through the emperor's embodiment of the nation's suffering in his speech, this defeated nation that lost its empire overnight seemed to have been able to forget the suffering of the victims of its aggression in China, Indonesia, Malaysia, the Philippines, and a handful of other countries in Asia and the Pacific. Thus, the fact that Japan was a perpetrator of millions of deaths in Asia was hardly recognized and continued to remain unacknowledged for several more decades in postwar Japan.

The OCCUPATION FORCES also had its share of this amnesia: it constructed the war as "a conspiracy of militarists and radical nationalists who were responsible for Japanese aggression," and excluded the emperor from this conspiracy (Orr 2001, 15). Put another way, the words of both the emperor and the OCCUPATION FORCES acquitted the Japanese public of its complicity in the nation's violence against the people of Asia. Note that, in this discourse of acquittal, Japanese soldiers occupied extremely precarious positions. They not only brought back their experiences of suffering both during and after the war but also transported their experiences of violence back into postwar Japan. Nevertheless, unlike Krebs, these "defeated" soldiers rarely told stories of atrocities in public due to national pride. Rather, they had to "whisper" them, or the public had to sense such stories in the soldiers' refusal to tell them, at least until the mid-1970s. These soldiers' experience of suffering in the aftermath of the war, then, became a "morally and methodologically difficult problem," precisely because "the suffering that [Japanese soldiers] experienced was the direct consequence of the violence they had first committed" in the territories of others (Biess 2006, 6).[4]

The soldiers who had been left behind in Japan's perished empire are called *zanryū Nihonhei* in Japanese. The Japanese Ministry of Health and Welfare (MHW), the institution that has been undertaking the repatriation of demilitarized soldiers and civilians since Japan's defeat, defines this term as referring to "soldiers of the Japanese military who left their military services without formally being demilitarized by the state's order" (Kōsei-shō 1997, 13; my translation). Soon after Japan's capitulation, the MHW initially categorized such soldiers as "the missing" (or "the fugitives," in some cases). When the missing made delayed returns, the MHW demilitarized them on paper. As of 1959, approximately 31,000 former soldiers and civilians were still missing. For the sake of the surviving family members of the missing soldiers who were still waiting for the soldiers' returns and were therefore unable to receive compensations, the MHW changed the category of "the missing" to "the deceased" in their household registries. Those ex-soldiers and civilians who made delayed returns after 1959 were indeed the "ghosts" from a dark past. I historicize the experiences of the returned soldiers to postwar Japan and of the Japanese public who received them by dividing the first three decades of sengo into two groups: from 1946 to 1959 and from 1960 to 1974.

Return of Japanese Soldiers to Postwar Japan: 1946–1959

Depending on how they returned and from where, the soldiers who made delayed returns to postwar Japan between 1946 and 1959 can further be divided into three groups. First are those who were detained as POWs by the Allied Forces—the U.S. military in this case. Second are the soldiers who were left behind in South and Southeast Asia at the end of the war, and third are those who were detained as POWs or war criminals by the Soviet Union or the People's Republic of China after 1949.

POWS BY THE ALLIED FORCES

Those who were detained as POWs by the Allied forces comprised about seventy thousand surrendered soldiers who helped the United States as laborers in the Philippines, Okinawa, and islands across the Pacific. These ex-servicemen made delayed returns some time in 1946. The repatriation of the majority of these soldiers was smooth as they were well protected by international treaties. Yet, once returned, they met with reproach from the public, who previously during wartime had enthusiastically celebrated their departure for battlefields with cheers and band music. One of those who returned was Noda Mitsuharu.

In July 1944, Japan and the United States were engaged in a fierce battle on the island of Saipan. In this conflict, which Noda later described as the battle "between tanks [that represented the United States] and bamboo spears [that represented Japan]," thousands of Japanese soldiers died for the sake of dying (1976, 142). Noda, however, survived this battle because he was captured as a POW, transported to Hawaii, and then repatriated to Japan in January 1946. Yet his family had already been notified of his "honorable" death. Hence, when he finally reached home, he was told that, as he was killed honorably well before Japan's capitulation, as many as 750 people came to his funeral. In January of 1946, those hundreds of people were nowhere to be found and the monk at his family temple looked confused about how to greet him (Noda 1976, 138). Recall here that the people of the Kansas town in Hemingway's story found the return of Krebs to be "ridiculous" years after the war was over (1996, 69). Whether it may have been ridiculous, awkward, or confusing, Noda's feeling and his village people's feeling toward him turned him against the war and his homeland. Recalling the time when he was captured and transported to the military hospital in Hawaii, he wrote: "[The U.S. military] transported me, an enemy soldier of no rank, to the military hospital by plane. At that moment, I was awakened to the importance of human life. I was ready to hate the Japanese military that had completely ignored my humanity" (142, my translation). But was Noda patriotic during wartime? If so, to what or to whom? What happened to his patriotism over the divide of 1945, the year of Japan's capitulation? To answer these questions, I must rely on one of the works by E. Herbert Norman, *Soldier and Peasant in Japan: The Origins of Conscription*, published in 1943.[5]

According to Norman, the universal system of conscription was hastily decreed in 1873, only six years after the end of feudalism in 1867 and before the establishment of a constitution or any representative institutions. To shed light on this rushed action of the modern Japanese government, Norman urges us to go back to the last decades of Japan's feudal era, in which the arms-bearing ruling class of lords and warriors and the oppressed and disarmed class of peasants were still rigidly separated (1943, 52; see also Sansom 1943, xi). After the arrival of Western imperial powers to Japanese shores, the feudal government saw the need for a radical change in its military power to be a bulwark against growing pressure from the West (Norman 1943, v). In addition, the martial quality of lords and warriors had already been blunted due to the long period of peace lasting from the beginning of the seventeenth century. In addition, the warriors' swordsmanship was of no use against Western gunboats. In other words, the feudal warriors were not the best candidates to be conscripted into a modern military. This led the Meiji government to "draw upon the deep, untapped reservoir of the peasantry" (Norman 1943, v). Here, Norman alerts us to the meaning of mobilizing peasants into armies at this critical juncture of history: by so doing, the leaders of the Meiji government could suppress peasant rebellions that by then had spread into every corner of Japan. In other words, the reform of the military system was to check the movement toward emancipation among peasants (Norman 1943, 36). The universal conscription system was thus hastily decreed. Hence, the Japanese modern military, according to Norman, was not an institution consisting of "patriotic" soldiers. Rather, its members were the emperor's subjects who were expected to defend the emperor. For this reason, soldiers were exonerated from protecting not only their compatriots, Japanese citizens, but also their comrades. Furthermore, they were not expected to value their own lives, for they were taught not to return home alive but to die for the sake of the emperor.

Yet for Noda the discovery of the nature of the Japanese military came too late. By the time of his delayed return, the Japanese public had already been "exposed to a steady flow of information concerning the shocking range of atrocities committed by the imperial forces in China, Southeast Asia, and the Philippines" (Dower 1999, 60). The defense of returned soldiers, that it was not them but the military cliques who were ultimately responsible for war and its conduct, was largely in vain. The historian John Dower offers us the reason why the public sentiments toward ex-servicemen changed so radically after Japan's defeat: the returned soldiers were after all "losers," and as such they quickly fell out of "proper" social categories in the immediate postwar era (1999, 61). While I agree with Dower, I add yet another reason for this change of public sentiments: the nature of the patriotism of these soldiers was now revealed in front of the public. These soldiers offered no contribution to the betterment of the nation of Japan; instead, they committed violence overseas in the name of the emperor. Furthermore, they failed to protect the citizens of Japan overseas and at home. What emerged at this historical juncture was the ex-soldiers' association with violence (they committed without the clear purpose of protecting their own compatriots), which made them "improper."

SOLDIERS LEFT BEHIND IN SOUTH AND SOUTHEAST ASIA

The conditions in Southeast Asia and South Asia during the Second World War call for our special attention. In these areas, the defeat of Japan was already sealed months before Japan's surrender (Kōsei-shō 2000a, 22–28). By the spring of 1945, most battalions stationed in Southeast and South Asia had lost a major part of their forces. Faced with starvation, those surviving soldiers who had been fighting in, for example, Burma, fled in increasing numbers to other parts of Southeast Asia, such as Thailand, Indochina, or Malaysia, in search of food, not enemies. Instead of surrendering to the enemies, these soldiers hid themselves in jungles while fighting starvation and disease (see Kōsei-shō 1997, 259–66). In Indonesia, an unknown number of Japanese soldiers, perhaps ranging from one to two thousand, participated in the war of the country's independence against its former colonial powers—the Dutch forces. These soldiers left the Japanese Imperial Army's order, became fugitives (*tōbō-hei*), and fought a guerrilla war (see E. Hayashi 2007, 2009). Indeed, more than half of the deaths among the soldiers stationed in Southeast and South Asia occurred in the last year of the war as the result of malnutrition, epidemics, and guerrilla war. In such conditions, the order of demilitarization and repatriation to Japan after August 1945 was slow to reach soldiers who had barely survived, which in turn delayed the return of some soldiers until the 1970s. Let me focus on the case of one individual soldier who returned to Japan in 1946 from colonial Indonesia. What delayed his return, however, was not starvation, epidemics, or guerrilla war: it was his relationship with a local woman.

Yamazaki Kenji was born to a relatively wealthy landowning family in Shizuoka in 1902. As a young man growing up in the era of Taishō democracy, he was introduced to the idea of socialism and ran successfully for a seat from the Social Mass Party (Shakai Taishū tō) at the local assembly several times beginning in 1931.[6] He then won the seat of the House of Representatives of the Imperial Diet (Teikoku Gikai) in 1936, albeit in 1942 he was no longer able to run for reelection due to the state's increasingly harsh persecution of the members of liberal political parties.[7] Having been deprived of the opportunity, he chose to run away to Japan's overseas empire to fulfill his dream to be on the side of workers and peasants. He thus enlisted himself into the Japanese Imperial Army, left for Borneo, and asked the army to appoint him as a governor of one of its prefectures. Yamazaki Toyoko (2008a, 2008b), on whose works I base my discussion, writes that, during wartime, high-ranking military officers such as Kenji were able to employ what they called "personal maids," who were in reality temporary wives, regardless of the officers' marital status. Though Kenji was married, he employed a local woman and eventually had two children with her. When Japan surrendered, he had two options: to remain in Borneo or to return home. He chose the latter and in 1946 returned to Japan with this woman and their two children without notifying his wife, Michiko.

Michiko, who had been waiting for his return in Japan, was not an ordinary woman: she was a liberal political activist during wartime, and after women obtained suffrage in the immediate postwar Japan, she successfully ran for the seat at the House of Representatives of the Imperial Diet. Shortly after Kenji's return in March 1946, Michiko exercised another right that Japanese women newly obtained—divorce. Kenji, now a husband of a woman from Borneo, tried to revive his career as a politician, but it was in vain. Having failed in every endeavor, he migrated to Brazil in 1953 to try to become famous there, a choice rather similar to the one he took when he decided to leave for Borneo. However, he soon died of illness in 1958. According to Yamazaki's articles (2008a, 2008b), after Kenji's death, Michiko helped Kenji's new legal wife to return to Japan and restored her life there. Like Kenji, Michiko too took responsibility for the welfare of this woman from Borneo.

Kenji's return was far more ridiculous: it was scandalous for he was a public man and a former high-ranking military officer. Furthermore, Michiko was also a public figure and the action she took toward Kenji's wife from Borneo made Kenji's delayed return more scandalous. I note here that most Japanese soldiers who maintained quasi-marital life with local women in such places as Indonesia and the Philippines either abandoned them and returned home alone (which in the postwar era had created the problem of their stateless children left in their mothers' countries) or stayed with them to raise families in lieu of returning.[8]

POWS BY THE SOVIET UNION

Another group of soldiers who made delayed returns before 1960 were those who were detained as POWs or war criminals by the Soviet Union. Approximately 575,000 of them were sent to labor camps in Siberia and other parts of the Soviet Union. By the Japanese government's estimate, about 55,000 of them died due to brutal working conditions. Most of the survivors were repatriated to Japan around 1949. This group of ex-servicemen who returned around this time also included those who were mobilized by the Communist forces to fight in the Chinese Civil War against the Nationalist forces. In addition, in 1950, about one thousand soldiers who had been detained in Siberia were extradited to China, where they joined approximately one hundred Japanese war criminals who had been banished there for fighting on the Nationalist side in China's civil war. These soldiers did not return to Japan until 1956, with some even having their returns delayed until 1964 (Kōsei-shō 1997, 257).

Like those returning soldiers from other regions, soldiers returning from the Soviet Union and the People's Republic of China were seen by the public as "improper people" and were met with the same opprobrium that their compatriots did. The following passage from a Japanese government report clearly indicates the reason why they became "improper people" in the society's perception.

> The ex-POWs under the Stalin regime participated in the so-called movement for democracy [minshu undō] at the labor camps under such slogans as "let us crash the anti-Soviet and anti-Communist demagogues," "it is the reactionary forces of Japan and the United States that prevent us from returning home," "the Red Army is the real army for ordinary people," "all the roads lead to Communism," or "there is no democracy [in Japan] without crushing the Emperor system." . . . Even though these former POWs were detained forcefully for as long as four years and were exploited for their labor without any legal protection, they hardly felt any grudge against the Soviet authority. On the contrary, many of them identified with the Soviet Union as their home country. This kind of phenomenon is unheard of in the history of humankind. We have to explore the reasons as to why they felt this way and must come up with the state-level policies to re-rehabilitate them. (Kōsei-shō 2000b, 30–31; my translation)

This notion that returning soldiers from the Soviet Union and the People's Republic of China were brainwashed by Communists and therefore posed a threat to the integrity of postwar Japan seems to have been widely shared among the Japanese populace.

Whether they were truly "communists" or not does not concern me here. What was more striking was that the postwar Japanese state's "re-rehabilitation" of the so-called red repatriates neither changed societal perceptions of them nor promised them a better life. For example, Inokuma Tokurō, a former Soviet POW who returned to Japan in 1947, writes:

> Since I was mobilized at the age of sixteen, I had no skills to survive [in postwar Japan]. I therefore returned to my school. There, my school principal, who saw me off with cheers [when I joined the army], looked so confused and told me, "since I will issue a certificate of graduation, go somewhere else [to continue your studies]."

He also told me not to mention that I returned from Siberia to anyone from now on. (Takahashi, Kaneko, and Inokuma 2008, 302; my translation)

Indeed, Inokuma had to change his workplace thirteen times after he returned to Japan, all because he was a red repatriate.[9]

DESPITE THE HARDSHIPS endured by the former soldiers of the Japanese Imperial Army, the official publication of the MHW occasionally depicted scenes of state officials (who enlisted local women near the port of entry) extending a warm welcome to the repatriated soldiers:

> Those who welcomed [ex-soldiers] were not only state officials but also local young women volunteers, including the students of Hijiyama High School. Upon seeing these young women, the soldiers still on board took off their hats and waved at them. They then tried to calm themselves, yet, clearly failing to do so, came down cheerfully ashore. "Hello, I will carry your backpack," one young woman said. "Oh, no, this is very light," one ex-soldier murmured. "Oh, no, I will, please let me carry it," said the woman. These women made such a commotion. Those who had succeeded in getting backpacks from ex-servicemen carried them cheerfully, though their appearance clearly suggested otherwise, as soldiers' backpacks were indeed quite heavy. Those women who failed to get backpacks evidently looked disappointed. (Kōsei-shō 2000a, 45; my translation)

At the same time, these reports also suggested that the state officials' devotion to the welfare of repatriated soldiers hardly went beyond the ports of entry. As noted earlier, both the state and the public had not been very accommodating toward these ex-soldiers who failed to fall into "proper" social categories in larger society, as was the case with many of them. Another category of people in a similar predicament in postwar Japan were war orphans (*sensō koji*). Being homeless, they were forced to beg for or steal food on the street. Commenting on the indifference of the Japanese public toward the war orphans, the celebrated wartime writer Hayashi Fumiko writes: "Japan, which failed to prepare any facility for these kids, can hardly be called 'a cultured nation' (*bunka kokka*)."[10] She also laments that, even the temples and shrines, which stood on spacious grounds, "failed to provide shelters to homeless children" (1988, 31, 32). Nonetheless, Hayashi makes no comments on the fates of homeless ex-servicemen due in part, I believe, to their association with violence, which she despised.

Return of Japanese Soldiers to Postwar Japan: 1960–1974 and Beyond

The end of the U.S. occupation of Japan in 1952 seemed to change the lives of the soldiers who had already been repatriated by then, at least in terms of their material gains. To discuss this, I must momentarily go back in time to the war period. Repatriated and retired soldiers received more than adequate benefits and pensions from the Japanese state. After Japan's defeat, the Occupation Forces reassessed the privileges offered to soldiers during the nation's militarism, issued a law named "Pension and Benefits," and ordered the Japanese government to terminate pensions and benefits for the veterans and surviving families of fallen soldiers by February 1, 1946.[11] Once the U.S. occupation was over in 1952, however, the Japanese state revived the pensions and benefits for the ex-servicemen, while civilian victims of atom bombs, aerial bombing, and the war in Okinawa were left to suffer in hardship and poverty without any compensation. Furthermore, in 1957, together with the surviving families of fallen soldiers, the ex-servicemen founded the Nihon Izoku-kai (Japan Bereaved Families Association). Due to this association's close ties with the conservative government of the Liberal Democratic Party, the group grew into a powerful lobby, which constantly demanded more and better benefits and compensations throughout the 1950s and 1960s.

As Tanaka Nobumasa and others have correctly pointed out, it was the soldiers' "special relation to the Japanese state," as well as their "suffering" upon return, that had transformed the "improper" losers into "powerful" lobbyists by the late 1950s (Tanaka, Tanaka, and Hata 1995, 106; my translation).[12] This does not necessarily mean that the material gains of ex-servicemen through the 1950s and 1960s made the society's contempt toward them entirely disappear. What it means, however, is that the suffering of ex-soldiers *after* the war abroad and in Japan was officially recognized, and it is in this context that several soldiers returned to Japan from Southeast Asia in the 1960s and 1970s. Among these soldiers who returned from the Philippines, Indonesia, and Guam, I focus on two individuals, Yokoi Shōichi and Onoda Hiroo, for each of them was considered to be "the last soldier" to be returned from the past.

On January 25, 1972, a short article was published in the morning edition of the *Asahi Shinbun* (Asahi newspaper) (and in practically every other newspaper nationally circulated) with the following headline: "Moto Nihonhei o Hakken ka" (An Ex-soldier of the Japanese Army Is Rumored to Have Been Discovered). This was followed by another article on the front page of its evening edition on the same day with this headline: "Kiseki no Moto Nihonhei: 28nen buri Hakken" (A Miracle Happened, an Ex-soldier of the Japanese Army Found in the Jungle of the Island of Guam after Twenty-Eight Years of Hiding). This ex-serviceman was Yokoi Shōichi.[13] When two local men found him while he was fishing, Yokoi was still armed, yet he followed them to their house for food. When they realized that Yokoi was a former soldier of the Japanese army, they brought him to the village headman. Yokoi was then transferred to the hospital. The Japanese consulate in Guam acted quickly and summoned a team of doctors from Tokyo to treat Yokoi, so that he would successfully reintegrate back into "civilization" when he returned home. Notably, Yokoi had to be discovered before he made a return to postwar Japan.

Between the day when Yokoi was found and the day of his return to Japan on February 2, 1972, an increasing number of Japanese journalists traveled to Guam from Japan to interview him, to the point where the hospital authority, considering Yokoi's psychological state, had to turn them away. Yokoi's narratives published in national newspapers sounded fragmented at best, even though they must have been heavily edited. Included were statements such as: "I feel as if I were still dreaming. I just do not understand what is going on now in my life"; "I would like to return to Japan, but I am also aware how shameful it is to return home alive"; "I was told again and again [during the time he served in the army] that I must return home dead"; "If I am able to return, I will first go to the temple in my village and console the spirits of all the dead soldiers"; and "To His Majesty the Emperor, I would like to convey at least the following, that I fought for the sake of the emperor, that I believed in you, and that I survived believing in the strength of Yamato spirits."[14]

It was not only the voice of Yokoi that was printed in national dailies. Commentaries of professionals, including those of writers, historians, anthropologists, psychologists, linguists, and medical doctors, who saw Yokoi as an object of research in their respective professions, were also published in the newspapers. Some quotes from these articles include: "[The return of Yokoi] reminds us, in the most miserable manner, that the last war is not yet over" (by a historian); "On the island of Guam, he had no shortage of proteins, the key to his survival, yet I wonder what substituted 'green leafy vegetables' in his diet" (by a medical doctor); "I am so happy to know that he has survived this long ordeal. He must be an extremely strong man equipped with every technique we can think of for survival. With his surprising return, all the surviving families of the missing, who have already given up on their loved ones, can rekindle their hope [of discovering them]" (by an anthropologist); "[The return of Yokoi] amply demonstrates the lesson we received during wartime, a soldier who does not surrender alive is by no means dead" (by a writer); and "I know no example like this. After twenty-eight years of solitude, he still remembers Japanese language" (by a linguist).[15]

The print media also featured the voices of ordinary people who sent in letters and called the press. Interestingly, these voices were more or less unanimous in criticizing the Japanese state. For example, one man wrote, "The Japanese government should not waste our tax money for trivial businesses of this and that but use it to search for such people as Mr. Yokoi who may still be living [in remote parts of Asia]."[16] Another wrote, "I am angry over the small amount of compensation Yokoi will possibly receive. Can the government do anything? Each member of the Parliament should contribute at least 10,000 yen [about USD 100] to him."[17] These voices were also unequivocal in criticizing the attitude of the Japanese emperor toward repatriated soldiers. For example, one man wrote, "The emperor [of Japan] must extend his apology to Mr. Yokoi for his suffering."[18] Another woman wrote, "His Majesty the Emperor, please see your soldier when he returns, and act like his father."[19]

Some of these letter writers felt that social problems facing Japan in the early 1970s, such as consumerism and environmental problems, were symptomatic of the wider, lamentable condition of Japanese society. One man wrote, "I am ashamed to show this country to Mr. Yokoi, for it has been plagued with all sorts of environmental disruption and political corruption."[20] Another man wrote, "I wear nice clothes, eat good food, and play around with girls, but I am now dismayed by myself. What have I been doing for these twenty-eight years?"[21] Some of these writers seemed to be jealous of Yokoi, who, in the words of one letter writer, "lived like Robinson Crusoe."[22] Another man also wrote, "The media claims that Mr. Yokoi has now regained his humanity. But what is the meaning of this 'humanity'? Is it 'we' who have already lost it?"[23] Two of these letter writers were former comrades of Yokoi's in Guam, but they returned to Japan in 1960. After they had visited him in Guam by invitation of a certain publisher who had planned to print their encounters with Yokoi, they were reported to have said the following: "When we returned [to Japan in 1960], the government official told us that we should just be grateful for the fact of being able to return home alive, and gave each of us as little as 10,000 yen [about USD 30 in 1960], train fare to go home, and another little sum of money to buy lunch."[24]

In fact, the government's payment accorded to Yokoi, calculated right after his return, amounted only to about 50,000 yen: while this was equivalent to the total salary he received for his twenty-eight years of service to the military from 1945 to 1972, the government apparently used his wartime rank and salary scale, which were quite low, in the calculations.[25] Since the benefits that Yokoi (who returned in 1972) and his comrades (who returned in 1960) received were not radically different, what made his former comrades compare their situations with Yokoi's had less to do with monetary compensation than with the media spotlight that Yokoi alone received. Nevertheless, in 1972, while some viewed Yokoi as a "primitive man" who knew nothing of modern civilization, most still admired his extraordinary skills of survival and his determination to abide by the emperor's order to not go home alive. He was indeed "a true Japanese," who could no longer be "found" in a Japan plagued with all the ills of modern society. In addition, Yokoi's return led the Japanese people to criticize their own government and the emperor, who, in their view, had been uncaring toward *his* soldiers.

The Yokoi fever, however, lasted for only a few months after his return to Japan. The reasons for the short-lived euphoria were several, but the most important one was the anger directed at Yokoi by ex-servicemen who had already returned to Japan. Although they had been receiving pensions and benefits since 1952, they were still critical of the use of a large sum of taxpayer money for treating Yokoi in a luxurious hospital room and transporting him from Guam to Japan by a chartered plane. Those who were particularly critical of the Yokoi fever were the families of fallen soldiers. In their view, Yokoi was by no means *gunshin*, an archaic word meaning "the god of soldiers" who kept his loyalty to the emperor beyond Japan's defeat. The god of soldiers should have killed himself when the emperor surrendered, so for the ex-servicemen, Yokoi was nothing but a traitor (*kokuzoku*). Here, we understand that the nature of patriotism did not radically change even in the 1970s but remained devoted to "emperor-ism." While Yokoi was able to build a spacious house because of the donations he received from the public (during the Yokoi fever), he was unable to build a career for the rest of his life. Instead, he named himself "the expert of sur-

vival" (*sabaibaru hyōronka*),[26] and in this capacity mounted a national circuit of lectures. Yet the survival techniques he used in the remote jungles
of Guam sounded outdated to the modern audience, who were already accustomed to the fruits of Japan's rapid economic progress. While at least
five biographies of Yokoi have been published, they were all written in 1972,
the year of his return (Asahi Shinbun Tokuhakisha-dan 1972; Itō 1972; Mainichi Shinbun-sha Henshû-bu 1972; Sankei Shinbun-sha Henshû-bu 1972;
Shimamura 1972). After all, the public was only interested in Yokoi's life in
Guam from 1945 to 1972, not in his postrepatriation life in Japan, and with
the return of another soldier in 1974 from the jungles of the Philippines,
Yokoi's popularity was rapidly eclipsed.

In the spring of 1974, news of yet another Japanese soldier, who was
discovered in the jungles of Lubang Island in the Philippines, spread like
wildfire in Japan. Unlike Yokoi, this former soldier, Onoda Hiroo, did not
hide himself in a cave to shut out communication with local people: he
continued to fight against "America," as personified in local policemen
and soldiers. Indeed, Onoda and his two comrades (who died in Lubang
before 1974) assaulted and injured more than thirty local people. Furthermore, when he was discovered and rescued by Japanese tourists, he did not
ask them for help, nor did he surrender to the order of the Japanese government. Instead, he made it clear to state officials in Japan that he was to
accept the order of demilitarization only from his former superior of the
Japanese army. Luckily (for both the Japanese and the Philippine governments), this man was alive and traveled all the way from Japan to the island
to order to disarm Onoda. Only then did Onoda agree to accept the protection of the Japanese government. The government, however, had to negotiate with the president of the Philippines, Ferdinand Marcos, to have him
pardon Onoda of his crimes committed after Japan's capitulation. Marcos
agreed (largely due to his country's reliance on Japan's economic assistance), and on March 12, 1974, Onoda finally made his return to Japan.

In the following passage from his autobiography, which he published
in 1982, Onoda wrote of his thoughts at the moment of return at Haneda
International Airport:

> I was utterly dismayed and did not know what to do or say. I was
> nothing but a former soldier who was defeated in the battle, surren-
> dered to the enemy, and returned to Japan. I was quite aware that I
> made a delayed return, but this is because I had adhered to the order
> given to me. . . . I lost two comrades of mine [in the Philippines]

who had continued to fight with me believing in the victory of our country. Had I been able to protect them from the enemy, we could have returned to Japan together. As a lieutenant who was entrusted two soldiers by His Majesty the Emperor, I wanted to return them to their parents alive. Nonetheless, I alone was standing on the glittering stage. (1982, 43, my translation)

Indeed, on this glittering stage where Onoda stood, he heard the sound of fanfare and the cheers of thousands of people waving the national flag for him. But Onoda was angry not only with the crowd, which was "agitated by [his] mere presence without thinking of what had happened to millions of fallen [Japanese] soldiers" (1982, 55), but also about the way he was treated at the hospital in Tokyo because the doctors acted as if he was a victim of starvation. They were not aware of the fact that, on Lubang Island, he had been "daily walking around carrying a backpack that weighed more than thirty kilograms [about seventy pounds] while eating an adequate amount of food to do so" (46). He was also angry about postwar Japan, which in his opinion was built on the idea of "the end of war" (shūsen) instead of "the defeat in war" (haisen), because in his view Japan had never faced up to the fate of fallen Japanese soldiers (46). Unlike Yokoi, then, Onoda had been fighting with the enemy until the moment of his return. For all these reasons, Onoda was quick to free himself from his "home," and only after about a year of stay in Japan, he left for Brazil on April 6, 1975, with the dream of becoming the owner of a large-scale cattle farm.

In his autobiography, Onoda lists several reasons why he chose to immigrate to Brazil. First, Brazil's climate is similar to that of Lubang. Second, during those thirty years on the island, he lived on beef as the main source of protein. Third, on Lubang he learned skills that might be useful for his life in Brazil. Fourth, while growing up in Japan, he often visited his maternal grandparents, who raised dairy cows. Fifth, one of his brothers, to whom Onoda felt closest, was already in Brazil; he was an ex-serviceman repatriated from China in 1946 and had migrated to Brazil several years later. Last but most important, Onoda no longer wanted to deal with "people": he badly wanted to work with "nature" (Onoda 1982, 70).

Onoda eventually fulfilled his dream. In his 1982 autobiography, he vividly describes his daily life as the owner of a herd of more than a thousand cattle in the State of Mato Grosso in Brazil. Onoda, however, did not sever his relationship with Japan. After all, he built his farm among a community of Japanese immigrants to Brazil, and became the head of the Japanese Brazilian association in Mato Grosso. Furthermore, due to the success of his autobiographies in Japan (Onoda 1974, 1982; Onoda and Sakamaki 1977; see also Onoda 1995a, 1995b), he frequently "returned" to Japan. Since the mid-1980s, he has been working with Japanese youths, teaching them the importance of preserving nature. In this sense, he has not abandoned Japan, yet he definitively established his home in Brazil, where he still lives today.[27] In other words, Onoda turned his delayed return into a proper one; to do so though, he had to leave Japan. It is his return from Brazil to Japan that has become more or less normal for both Onoda and the Japanese public.

War, Migration, and "Ridiculously" Delayed Returns

I have dealt with three main agents—the Japanese state, Japanese society, and Japanese soldiers who made delayed returns to postwar Japan between 1946 and 1974. These agents were put in relation to central questions: what kinds of political and cultural logics were working behind Japan's struggles with the last military conflict in the course of the nation's reconstruction, and how did these logics relate to the changing meanings and practices of return from the fallen Japanese empire? What is clear is that the passage of time did many things to the minds of Japanese soldiers, the society, and the state. Depending on when, how, and from where they returned, the soldiers' delayed returns became ridiculous, confusing, awkward, scandalous, threatening, or normal. Generally speaking and at the risk of greatly simplifying complex stories, postwar Japan did not extend sympathy to ex-servicemen and their suffering during and after the war until at least the late 1950s. Instead, the Japanese society had, for the most part, despised the ex-servicemen, which added to their suffering. My discussion of the Japanese soldiers who returned between 1945 and 1959 relies on the idea of violence (as defined by the Japanese public), violence that they committed during wartime. However, it is not only the violence that made their delayed returns ridiculous, confusing, awkward, scandalous, or threatening. Rather, it is the combination of violence with its varying consequences. For some it was the realization of the nature of patriotism in prewar Japan. For others it was the stark difference in military power between Japan and the United States or the effects of brainwashing by Soviet Communism. For yet others it was the soldiers' relationships with local women overseas.

By the late 1950s, when Japan began to see the fruits of rapid economic progress, the repatriated soldiers amassed a certain political power with adequate compensations coming from the conservative government. The society, however, still anxiously waited for the return of the "last" soldier from the perished empire. When Yokoi and Onoda finally returned, both created a fever in Japan, but their sensationalism was short-lived. The public admired these two men for their suffering after the war's end and their extraordinary skills in overcoming the difficult conditions of survival in the jungles of Guam and Lubang Island. Onoda's claim that the Japanese society remembered "the end of the war," but not "Japan's defeat" is noteworthy, for it illuminates a key logic that postwar Japan relied on in the 1970s to face its past. Now that the last soldier had returned, the war really ended, and because it ended completely, both Yokoi and Onoda were soon forgotten. The return of Yokoi and Onoda, however, caused a different reaction among the families of fallen soldiers and those soldiers who had been repatriated to Japan before Yokoi and Onoda: Yokoi and Onoda should have committed suicide for the sake of all the soldiers who died for the emperor. To the families of fallen soldiers and the ex-servicemen, Yokoi and Onoda brought home only shame.

Throughout the first three decades of the postwar era, the violence committed by Japanese soldiers in Asia, and the complicity of the Japanese people in the violence, were largely forgotten. Indeed, this amnesia—that is, the attempt to push the dark times of war into the past and to sever its relationship with the living reality of the nation's economic reconstruction—seems to have been sealed since the time the emperor uttered those words of unconditional surrender to the Allied Forces on August 15, 1945. This is why, even as early as January 1946, the sudden return of Noda reminded the people of his home village of the period they desperately wanted to leave behind. Noda's reappearance brought back the memory of the villagers' complicity in the war. Their participation in Noda's funeral as the emperor's martyr even before the war ended was only telling of the experiences that they were so eager to forget.

This amnesia about the past was also related to another cultural strategy that postwar Japan engendered while dealing with the history of the war: the discourse of suffering. According to this strategy, the Japanese people, save for a handful of high-ranking military officers and politicians who had either passed away or been executed, were all victims of the war. Indeed, even the emperor presented himself as one such sufferer, for he claimed that he suffered most because of the suffering of his subjects. However, the question posed to Japanese society, and later to the returned soldiers themselves, was how to fit ex-servicemen into the discourse of suffering. Eventually, it was their suffering *after* Japan's defeat that mattered. Japanese society thus condoned the handsome pensions handed out to former soldiers by the government, and soldiers themselves began emphasizing their contributions, not to the war that Japan waged and lost, but to Japan's postwar economic recovery. Put in another way, the perpetrators of violence soon became so-called victims of discrimination in their own society, and later they became powerful lobbyists with the conservative government. In this way, society ceased to question the millions of deaths among Japan's former enemies.

When, then, did the former soldiers of the Japanese Imperial Army begin openly recounting what Hemingway called "atrocious stories"? Not until the early 1990s. In this fairly late development, the so-called red repatriates played a major role. For example, about 1,100 of those ex-servicemen, who were once POWs and war criminals in the Soviet Union and China, formed an organization called Chūgoku kikansha renraku kai (or Chū-ki-ren, the Network of the Returnees from China) in 1957. Although it was disbanded at the time of China's Cultural Revolution in 1966, due in part to the worsening relations between the Chinese and the Japanese Communist Parties, it was revived in 1986 and survived until 2002. Two others were Nic-Chū yūkō moto gunjin no kai (the Japan-China Friendship Society of Former Soldiers), founded in 1961, and Fusen heishi no kai (the Association of Soldiers Who Shall Never Fight) established in 1988. In the late 1980s and 1990s, members of these three organizations devoted much of their time to speaking out about the violence that they had committed against the people of Asia. But in 2008, when the leaders of these groups were invited for an interview by the editors of a progressive journal, *Sekai* (The world), they all lamented that there were decreasing opportunities to do so in Japan (Takahashi, Kaneko, and Inokuma 2008).

I do not argue, however, that their efforts were in vain. Since the late 1980s, their voices have certainly diversified the opinions of Japanese society, including those among state leaders. In 1995, Japan's prime minister then went so far as to make an official apology to the "neighboring countries of Asia," using such words as "During a certain period in the not too distant past, Japan, following a mistaken national policy, advanced along the road to war, only to ensnare the Japanese people in a fateful crisis, and, through its colonial rule and aggression, caused tremendous damage and suffering to the people of many countries, particularly to those of Asian nations."[28] Nonetheless, this apology has since been radically shortened and become an apology solely for "tremendous damage and suffering to the people of many countries, particularly those of Asian nations." Such a standardized text used by every succeeding prime minister since 1995 has little to do with history in terms of clarifying what happened to whom, when, and where. As Alexis Dudden has persuasively argued, it seems to have been co-opted by state leaders in order to make national apologizing work toward strengthening the state. Furthermore, the official apology has merely helped generate and spark an unstable presence in East Asia (Dudden 2008, chapter 2). After all, this official apology is today associated with a significant number of high-ranking politicians, bureaucrats, and conservative intellectuals who otherwise refuse to acknowledge Japan's perpetration of violence during the war. Of course, apologies, whether offered by emperors, prime ministers, or ordinary citizens of Japan, should not have so easily placated victims of the war. This idea gets further complicated when the perpetrators of violence insist on their own victimhood.

Does this mean, then, that there is a better time to apologize? Did the Japanese political leaders apologize to the victims of Japan's aggression in Asia at the right time? In the same manner, is there the right time for a Japanese soldier to return home? Is that time over or is it still to come? I have no answers to these questions. Yet by examining the history of delayed returns among former Japanese servicemen, we can understand much about the changing meanings and practices of patriotism and nationalism in postwar Japan. This process not only dates back to the time of Japan's surrender, when these soldiers, officially at least, began to return home, but also continues to this day.

Notes

1. The chapter is not able to deal with all the soldiers in Japan's Imperial Army. As the people of the Japanese empire were also considered to be the Japanese emperor's subjects during wartime, some of them were forced to join the Japanese military. This included a large number of Korean and Chinese (including Taiwanese) soldiers. After Japan's defeat, they too tried to return home but encountered difficulties due to the postwar political conditions in Asia. They often ended up returning not to their homes but somewhere else in the Far East such as Sakhalin. In addition, their returns were almost always delayed for months and years.

2. I note, however, that Arjun Appadurai, as a prelude to his discussion on the glob-

alization of patriotism, writes about the change in meaning of the term over the divide of 1945, two years before India's independence from Britain. Before 1945, his father served an expatriate of the Indian nationalist Subhas Chandra Bose, who split with Gandhi and Nehru and gained support from the Japanese military. Appadurai's father was a "patriot," yet when he returned to India after Japan's defeat, he became nothing but a "pariah patriot" due to Bose's position against the nonviolence advocated by Gandhi and the Fabian Anglophilia of Nehru (1993, 413).

3. The "fifteen-year" of the Fifteen-Year War refers to the period between the Manchurian Incident of 1931 and Japan's defeat against the Allied Forces in 1945.

4. Here, by citing a passage from the book by Frank Biess, *Homecomings: Returning POWs and the Legacies of Defeat in Postwar Germany* (2006), I made an analogy between the Japanese and the German soldiers in the postwar era.

5. E. Herbert Norman was born in Japan to Canadian Methodist missionaries and studied at Victoria College of the University of Toronto, Cambridge University, and Harvard University, from which he received a doctorate in 1940. Except for the three years between 1942 and 1945 when Canada entered the war against Japan, Norman lived in Japan as a Canadian diplomat while continuing to pursue his academic interests in modern Japanese history. In the 1950s, however, he became one of the unlikely suspects of McCarthyism in the United States. This eventually led to his virtual diplomatic exile in New Zealand and Egypt and his death by suicide in Cairo in April of 1957. See Norman's biography posted by the University of Victoria at http://web.uvic .ca/ehnorman/Pages/Biography.html (accessed January 25, 2013).

6. "Taishō democracy" refers to the period between the two world wars. This was a period when (male) citizens, energized by the post–First World War economic boom, were allowed to express their political views to a certain extent. John Dower describes Taishō democracy as a period in which "deviance was tested against the polestars of respect for the emperor and for private property" (1979, 306).

7. The Imperial Diet, established in 1890, is the direct predecessor of the present Diet in postwar Japan. Like the present Diet, the Imperial Diet was also a bicameral institution that consisted of a House of Peers and a House of Representatives. Unlike the present Diet, however, the power of legislation was vested in the emperor because the cabinet was responsible to the emperor rather than to the Imperial Diet (see Baerwald 1983, 94).

8. Among the Japanese citizens who tried to settle in northeast China (Manchuria) as farmers, a story such as Kenji's was not uncommon. However, those who recounted such stories were not male but female Japanese citizens. Of the total of about 388,000 Japanese farmers who migrated to Manchuria after 1932, when Japan built its puppet state of Manchukuo, the men among them became targets of the Japanese army's mobilization toward the end of the war. For this reason, their wives and children were left to themselves, and many of them married local men to survive the Soviet invasion of Manchuria and the end of Japanese empire. These women were called Chūgoku zanryū fujin (the women who had been left behind in China) in postwar Japan. After the normalization of diplomatic ties between Japan and the People's Republic of China in 1972, these women began to return home with their Chinese husbands. By then, their Japanese husbands had already remarried (see Tamanoi 2009). While these women

were noncombatants, their stories, like Kenji's, were the product of war and migration. These events had transformed the allegiance of the returnees toward their home, often to the point of losing, usually by force, their faithfulness to their partners.

9. According to the survey conducted in Hiroshima in 1949, only thirty-four among the group of one hundred red repatriates led more or less stable lives (with small but regular income), while twenty-seven of the same group received state welfare; thirty-five of these one hundred repatriates were unemployed because they were viewed as Communists, and the bottom ten on the income scale relied on the wages of their wives, who worked as day laborers or domestic maids (Kōsei-shō 2000b, 45). The source of their hardship is obvious: the societal perception of them as carriers of improper ideology.

10. Hayashi Fumiko was a poet and writer who was best known for being the author of *Hōrōki* [Journal of a vagabond] (1935), her first novel. A wanderer since her childhood, she continually traveled after her fame had been established and visited Europe, China, Manchuria, and Southeast Asia as a reporter. In her numerous works, Hayashi "repeatedly and compassionately [captured] the dark misery of war, of rootless women, or of couples tortured by stale marriages" (Selden 1983, 116).

11. A notable exception was the so-called *shōi gunjin* (the crippled and maimed veterans). They were included in the category of "the disabled (due to nonmilitary reasons)" and continued to receive benefits for treatment of their physical conditions and for maintenance of their daily lives.

12. On the notion of victims, Jean-François Lyotard argues, "It is in the nature of a victim not to be able to prove that one has been done a wrong. A plaintiff is someone who has incurred damages and who disposes of the means to prove it. One becomes a victim if one loses these means" (Lyotard 1988, 8; see also Das 1995, 174). In other words, the former soldiers of Japan's army became plaintiffs and ceased to be the victims.

13. The evening edition of *Asahi Shinbun* (Asahi Newspaper), published on January 25, 1972, reported that in 1944 the Japanese Imperial Army reported to Yokoi's family that he died in the battle against the United States on September 30 of that year.

14. See *Asahi Shinbun* (Asahi Newspaper), evening edition, January 25, 1972; morning edition, January 26, 1972; morning edition, January 27, 1972; and morning edition, January 29, 1972; my translations.

15. See *Asahi Shinbun* (Asahi Newspaper), evening edition, January 25, 1972; morning edition, January 26, 1972; and evening edition, January 26, 1972; my translations.

16. See *Asahi Shinbun* (Asahi Newspaper), morning edition, January 25, 1972, my translation.

17. See *Asahi Shinbun* (Asahi Newspaper), morning edition, January 27, 1972, my translation. This letter writer seems to believe that because of the lateness of his return, he would receive far less compensation from the government in comparison to those who returned to Japan immediately after Japan's capitulation.

18. See *Asahi Shinbun* (Asahi Newspaper), evening edition, January 27, 1972; my translation.

19. See *Asahi Shinbun* (Asahi Newspaper), morning edition, January 29, 1972; my translation.

20. Ibid.

21. See *Asahi Shinbun* (Asahi Newspaper), morning edition, January 27, 1972; my translation.

22. See *Asahi Shinbun* (Asahi Newspaper), morning edition, January 26, 1972; my translation.

23. See *Asahi Shinbun* (Asahi Newspaper), morning edition, January 27, 1972; my translation.

24. See *Asahi Shinbun* (Asahi Newspaper), evening edition, January 25, 1972; my translation.

25. Ibid.

26. This term, *sabaibaru hyôronka*, has appeared on numeous internet sites on Yokoi Shōichi since 1972. While many such sites are no longer available, the two sites that I could access recently are: "guambeach.com" at http://guambeach.com/history-3.html (accessed January 27, 2013) and "musinan" at http://geocities.jp/urbanivjp/musinan .html (accessed January 27, 2013).

27. Toward the end of 1974, another soldier was discovered in Indonesia. This ex-soldier, whose Japanese name was Nakamura Teruo, was from Taiwan: he served the Japanese army as a civilian employee due to his status as a colonial subject. In his case, the Japanese government returned him to Taiwan, not Japan, without drawing any attention from the Japanese media (see Kawasaki 2003).

28. Quoted from "Statement by Prime Minister Tomiichi Murayama 'On the occasion of the 50th anniversary of the war's end' 15 August 1995" at http://www.mofa .go.jp/announce/press/pm/murayama/9508.html (accessed January 25, 2013). Translated by the office of the Ministry of Foreign Affairs of Japan.

Guiqiao as Political Subjects in the Making of the People's Republic of China, 1949–1979

⌃ WANG CANGBAI

The 1979 movie *Haiwai chizi* (Red sons overseas) was one of the first in the People's Republic of China (PRC) to include returnees from overseas, a hitherto marginal political subject, in representations of nationalism in popular arts.[1] The protagonist, Huang Sihua (in Chinese, *si* means "missing" and *hua* refers simultaneously to Chinese "nation", "culture", and "ancestral origin"), is the China-born daughter of patriotic parents working and living in one of the Overseas Chinese farms (*huaqiao nongchang*) established by the PRC government exclusively for post-1949 returnees.[2] Sihua passes the examinations for admission to a cultural troupe of the People's Liberation Army (PLA) with outstanding scores,[3] but she is rejected because of the overseas connections of her family as noted in her personnel dossier (*dan'gan*).[4] A party cadre, Han Shan, is sent to the farm to conduct a political investigation (*zhengzhi shencha*) of her family.[5] It transpires that both her parents, Huang Dechen and Lin Biyun, were born in Southeast Asia.[6] They had met during a fundraising campaign for China's anti-Japanese war effort, when Dechen saved Biyun from attempted rape by Western sailors (rather obviously symbolizing the Chinese standing up to the humiliation of the motherland by Western imperialist powers). With the news of the PRC's founding, Dechen and Biyun left for China without any hesitation, leaving their baby son Siguo (again, *si* is "missing," and *guo* could be interpreted as "homeland," "territory," and "nation") behind with relatives. Although Dechen and Biyun worked hard in the *huaqiao* farm, where Sihua was born, and devoted themselves wholeheartedly to the socialist project, their overseas background subjected them to suspicion and discrimination. In the late 1970s, when the PRC loosened its controls over the exit of returnees and visits of Overseas Chinese, Siguo, their now grown-up son, comes to visit and asks his sister to join him overseas so that she might get a better education and have a better life. But Sihua turns down his offer because of her undiminished love for China. Happily, all wrongdoings against returnees are rectified after the Cultural Revolution (1966–76). Sihua becomes a professional singer and the film comes to a rousing close with her passionate stage performance of "I Love You, China."

The film's depiction of how Overseas Chinese returnees were perceived and categorized in the period conventionally called Mao's era (1949–79) highlights the complex relations between ethnicity, culture, territory, and politics in the socialist nation-building process. Without presuming European inspirations, the dynamics and complicities in making the modern Chinese nation (and nationalism) have been variously traced to the cohesions as well as cleavages between political nationalism, Han chauvinism, a (historical) Chinese ethnic identity, and sentiments of cultural superiority rooted in narratives of an uninterrupted and undivided Chinese civilization (Townsend 1996, 28). As Prasenjit Duara proposed, Chinese national identity should be viewed "as founded upon fluid relationships; it thus both resembles and is interchangeable with other political identities. . . . What we call nationalism is more appropriately a *relationship* between a constantly changing Self and Other, rather than a pristine subject gathering self-awareness in a manner similar to the evolution of a species" (1996, 31, 39).

Along a similar line, John Fitzgerald (1996, 57) rightly identifies disjuncture in the "distinctive and often competing definitions of the nation" in successive twentieth-century Chinese state formations, advocated respectively by Confucian reformers, liberal republicans, Nationalist revolutionaries, and then Communists, which exclusively associated the national self with a distinctive Chinese civilization, a body of citizens, a Chinese race (*zu* or *minzu*),[7] and social class. Therefore, in modern Chinese nationalism, Fitzgerald argues, "nation is an essentially-contested concept in the political discourse concerned with the assertion of state unity, sovereignty and independence within the international state system," which invites close investigation of the "process of representation, or nation-defining, in state-building" (58, 59). Thus, in understanding the PRC's nation-building process, we need to move away from the predominant conceptualization that sees the nation-state as a territorialized entity autonomously emerging from modernization. We should instead pay special attention to the fluid and complex interactions between multilayered, historically formed social forces both within and beyond the Chinese border (Duara 1995, 2008), and the decisive role that the state played in making a nation from above. Migration and return, driven by various motivations and assigned different meanings, as metaphorized by the highly symbolic and ambiguous names of the protagonists of *Haiwai chizi*, provide a critical lens for discerning the multifaceted social and political processes of making the new political order in the mid-twentieth century.

Bearing these historical and theoretical concerns in mind, this chapter explores how Overseas Chinese returnees were mobilized, categorized, supervised, and controlled by the party-state for nation-building purposes in the period from 1949 to 1979. In the constant political struggle to define the socialist nation *and* the criteria for membership in the category of *renmin* (the people), Overseas Chinese returnees were constituted as a political Other. Central to this were *the routine practices of state power* in defining the constituents of the nation. As Thomas Hansen and Finn Stepputat point out, sovereignty "needs to be performed and reiterated on a daily basis in order to be effective and to form the basic referent of the state," and the performance of sovereign power "can be spectacular and public, secret and menacing, and also can appear as scientific/technical rationalities of management and punishment of bodies" (2005, 7, 3). Specifically, I focus on the invention of the policy category *guiqiao*, which refers to returnees who were born and had resided overseas, in the politics of making a class-based rather than race-based Chinese nation. Even though the PRC remains a party-state, state policies in the post-1979 reform era no longer ideologically discriminate between *renmin* as the fundament of the nation and contemporary waves of educated returnees, mostly from the West. In a seeming historical reversal, the returnees are accepted as returning nationals within a more "cultural" definition of belonging to the Chinese nation. Return migration to China in the period under this study, however, took place in politically and ideologically volatile contexts that had no historical precedence.

This chapter is based on extensive studies of governmental documents, official publications on Overseas Chinese affairs, and newspaper and journal articles on Chinese returnees published in both mainland China and Hong Kong. Archival sources are complemented by oral history interviews with returnees, who returned to China from Indonesia in the 1950s and 1960s but moved to Hong Kong in the 1970s and 1980s. I conducted these interviews from 1999 to 2003 as part of a larger project on the identities of Indonesian Chinese in Hong Kong (see Wang C. 2006; Wang and Wong 2007).

Return Migration and Nationalism in Historical Context

Guiqiao comprised but one of the many streams of return migration in modern Chinese history, each of which resulted from a complex combination of pull and push factors in a specific context. From a pull-factor perspective, the return of Overseas Chinese in different periods was closely related to the ways China was imagined and defined in that particular historical context. During much of the imperial Manchu Qing dynasty, particularly between 1680 and the 1840s, the Chinese polity was positioned within the concept of *tianxia* (all under heaven), "a globalistic idea of how to structure the world" (Meissner 2003, 205), which assumed the superiority of Chinese culture over the cultures of outside population. With this culturalist cosmology, the idea of racial difference, though traceable to an ancient China according to some scholars (e.g., Dikotter 1990), was subsumed by cultural affiliation. The Manchu leaders, with a barbarian origin in the eyes of Ming loyalists, legitimated their rule through emphasizing Confucianism as the ruling principle and established a unified multiethnic empire referred to as both Da Qing Guo (Qing empire) and Zhongguo (Central State) (Barabantseva 2011, 20). Until the mid-nineteenth century, migrating abroad was seen as an unforgivable betrayal to the heavenly imperial authority — the representative of superior Chinese civilization — and thus prohibited by the Qing court; emigration was difficult and returning was fraught with the danger of a death sentence (Zhuang 1989).

After the defeat in the Opium Wars, the Qing court was forced to allow subjects to travel to the European colonies in Southeast Asia to meet the increasing demand of labor, mostly in mines and cash-crop plantations, as a result of European expansion (Wang G. 1992, 25). This marked the beginning of large-scale outflow of Chinese and catalyzed constant waves of out-migration and return migration. More importantly, Western penetration gave rise to a modern, racially based conception of the nation-state, which redefined the relation between China and Overseas Chinese and gave new meanings to return. In confronting Western imperialist oppression in the wake of the 1840 Opium War, Chinese intellectuals developed the concept of *minzu*, from the Japanese term *minzoku*, created by the Meiji-era Japanese modernizers to refer to "nation" in Western works (Li Y. 1971, 97). However, the term *minzu* in Chinese could simultaneously refer to people, clan, and race. Thus the term *zhonghua minzu* (Chinese nation) was initially defined by Sun Yat-sen, the founder of the Republic of China, to construct a single unified race comprising the majority Han centered in north China since the Xia dynasty (c. 2100–1600 BCE).[8] By this definition, "*Hua, Xia,* or Han could be used interchangeably to mean China the nation-state, Chinese the race (or tribe), and China the geographic location" (Wu 1991, 161). This ambiguous, all-embracing notion aimed at breaking entrenched linguistic and regional divisions was deliberately created by Sun in his move to overthrow the barbarian (non-Han) Qing ruler.[9] "The overriding purpose of the rhetoric is clear: a call for the unity of the Chinese nation based on a common charter of descent" in opposition to insignificant minorities and Western invasions (Gladney 1998, 116). Thus, from its inception, modern Chinese nationalism "displayed a strong ethnic, even xenophobic, strain in opposing imperialism and Manchu rule" (Townsend 1996, 16).

This racially defined and deterritorialized conception of the nation naturally included the Overseas Chinese. Compelled by a racialized notion of the Chinese nation and the need to resist humiliation by Western imperialism, Overseas Chinese became actively involved in China's anti-imperialist movements beginning in the late nineteenth century. They were the backbone of the anti-Qing military rebellions led by Sun, who hailed Overseas Chinese as "the mother of the (republic) revolution" (Hong 1989, 147) and of the later 1911 revolution. The Japanese invasion in the early 1930s and especially in 1937 dramatically aggravated the broadly based, geographically dispersed but China-centric sense of Chinese solidarity. More than forty thousand Overseas Chinese returned, mostly from Southeast Asia, during the anti-Japanese war. They were found in the Communist headquarters (Yan'an) and the Nationalist capital (Chongqing), as well as battlefronts across China. The Overseas Chinese worked as translators, engineers, doctors, and nurses behind the enemy lines, or as battle plane pilots, ground army soldiers, and guerrillas fighting alongside their local compatriots (Huang, Zhao, and Cong 1995).

The founding of the PRC in 1949 marked the climax of the century-long return migration of Overseas Chinese. In the early years of the PRC when it was still in the presocialist stage of New Democracy, the Chinese Communist Party (CCP) employed moderate and flexible policies to mobilize various forces with diverse social, economic, and ethnic affiliations to consolidate the new regime. Under this circumstance, Overseas Chinese were seen as a much-needed source of manpower and capital for restoring and rebuilding the war-torn national economy and a unique force in building friendly relations between the new republic and their host countries. Representatives of Overseas Chinese were invited to attend the first National People's Political Consultative Conference, held in 1949, and the first National People's Congress (NPC), held in 1954. In addition, the first constitution of the PRC issued in 1954 claimed, in the ninth chapter, regarding citizens' rights and duties, that the PRC government would protect the proper rights and interests of Overseas Chinese. Clearly, the Communists steadily followed the ethno-nationalist principle as defined and practiced by the previous Republican leadership, and through a set of policies termed by Elena Barabantseva (2011, 46) as "ethnic internationalism" claimed an extraterritorial commitment of Overseas Chinese to Socialist China. Many of my returnee interviewees revealed that their migration to China had been heavily influenced, though indirectly, by the call of the underground CCP.[10] This policy continued up to the mid-1950s, when it became obvious that further attempts of mobilization could possibly harm China's diplomatic relationship with Southeast Asian countries, where the majority of Overseas Chinese resided, and endanger international recognition of the new China. In 1952 the CCP canceled its overseas extension and recalled overseas party members (Zheng 2005, 295). Three years later, the Chinese government officially discarded the policy of dual citizenship in Indonesia and then in all foreign countries, which encouraged Overseas Chinese to settle down where they were and be naturalized to host societies. However, the leftists remained dominant in Chinese embassies and the influence of the CCP in Overseas Chinese communities continued to the early 1960s (Zheng 2005, 289–97). The high-rising nationalist sentiment was vividly demonstrated in a poem titled "Beijing de shengyin" (Voice of Beijing) published in a Jakarta-based Chinese newspaper *Zhongcheng Bao* (Loyalty Newspaper) (May 10, 1964; my translation):

Sitting by the radio,
from where comes the voice of Beijing.
My heart throbs with joy, and
light flashes in front of my eyes.

I hear the bugle calling for battle, and
acclaim of victory.
The storm of revolution encourages me, and
the trend of the times propels me to forge ahead.

Following the "calling for battle" and the "storm of revolution," about 250,000 Chinese from Southeast Asia, mostly students and teachers, migrated to the PRC in the early and mid-1950s (Godley 1989). At the same time, some 2,500 Chinese scholars and students, together with their families, returned from the West and Japan to the new China (Li T. 2000). The return migration from Southeast Asia continued after the mid-1950s, but for more complicated reasons. While nationalist sentiments continued to be a major force behind the return of young students, many others, including shopkeepers, traders, and laborers, were forced to join the waves of return, usually with their entire families, due to the intensified racial tensions and riots in some Southeast Asian countries, especially Indonesia.[11] In the period between 1960 and 1966, around 200,000 Chinese, many of whom were received by the Chinese government as refugees, returned from Indonesia and some other Southeast Asian countries (see Coppel 1983; Mackie 1976). In the late 1970s, a further wave of about 160,000 Chinese refugees from Vietnam moved to China at the end of U.S. war in Vietnam, driven by the persecution and expulsion policies of the Vietnam government (Huang X. 2005, 56).

It is estimated that about one million Overseas Chinese returned to Mao's China in different periods, of which those from Indonesia constituted the largest group.[12] These returnees ended up in different places in China. Initially, the majority settled in the coastal provinces in southern China, including Guangdong, Fujian, and Guangxi, which were the traditional sending areas and thus preferred by returnees and the government.[13] The continuous and large influx of return migration in the 1960s forced the government to turn to a more centralized way of settlement. Except for a small percentage of returnees who were wealthy enough to invest in China, or who had the required skills or tertiary qualifications and were settled in cities, the rest were centrally allocated to designated rural areas.

The experience of returnees in the post-1949 China was qualitatively different from any before or since. Except for the early years of the PRC, Mao's China was essentially imagined as a "class nation" and membership was defined exclusively by class status (J. Fitzgerald 1996, 59). As James Townsend points out: "Class-based definitions of the 'people' and recurring movements of class struggle divided the Chinese nation up to 1979, in effect revoking the citizenship of millions of its members by labeling them as enemy classes, devoid of political rights" (1996, 19). Because of the PRC's primary concern with class relations in its nation-building project, returnees—once unquestionably "one of us"—were now a classed Other. As the radicalization of the politics within the PRC and the deepening of the Cold War cut off China from the outside world and put a halt to voluntary return migration and out-migration, state policy decisively shifted toward transforming or rehabilitating returnees into acceptable political subjects within the revolutionary party-state.

The Invention of Guiqiao as a Classed Other

Whereas Sun Yat-sen had propounded the notion of the Han as the subject of national salvation from Manchu degradation and Western encroachment (Gladney 1998, 117–18), Mao Zedong's continuation of the nationalist project employed the concept renmin (the people) to mobilize different linguistic and regional groups into an overarching whole, standing in opposition to Western imperialists as well as domestic antirevolutionary classes. The constituents of renmin were not fixed but dependent on which social classes the Communist Party wanted (or needed) to rally. By the late 1950s, when CCP announced that the transformation from New Democracy to Socialism had been completed in China and the dictatorship of the proletariat had replaced democratic dictatorship, the so-called exploitative social classes (landlords, urban petty bourgeoisie, national bourgeoisie, and bureaucrat bourgeoisie), once tolerated under the democratic dictatorship, were eliminated. Thereafter renmin referred strictly to peasants and workers, the majority working classes. To maintain the purity of renmin and strengthen the solidity of the people's republic, continuous class struggle against surviving reactionary elements became an imperative. It fell on the party to identify, supervise, and control suspicious or enemy elements within the Chinese population, which in practical terms was tantamount to disenfranchising them of political rights.

It was in this context that realizing a purified class-based nationhood soon became the central mission of the special policy domain *qiaowu* (Overseas Chinese affairs) that was created shortly after the founding of the PRC. As the Cold War had put a freeze on direct dealings with populations overseas, it was their relatives and dependents residing in China and the returnees—the "domestic Overseas Chinese" (S. Fitzgerald 1972, 52)—who were the core subjects of these policies during the Mao era. The two major pillars of *qiaowu*, the Zhongyang Qiaowei (State Commission of Overseas Chinese Affairs; hereafter State Commission), established in 1949, and the Zhongguo Qiaolian (All-China Federation of Returned Overseas Chinese; hereafter All-China Federation), established in 1956, both set up branches at the provincial and municipal levels.[14] The State Commission's flagship propaganda newsletter, *Qiaowu Bao* (Qiaowu News; hereafter QWB), launched in 1956 and disseminated party-state policies concerning returnees.[15]

Under preceding Chinese imperial and Republican administrations, return migrants and Chinese populations overseas had been lumped together generally as *huaqiao* or *qiaomin*, both terms simply meaning "Overseas Chinese"; there had been no official distinction between the returned and nonreturned Overseas Chinese. Even in the early years after the establishment of the PRC in 1949, the term *guiqiao* (returned Overseas Chinese) was not an officially defined category differentiated from *huaqiao* (Overseas Chinese). This can be seen from the naming of the representatives of the first National People's Political Consultative Conference, in which Overseas Chinese (including both returned and nonreturned Overseas Chinese) were counted as one of the participating units, which was named "overseas *huaqiao* democratic personages" (later changed into "foreign democratic personages") (Zhonguo Renmin Zhengzhi Xieshang Huiyi Quanguo Weiyuan Hui Wenshi Ziliao Yanjiu Weiyuanhui 1994). Similarly, in the first NPC, the term *huaqiao* was still applied to categorize representatives of Overseas Chinese if they had returned for residence or still lived abroad (Quanguo Renda Changweihui Bangongshi 1987; Quanguo Renda Neiwu Sifa Weiyuanhui Bangongshi 1992). This occurred for the first time when, to further the establishment of the *qiaowu* system, the party-state of the PRC invented a separate category for returnees. The term *guiqiao*, referring to any Overseas Chinese who had returned to China, first appeared in a 1957 document titled "Guanyu *huaqiao, qiaojuan, guiqiao* and *guiqiao xuesheng* de shenfen jieshi" (Explanations for the statuses of Overseas Chinese, dependents of Overseas Chinese, returned Overseas Chinese and returned Overseas Chinese Students),[16] issued by the State Commission to distinguish between different categories of Overseas Chinese for policy purposes (Lu and Quan 2001, 2).

The semantics of the term are pertinent. In Chinese, the word *gui* (return) has meanings beyond spatial movements, signifying a renewing or conversion of allegiance after departing or deviating from orthodoxy.[17] The word *qiao* (sojourner) was never a neutral term in official discourse but had connotations of being outcast or exiled, commonly referring to dissenters and potential threats to stability and authority. In a nutshell, *guiqiao* as a category was created by the party-state to aid its nation-building purpose by emphasizing the returning of Overseas Chinese to a pledge of allegiance and obedience to the new party-state sovereignty (regardless of whether the *guiqiao* had even been to China before). As such, given a tainted past in Western capitalist and colonial societies, Overseas Chinese could not be considered members of *renmin*; instead they were were subjects for transformation.

The labeling and identification as *guiqiao*, once confirmed through various registration processes (*shenfen rending*), was a lifelong political marker recorded in returnees' personnel dossiers (*dan'gan*) and continually referred to by work-unit officials to investigate the political life of individuals; some provinces issued certificates (*guiqiao zheng*) to register and keep tabs on the returnees under their control (Lu and Quan 2001, 5). The party-state's justification for institutionalized policing of Overseas Chinese returnees (*guiqiao*), and their dependents (*qiaojuan*) in China, was spelled out in a 1958 *QWB* editorial:

> Considering the fact that most *guiqiao* come from capitalist countries and were influenced by bourgeois ideology, they must go through transformation. As many *qiaojuan* have been living on remittances and have never engaged in manual labor, they must be remolded into working people living on their own labor; as they have relatives overseas, they must be under the continuous influence of capitalist thoughts. Therefore, the transformation of *guiqiao* and *qiaojuan* is long lasting and arduous. (Benkan Bianjibu 1958; my translation)

Transforming Guiqiao into "New Socialist Persons"

The policy matrix put in place for transforming the *guiqiao* into national-ist *renmin* consisted of both hard and soft and negative and positive mea-sures. Hard measures included participation in organized political studies and campaigns and institutional arrangements that determined their ma-terial lives. Soft measures referred to some privileges in daily lives and politicized leisure activities, such as the specially organized film receptions or celebration parties for the returnees and their families during major public holidays, hosted by the national and provincial chapters of the All-China Federation. Incentives aimed at eliciting the returnees' loyalties in-cluded the awarding of privileges and honors, while negative sanctions were meted out to those deemed to be hanging on to bourgeois outlooks. A recurring political task effected through *qiaowu* institutions was to train cadres to understand "how to balance privilege against participation, free-dom against control, and persuasion against force" (S. Fitzgerald 1972, 20). Acquiescence to party-state controls was reinforced through constant oscillation in the application of these measures.

HONORS AND PRIVILEGES

In the 1950s, when the newly founded PRC was in urgent need of skilled manpower and remittances from Overseas Chinese, the return of Overseas Chinese was actively encouraged and honored. Returning to the home-land was regarded as exemplary patriotic behavior. Numerous articles with such titles as "Warm Welcome to Motherland's Great Children" and "Motherland Is a Big Warm Family" in mainstream newspapers reported on the devotion of Overseas Chinese returning to the motherland (see Benkan Bianjibu 1966; Chen G. 1960). As a way of honoring Overseas Chi-nese, elites and respectable representatives selected from Overseas Chi-nese communities were appointed to leading positions within *qiaowu* in-stitutions. For example, Tan Kah Kee, a Fujian-born Chinese tycoon from Singapore, was appointed the first chairman of the All-China Federation, and Zhuang Xiquan, a *guiqiao* elite from Malaya, was appointed vice chair-man. Other elite figures were politically honored as *renda daibiao* (repre-sentatives of the People's Congress) or as *zhengxie weiyuan* (members of Political Consultative Conferences) at the national or local level.

During the 1950s and early 1960s, the returnees as a whole benefited from a *qiaowu* policy that was briefly summarized as "Yishi tongren, shi-dang zhaogu" (to treat equally but make appropriate preferential arrangements). This policy, seeming to contain a "non-antagonistic contradiction" (S. Fitzgerald 1972, 54), meant that returnees were asked to participate in Socialist construction together with the *renmin* in the common pursuit of a class-based new Chinese nation, but, at the same time, returnees were granted exemptions from participating in political and social movements and permitted a number of daily-life privileges, including receiving remittances, which brought precious foreign currency into the economy when the PRC was cut off from the outside world. In return, *guiqiao* were allotted extra rations (*qiaohui quan*) for daily goods, such as certain amounts of sugar and butter, and even luxury items, such as bicycles and watches at special shops. In the 1950s, *guiqiao* were also encouraged to establish private businesses, build their own houses, and purchase private properties. So-called *huaqiao cun* (Overseas Chinese villages) in Guangzhou, Xiamen, and Beijing were districts congregated with quality private apartments and houses of wealthy returnees or *guiqiao* elites allowed to live there. They were thus privileged suspects. Such preferential treatment, ostensibly to help *guiqiao* adjust to their new lives in China, served the party-state agenda. A QWB editorial clarifies this: "It is incorrect to break away from the general principle of socialist construction and the whole Chinese people to emphasize the preferential treatments toward *guiqiao* and *qiao-juan*. . . . To give them preferential treatments was for the purpose of fully mobilizing their initiatives" (Benkan Bianjibu 1958; my translation).

HUAQIAO FARMS AS POLITICAL SPACE

Returnees to the PRC before 1979 did not expect that they would have little choice in where and how to live. Official policy guidelines were "*anji anzhi*" (to settle the returnees in their places of origin, my translation).[18] However, for the considerable numbers who had lost connections with home and ancestral villages, particularly those from families settled overseas for a few generations, "place of origin" might as well be anywhere that the government decided. As a result, except for returning students who arrived in the 1950s and were lucky enough to find jobs in cities after graduation from university, the large majority of *guiqiao*, particularly those who arrived in the 1960s and 1970s, were placed in the specially established *huaqiao* farms, mostly located in remote mountain areas of Guangdong, Fujian, and Guangxi provinces, which were sparsely populated because of barren land and inconvenient transportation.

Before 1960 there were only eight *huaqiao* farms settled by 11,112 returnees, excluding those returnees who settled with their relatives in their hometowns (Benkan Bianjibu 1959). The sudden influx of Chinese immigrants from Indonesia in 1960 and after 1966 prompted the government to centralize all new settlements in farms. In 1960 alone, between sixty thousand and seventy thousand returnees, out of more than ninety thousand nationwide, were assigned to *huaqiao* farms. The number of *huaqiao* farms increased to thirty-two within a year (Benkan Bianjibu 1962; Fang 1961). It was not uncommon for a whole ship of returnees to be allocated to the same farm, regardless of their putative places of origin. By 1978 there were forty-one *huaqiao* farms, and an additional forty were built to receive the influx of returnees from Vietnam after 1978. According to an official figure, there were eighty-six *huaqiao* farms inhabited by about 210,000 returnees in 1985 (Huang X. 2005, 69).

The *huaqiao* farms were more than places for living and working; they were also invented space for "settling, educating, transforming and organizing *guiqiao* for their participation in socialist construction." It was thus "not just an economic task to manage the farms well"; it was also "a political undertaking" (Fang and Feng 2001, 255).[19] Initially, the farms were under the State Commission's charge, with daily management overseen by the provincial-level offices and county governments where the farms were located. With their rapidly increasing numbers, however, the central government transferred the responsibilities of local authorities to a specially created Farm Management Department within the State Commission in 1963. To ensure the success of its political agenda, the government pledged enormous investments to the infrastructure and agricultural productivity of *huaqiao* farms, together with provisions of financial subsidies, tax reductions, and exemptions in agricultural production. Working as de facto state employees, returnees received monthly salaries (albeit meager) and enjoyed welfare benefits that were not available to most rural populations, such as health care, children's education assistance, and pensions. Standing apart from the formal urban-rural structure, *huaqiao* farm settlements were administratively, socially, and politically separate from their neighboring villages (Li M. 2005, 165–71). But the strict control, bureaucratic misconduct, and frictions with local governments also created many problems. From the returnees' point of view, the farms were places where they suffered from social isolation, excessive political control, and material impoverishment during the Mao era (Li M. 2005; Naicang 2010).

Education was another policy domain where returnees were kept apart from the mainstream *renmin*, at once a privilege and a means of surveillance. Parallel to policies of concentrated settlement, the Chinese government determined that returnee students should be "received in a centralized manner, sent to different schools, and admitted with preference" (*jizhong jiedai, fensan ruxue, youxian luqu*) (Huang X. 2005, 49; my translation). Between 1950 and 1953, offices in Guangzhou that were specially set up registered an estimated nineteen thousand returned Overseas Chinese students and sent them to special *Huaqiao xuesheng buxi xuexiao* (Returned Overseas Chinese preparatory schools) managed by the State Commission (Huang X. 2005, 49). These schools were first set up in Beijing, Jimei, and Guangzhou (in 1950, 1953, and 1954, respectively). In 1960 there were as many as 3,500 students in the Beijing Huaqiao xuesheng buxi xuexiao (Beijing preparatory school for returned Overseas Chinese students); over the period 1950–66, 22,250 students had spent varying lengths of time studying there (Beijing Huawen Jiaoyu Zhongxin 2000, 29). To cope with the influx of Indonesian Chinese students in 1960, four more preparatory schools were set up in that year; they were in Shantou, Kunming, Nanning, and Wuhan (Zhou 1999, 100–101).

Returned students usually attended the preparatory schools for one to two years before being admitted to ordinary state universities or colleges. Those who did not pass the entrance examinations were allocated work in factories or farms. The preparatory-school curriculum included Chinese language and culture but was primarily aimed at the indoctrination of Marxist-Leninist theories and Mao's thoughts and at encouraging moral cultivation through pedagogy for the making of socialist new persons. In the radicalized politics of the Anti-rightist Movement (1957), the Great Leap Forward (1958), and the subsequent "Three Difficulties Years" (1959–61),[20] returned students spent most of their time attending political campaigns or farming in the rural areas. To accommodate the growing numbers of Overseas Chinese university-level students, the PRC government reopened Amoy University (1957) and Jinan University (1958) in Fujian and Guangdong, and in 1960 set up Huaiqao University in Quanzhou, Fujian.[21] These universities were administered directly by the State Commission and, along with the preparatory schools, served as a special educational channel for Overseas Chinese students.

Toward the late 1960s when China's domestic politics became increasingly radical, *qiaowu* policy turned harsh and preferential treatment was replaced by discrimination and even persecution during the Cultural Revolution (1966–76). Even in the 1950s, when the returnees and their relatives were generally treated favorably, returnees were often victims of political campaigns. In the land reform (1950–52) and Socialist transformation period (1953–56), for example, some were classified as *huaqiao dizhu* (Overseas Chinese landlords) and their lands and houses were confiscated. During the Anti-rightist Movement, many were labeled "rightist elements" and sent to labor camps in remote areas.[22] More broadly, these returnees' overseas connections became a political stigma that meant relegation to inferior sociopolitical positions and that precluded recruitment into key sections in the party-state apparatus, and into the ranks of the CCP and PLA (Gao 1956; Lu X. 1956).

Whenever domestic politics became radicalized, especially during the purifications of the Cultural Revolution, the returnees were frequently cast as the class enemies within and subjected to intense personal suspicion, denunciation, and persecution. Many people I interviewed recalled how their everyday habits, such as dressing and diet, were taken as evidence of their capitalist leanings and of being worshippers of things foreign. Their houses, remittances, and other private properties were confiscated, and mundane communications from relatives overseas became a liability and sometimes were regarded as a danger. The deputy head of the Zhongyang Wenge Xiaozu (Cultural Revolution Group), Chen Boda, went so far as to label the party-state-controlled *huaqiao* farms and villages as "the United Nations of enemy agents" (quoted in Godley 1989, 348). One of my interviewees put it in this way: "We *guiqiao* were the unwritten seventh bad element, after the landlords, rich peasants, criminals, counterrevolutionaries, rightists, and capital roaders."[23]

No accurate figures are available on how many returnees and their families were persecuted or imprisoned as spies or counterrevolutionaries during the Cultural Revolution. However, according to an official report by the director of the Office of Overseas Chinese Affairs of the State Council, Liao Hui (1982–1992), "in the Cultural Revolution, there were over 64,500 cases of 'wrongful accusation' against *guiqiao* and *qiaojuan* in China, 25,000,000 square meters of *guiqiao* and *qiaojuan*'s residences were taken, and 650,000 of *guiqiao* and *qiaojuan*'s dossiers had discrimination records" (Liao 1989; my translation).This hints at the type of persecution returnees endured, though the reality could have been far starker.

Overt state control, imposed segregation, discrimination, and persecution made returnees feel like "orphans at home" (*hainei guer*), as a returnee author described the *guiqiao*'s experience during the Cultural Revolution (Bai 1983, 22; my translation). In order to protect themselves, many returnees maintained distance from the mainstream society, and instead retreated to small circles of trusted friends and relatives who were often fellow *guiqiao*. The strong shared sense of alienation can be discerned from the high rate of marriages within the group. A survey of 359 returnees from Indonesia residing in Beijing found that about 50.4 percent of the respondents were married to other returnees (Huang J. 1999, 50). My own interviews revealed that a significant number of returnees also married mainlanders from similarly politically questionable or stigmatized backgrounds, such as landlord or urban bourgeois families.

What was most hurtful for the returnees was the discrimination faced by their descendants. A returnee from Indonesia in the early 1950s, who now lives in Hong Kong, recalled how miserable he felt on discovering that his China-born son was refused membership of Shaoxiandui (the League of Young Pioneers) at primary school because of his overseas connections. Another returnee from Indonesia in 1960, now a retired civil servant in Beijing, described his sadness when a friend, another Indonesian returnee from a Peranakan family and a renowned doctor at Beijing Tongren Hospital, decided to leave China in 1973 to spare his children any further political persecution after they had all been sent to the countryside when they were in middle school. Beginning in the early 1970s, when the Chinese government relaxed exit controls, large numbers of returnees began to leave for this very reason—to safeguard the future of the next generations—as well as their own welfare. In a decade from the mid-1970s to mid-1980s, some 250,000 returnees and their families left for Hong Kong and Macau (Godley 1989). According to an official source, about 60 percent of the returnees in Beijing left in the period between 1972 and 1980 (Benkan Bianjibu 1980). Among the returnees from Indonesia in Beijing, mostly the once patriotic students who returned in the 1950s after responding to the call of motherland and who supposedly enjoyed much better treatment than their counterparts assigned to remote *huaqiao* farms, more than 11 percent admitted that they regretted returning to China, and about 30 percent stated that they would opt to stay in Indonesia if they could choose again (Huang J. 1999, 52).

A New Generation of Returnees in the Reform Era

This chapter has explored how *guiqiao*, a special political category, was created in the Mao era, both discursively and in practice, as part of the class-based nation-building project. It reveals that the CCP's *qiaowu* policy "veered from left to right, and alternated between severity and leniency" throughout the Mao era in accordance to shifting definitions of who constituted *renmin* in the PRC (S. Fitzgerald 1972, 54). Returning to the ancestral or assumed cultural homeland of the Chinese nation, where distinction between classes was replacing the notion of the monolithic Chinese race or culture as the basis for defining the nation, the returnees found themselves excluded from the category of *renmin* because of their past connections with the colonial and capitalist world. The returnees were subjects to be re-educated and transformed and were regulated, discriminated against, and even persecuted. Their return journey coincided with a major historical shift in what the Chinese nation and subsequently what being Chinese meant. The returnees' experiences cast in sharp light how the party-state exercised its power through selective and differential subjectification.

Toward the end of the 1970s, as China opened up to the outside world, Deng Xiaoping and other Chinese leaders declared that "overseas connection is a good thing" (quoted in Guowuyuan Qiaoban ji Zhongyang Wenxian Yanjiushi 2000, 6; my translation). All of a sudden *guiqiao* became a positive category again and a new policy area (Wang G. 1985). *Guiqiao* are now seen as a strategic bridge to help establish linkages with Hong Kong, Macau, Southeast Asia, and, increasingly, Western countries. Moving away from the class-based definition of the nation-state, the Communist party-state has enthusiastically promoted the imaginary global China that is based on the common Chinese race, Chinese language and culture, and Chinese roots (*tong zhong, tong wen, tong gen*). High-profile initiatives to this end include the annual commemoration ceremony of the legendary Yan and Huang emperors, the establishment of the Confucius Institutes aimed at promoting Chinese language and culture worldwide, and the hosting of the World Chinese Entrepreneurs Convention in 2001, among many others. Overseas Chinese, defined in racial and cultural terms, are counted on for their contributions to economic development, to territorial reunification (with Taiwan), and to what the former Chinese president Jiang Zemin (2001) called the "great revitalization of the Chinese nation." A new generation of returnees has emerged since the 1990s in the context of the new round of globalization. Dubbed *haigui*, they are mostly China-born students or scholars who return from overseas to take advantage of the opportunities afforded by China's rapidly expanding economy (see Li C. 2005; Wang, Wong, and Sun 2006; Zweig, Chen, and Rosen 2004).

Many China observers have noted the revival of the sometimes triumphalist Overseas Chinese nationalism (Liu 2005; Nyíri and Breidenbach 2005; Wang G. 1996). However, unlike the sentiments prevalent among the Overseas Chinese in the 1950s and 1960s, present-day emigrants seem to have more diverse perceptions about China and are more circumspect in their attitudes toward the state. On the part of the party-state, its move away from class politics to a culturalist interpretation of the nation by no means implies the replacement of the politics of differentiation with one of unity. For example, the party-state's emphasis on individuals' economic success and professional capability, which underlies the official discourse about the *haigui* returnees, introduced a new mode of differential subjectification (see Xiang 2011; Xiang and Shen 2009). It is still too early to assess how relations between contemporary returnees, the party-state, and the larger society may evolve. In any case, as the *guiqiao* episode demonstrates, returnees' fate may serve as a sensitive window in revealing how Chinese politics change in relation to the outside world.

Notes

1. The English title of the film was officially rendered as *A Loyal Overseas Chinese Family* or as *Hearts for the Motherland*. It was one of most popular films in mainland China at that time and was awarded the Outstanding Movie Prize by the Ministry of Culture.

2. The term *huaqiao* first appeared in the late nineteenth century and became a popular term with a political flavor after the 1911 revolution, referring to Chinese nationals residing abroad. Its equivalent in English is Overseas Chinese. See Wang G. 1992. These two terms are used interchangeably throughout this chapter.

3. PLA art troupes came under the leadership of major departments of the Central Military Commission and served to indoctrinate PLA soldiers through creating and performing works celebrating and exhorting loyalty to the Chinese Communist Party.

4. *Dang'an* is a confidential file that is created and updated by schools or working units. The file contains information about a student's or employee's family background, political attitude, education, employment history, performance in work and political campaigns, and so on.

5. Political investigation was an essential part of the recruitment and promotion process in the Mao era. Its main purpose was to double-check the candidates' political backgrounds and to ensure that they and their families did not have exploitive class backgrounds or dubious overseas connections.

6. Both Huang and Lin are typical surnames of the Overseas Chinese from Guangdong and Fujian, the two major emigration provinces of China.

7. As a modern Chinese political conception, race was imagined to be biologically determined and defined by blood ties. Sun Yat-sen argued that all Chinese people shared the same ancestral origin and thus belonged to a single race that was distinct from all other races in the world. Based on this racialist conceptualization of the nation, Sun maintained that to save the nation was to fight for racial survival among races in the modern world.

8. Later Sun extended the content of *zhonghua minzu* to include four major non-Han peoples—the Man (Manchus), Meng (Mongolians), Hui (a term for Chinese Muslims), and Zang (Tibetan)—who were viewed as subbranches of a single race and had to be incorporated into a broader notion of the Chinese nation by the core Chinese, the Han. See Barabantseva 2011, 31–32.

9. Sun's racial interpretation of nationalism was categorically evidenced by his slogan "quchu dalu, huifu zhonghua" (expel barbarians, restore China), with *dalu* referring to the barbarians from northern China, here particularly the Manchu monarchy, and *zhonghua* being Han China.

10. It is hard to establish the full picture of the history of return due to the lack of information, but it is perhaps safe to say that Communist Party members had a certain influence on students and inspired them to go to China. For example, one of my interviewees, now a retired government official, was an underground party member in Indonesia. He disclosed to me that there were about eight underground party members in his city in the 1950s, most of whom were workers, clerks, and teachers. They organized "study groups" among workers and students to read Lenin and Mao Zedong. However, the role of the underground CCP in motivating students to go to China should not be overestimated. According to the same interviewee, the party members neither motivated students to go to China nor subsidized their trips (interview, Beijing, August 10, 2002, in Chinese). I found no direct organizational links between the underground CCP and return migration.

11. With the rise of indigenous nationalism starting in the late 1940s, ethnic Chinese became targets of attacks due to their perceived economic dominance in some fields and privileged status given by the colonial authorities in the past. The tension was particularly high in Indonesia. Various discriminatory legislations against ethnic Chinese were introduced, accompanied by racial riots, after the implementation of the dual-nationality agreement in June 1955. The ban of alien-owned small or retail stores in rural areas after January 1960 led to a new exodus of Chinese. All Chinese schools were closed down and massive repatriation of Chinese refugees occurred after the incident on September 30, 1965. See Coppel 1983, 52–72; Mackie 1976, 77–138.

12. Estimates of the number of returnees vary according to different sources. An official estimation made in the mid-1990s suggests that there are 1,135,065 returned Overseas Chinese (excluding their families) in China, and among them, about half are from Indonesia. See Lu and Quan 2001, 284–85.

It is noteworthy that most returnees were from families who left China relatively recently (known as *totok* or *singkeh* in Indonesia), who spoke Mandarin or Chinese dialects, and who maintained some connections with China. In contrast, Peranakans, descendants of early Chinese immigrants who married indigenous women, more often considered themselves natives or were more Dutch East Indies–oriented, and they were thus prone to stay in Indonesia or move to Western Europe. However, because of the re-Sinicization process triggered by the influx of China-born immigrants and the rise of Chinese nationalism inspired by Sun Yat-sen, a substantial number of Peranakans became China-oriented and returned to China as well. For detailed accounts of social and political transformation of Chinese communities in Indonesia in the first half of the twentieth century, see Skinner 1963; Suryadinata 1978a, 1978b; Willmott 1961.

13. See Zhongguo Qiaolian 1996, 73–101.

14. The State Commission fell directly under the leadership of the central government while the All-China Federation was nominally a voluntary body of returnees and dependants of Overseas Chinese. During the chaotic years of the Cultural Revolution, the State Commission was shut down, restored, and renamed in 1978 as Guowuyuan Qiaowu Bangongshi (Office of Overseas Chinese Affairs of the State Council).

15. *Qiaowu Bao* was closed down in December 1966 during the Cultural Revolution. The Office of Overseas Chinese Affairs of the State Council set up *Qiaowu Gongzuo Yanjiu* (Research of Overseas Chinese Affairs) in 1985 as the new flagship magazine to propagandize the party-state's *qiaowu* policies.

16. Apart from *huaqiao* and the newly coined term of *guiqiao*, this document also defined the categories of *qiaojuan* (dependants of Overseas Chinese, usually including grandparents, parents, siblings, spouse, children, and their spouses and grandchildren) and *huaqiao xuesheng* (returned students who had studied in Chinese-medium secondary schools overseas and hoped to continue their education in China).

17. For example, *guixiang* means to surrender, and *guishun*, *guiyi*, and *guifu* all mean to pledge allegiance to the authorities.

18. For the details of this policy, see Mao and Lin 1993, 213.

19. After the State Commission was abolished in 1969, the management of *huaqiao* farms was temporarily taken over by the provincial government until the commission was revived in 1978 as the Office of Overseas Chinese Affairs of the State Council.

20. This is called Three Years of Natural Disasters, which refers to the period from 1959 to 1961, when the PRC experienced a severe famine due to both natural disasters and implementation of the wrong economic policies.

21. Amoy University was originally established in 1921 by Tan Kah Kee. Jinan University was developed on the basis of Jinan Xuetang (Jinan College) that was established in 1906.

22. For example, in this period, thousands of returnees were sent from coastal China to Inner Mongolia for re-education in labor camps. They were forced to stay on the reform farms afterward. There were still 2,356 returnees living in different parts of Inner Mongolia in 2004. See Huang X. 2005, 250.

23. Interview, Hong Kong, March 20, 2002, in Chinese; my translation.

> > > > > > > > > > > > > CHAPTER FOUR

Transnational Encapsulation

Compulsory Return as a Labor-Migration Control in East Asia

▲ XIANG BIAO ▼

Tanimura Shinji, the owner of a garment factory in Kobe, Japan, who is also the president of the local association of small garment factories, has employed about ten female Chinese workers at any point of time since 1996. One of the most difficult aspects of the management of foreign workers is seeing them off at the airport. Not because this involves sad farewells but because ensuring that the workers leave Japan to return home when their contracts expire or are terminated is, Tanimura said, like "fighting a battle." To send off two workers, he had to enlist five association members (other garment factory owners in Kobe). At the airport the Japanese team holds hands to form a human cordon encircling the women and, step by step, move them across the departure hall, through the throng, toward the immigration checkpoint.

At the checkpoint, Tanimura hands each worker a neatly wrapped package containing the air ticket, passport—which Tanimura (as most other employers) has retained since the worker's arrival—and the unpaid salary accumulated over the past year or two. It is a standard practice for employers in Japan (and other countries, such as Canada and Australia) to pay migrant workers a monthly living allowance of between 10 and 50 percent of their wages, and pay the rest immediately before their actual departure. Since the amount of cash is so large, the women normally place it in pockets purposefully sewn onto their underwear for safekeeping. It is awkward, Tanimura admits, to see them do so in the midst of the busy airport. He is also genuinely concerned that their families in China stand to lose everything in case of an air crash, but he cannot remit the money directly to them, an option he has obviously thought through: "If we remit the money after [workers] return, they won't agree. They are worried that we won't remit. But if we remit the money before they go home . . . workers will insist that they leave only after receiving the confirmation [of receipt] from their family. During that time, they can plan to run away and overstay."[1] Such an obsession about guaranteeing the return of unskilled labor migrants on termination or expiry of their contracts is not unwarranted, because employers and recruitment agencies in Japan (as in South Korea and Singapore) will be fined or banned from bringing in more migrant workers in the future if their workers go missing or overstay. Hence the nightmare that workers might abscond as a group, even at the airport. From both the sending and receiving states' regulatory perspectives, compulsory return brings the migratory journey to a definite end. This chapter turns this end point of policy into the starting point of an inquiry about how compulsory return serves as a linchpin for controlling unskilled labor migration in the East Asian states of Japan, Korea, and Singapore.

The institutionalized practice of compulsory return leads to a phenomenon of "transnational encapsulation," whereby migrants are isolated from broader social relations and access to social resources even though they physically move across national borders. Transnational encapsulation has two aspects, international rupture and transnational policing. By rupture I mean that compulsory return decisively and abruptly removes migrants from a milieu in which they have been working and living, cuts them off from their social networks, and tears down the solidarity that they develop with other workers and local society in time. Crucially, the rupture is *inter*national because it is implemented by drawing on authority from state sovereignty (for instance, visa regulations), and furthermore the rupture is aimed at subjugating migrants to strict border control and discrete state regulations. For example, since legal systems are exclusively tied to nation-states, compulsory return effectively deprives the migrants of the possibilities of redressing any injustice that they had suffered in the host country by physically moving them back across the border. This international rupture, however, does not contradict the general trend of intensifying *trans*national connections and networks. Temporary labor migration to Japan, South Korea, and Singapore, including the compulsory return, is managed transnationally in accordance with terms set out in various bilateral agreements.[2] Furthermore, recruitment agents and employers work closely across state boundaries, effectively creating a transnational space of surveillance and policing. Thus, despite their physical mobility, unskilled migrant workers remain local and at a disadvantage in relation to the transnational reach of recruiting and employer institutions. In sum, compulsory return is an instance of international rupture made possible through transnational policing.

Compulsory return is not just an action, nor merely a result of particular policies, but is implemented by a spectrum of actors (state agencies, recruitment agents, employers, and so on) located at different levels (transnational, national, and local) through various means (see Lindquist, this volume). Return is a legal obligation of the migrants given their visa status, and also a contractual agreement, but the actual return is enforced by both contractual and extracontractual means. As we have seen in Tanimura's case, the combination of legal, extralegal, and illegal methods is crucial. Thus, international rupture is different from Catherine Nolin's (2006) "transnational rupture" that denotes the experiences of separation and displacement of Guatemalan refugees in Canada and Arjun Appadurai's (1996) emphasis on the "disjunctures" in the globalization effects of media and migration that create potentially destabilizing gaps between flow of ideas and movement of people. International rupture is essential for the perpetuation of a tightly integrated regulatory system. Compulsory return provides a critical means that enables the nation-states to reassert their status as the ultimate authority in maintaining public order in the face of increasing mobility.

This chapter forms part of my larger project on labor migration from China to Japan, South Korea, and Singapore for which I have interviewed more than two hundred informants in the four countries over four years (July 2004 to November 2007). In Japan and Korea, Chinese made up the largest nationality group among unskilled and semiskilled foreign workers (nearly 70 percent and more than 40 percent, respectively); in Singapore, Chinese were one of the four largest groups, probably second after workers from Malaysia (CHINCA 2004, 16–17, 40–48). Apart from being numerically representative, the experiences of these migrant Chinese workers are reflective of general state practices (except for migrant workers from Malaysia in Singapore, who can come and go more freely).

I first situate compulsory return as a central concern in regulating unskilled labor-migration flows in Japan, South Korea, and Singapore (notwithstanding differences in their labor policies), notably to respond to economic fluctuations, to minimize welfare responsibilities, and as a quick fix to defuse tensions. I then demonstrate how employers (whether in the private or public sector), private repatriation companies, and particularly recruitment agents operate a transnational policing to ensure return. This is followed by a discussion of three strategies adopted by migrant workers to thwart such tight controls. Finally, I highlight the characteristics of compulsory return and contemporary East Asian labor migration in the larger global and historical context.

Return as International Rupture

Compulsory return has been built into the design of labor-migration policies in East Asia. Japan, for example, admits Chinese workers as "industrial trainees" rather than employees, a categorization that neatly evades labor regulations for minimum wages, unemployment insurance, and so on. Moreover, "trainees," ostensibly permanent employees of an enterprise in China sent to Japan, clearly must, by definition, return when their contracted "training period" is up (Tsuda 2005, 40; see also He 1994, 108–9).[3] Singapore adopts a more liberal labor-migration policy. In theory anyone in possession of an employment contract is allowed entry. However, employers deposit a security bond of SGD 5,000 (USD 3,500) with the government for each unskilled worker, which will be forfeited if workers are not sent home within seven days of termination or contract expiry.[4] Furthermore, according to my informants, companies with more than one worker missing for more than a year risk being banned from recruiting foreign workers altogether. South Korea's Employment Permit System combines elements of the Japanese and Singaporean models: employers who fail to ensure that their workers exit Korea within a stipulated period will not qualify for replacement quotas to bring in new workers.

It is to be expected that governments of receiving countries would attempt to treat unskilled migrant labor flows as controlled and dispensable, especially in times of economic uncertainty. But why does return have to be enforced within a strictly defined time frame if, by definition, the status of temporary migrant prevents permanent settlement anyway? The answer given by my informants was simple: if migrant workers were not forced to return within a given time, they may never return and may somehow find a refuge locally. Compulsory return is aimed at rupturing migrants' ties within the local social milieu. A telling example of this rationale can be adduced in the cases of both South Korea and Japan, which, until recently, banned former migrant workers from reentering the country for work, fearing that those with previous experience in the country may be savvy enough to complicate the project of compulsory return. Since March 2003, the South Korean government has launched periodic crackdowns to round up and deport overstayers: those overstaying for less than a year are given a grace period to exit voluntarily without punishment; those who overstay longer than this are detained, fined, and deported immediately. In effect, those who have proved themselves to be more employable and better integrated into Korean society are targets of punishment and prioritized for return.

It is precisely for the purposes of cutting off social relations and minimizing social responsibilities that the sick or pregnant migrant bodies become prime subjects of deportation, because receiving medical treatment and giving birth may have complicated social repercussions. It is a common clause in job contracts that the worker has to return if he or she becomes unable to work, and must be deported immediately in case of infectious diseases, especially sexually transmitted diseases. In Singapore, all unskilled female migrant workers undergo a compulsory pregnancy check every six months, and those found to be pregnant have to return. One of the most difficult moments emotionally in my five-year research was when Zhang Song, a migrant worker from northeast China in Singapore, called me for urgent advice after he found out he had impregnated his wife, Li Na, also working in Singapore. Li's contracts with the recruitment agent in China and the employer in Singapore clearly stated that in cases of pregnancy, workers would be deported at their own cost and the bond deposited with the agent would be forfeited (Li paid RMB 20,000, or USD 3,000, before leaving China). Li had to go for an abortion before the next pregnancy check but did not dare go to a hospital as Zhang said this would be like "throwing oneself into a trap" (zitou luowang). According to their understanding, even if the authorities or employer found out about her pregnancy *after* the abortion, Li would be deported as a measure not only aimed at preventing unwanted births, but also as punishment for having sexual intercourse. I was referred to two clinics that did not require proof of patients' identities but charged a fee of USD 300, which they could not afford. In the end Li's family in China bribed a nurse to buy an aborti-facient (mifepristone) that Li had taken before, and sent it to her through another migrant worker. Li bled for three days, and both she and Zhang were relieved.

Return serves as a convenient means of dealing with disputes for em-ployers since, in Japan, South Korea, and Singapore, workers' visas can be canceled anytime. As immigration law supersedes employment and other legislations, migrant workers without visas cannot pursue justice and have to leave unconditionally. Once they return, however, they are effectively deprived of their basic capacity to seek legal redress because of differences in national legal systems, and the territory-bound legal and social respon-sibilities (particularly of agents and employers). Everything depends on the work permit, so the cancelation of work permits is seen as a magically quick fix, if also a violent act, which Chinese workers in Singapore called *ga*, a colloquialism to describe cutting heavy metal plates by guillotine.

The anxiety to repatriate workers at the earliest sign of trouble is also fueled by employers' concerns about keeping a "clean record": "trouble-some" workers might seek help from NGOs, engage lawyers, or lodge com-plaints with government agencies.The deputy manager of a repatriation company in Singapore told me: "We [the Singaporean society] have a very strict merit system. If these kinds of things [workers complaining to the government] happen, people will ask what is your security system? Where is your safety measure [to prevent workers from causing trouble]? What is your reputation then? People don't want to do business with a com-pany that has a bad name." In other words, the worry is not only about being taken to task over wrongdoings; it is equally about being questioned about failing to cover up wrongdoings! Because of their preoccupation with maintaining a clean record, Singapore employers sometimes convince the Ministry of Manpower to blacklist particular workers after their depar-ture, which will prevent them from reentering Singapore for a number of years and thus ensuring that no past misconduct will surface.

Under pressure from civil society and from migrant workers them-selves, state agencies in the three countries also crack down on abusive employers and recruitment institutions; ironically enough, the most com-mon penalty involves forced repatriation of affected workers. In Japan, for example, if an employer or employers' recruitment association is found to violate rules, the so-called foreign trainees have to be sent home and the cases are thereafter often regarded as solved. Out of sight, out of mind. For this reason, between 2003 and 2006, Chinese authorities also identified the large-scale deportation of Chinese trainees by the Japanese government on account of irregularities in conduct of employers or their associations as a major concern in Chinese labor migration to Japan (Pang 2006).

Forced return is arguably violently disruptive to migrants' lives. International labor migration is not only expensive (the minimum agent's fee in northeast China for work in Singapore, Japan, and South Korea was USD 5,000 in 2007) but also a highly emotionally charged investment that is expected to change one's fate once and for all. Premature return turns this dream into a nightmare. While Li's abortion allowed her to escape this, her husband, Zhang, decided not to see his contract through because the work regime was harsh and the wages were too low to even cover his agent's fee. I attempted to comfort them with the prospect of seeing their one-year-old daughter soon, but Zhang gave me a weary smile. He would not even be able to let their families know of his return: "Our parents won't be able to take it [his early return, after shelling out nearly USD 10,000]. It is so difficult for us already; this will be too much for them." Zhang would not be able to return to his home district where some of his friends were still waiting to hear from him about Singapore, because if they saw him back so suddenly it would create, as Zhang put it, "a bad influence" on his reputation (*yingxiang buhao*, a term used in official documents to describe actions with undesirable public impact). The couple was deciding which friend's home Zhang should stay at until he got a partial refund from the agent in China. In another case, Yan Lei, a twenty-one-year-old Chinese worker, broke down in tears when I met him through an NGO in Singapore just before he was forced to return home early, after a dispute with the employer. He condemned himself again and again for letting his parents down (*duibuqi*) because of this, and for bringing them so much shame that they would not be able to "go outside [of the home]" after his return.

The fear of arbitrary forced return severely undermines migrant workers' bargaining position. This is clearly evidenced in how nine Chinese women reacted to the discovery of a hidden camera installed by their employer in their changing room in Tokushima, Japan, in 2004. When this was reported in the Chinese media, it triggered a huge national outcry. The government of Liaoning province, where the nine workers came from, sent a delegation to Japan to investigate the incident. However, despite the extremely rare public attention and political support that they as migrant workers attracted, they decided not to bring the case to court because, if the employer was convicted, the factory would be closed down and all the workers would have to return to China.[5] The threat of forced return also undermines solidarity among workers. In another exceptional case, three female trainees in their last year in Aomori, Japan, demanded that the employer compensate them for poor working conditions. They had left the factory one night and stayed in a hostel, and they faxed their demand to the employer, at the same time contacting an NGO in Osaka. They did so partly to avoid opposition from fellow Chinese trainees in their first and second years who would expect to be sent home because the employer might either dismiss all the Chinese workers as punishment (which had happened before) or, if the compensation demands were satisfied, simply declare the factory bankrupt.[6] In sum, forced return—or even the possibility of forced return—effectively ruptures migrants' accumulation of social resources.

Transnational Policing and Encapsulation

Compulsory return aims not only to end a migration project but also to define a series of social relations between the migrant and the host society. Furthermore, the enforcement of return relies on collaborations—not always explicit—between employers, business associations, recruitment agents, and private security companies. Thus, return entails socially complicated and institutionally embedded processes. Preemptive arrangements for compulsory return affect migrants' living and working conditions and place them in tight social encapsulation throughout their employment contracts.

At the frontline of enforcing compulsory return are employers. In all three countries, although bilateral governmental agreements allow migrants to work up to two or three years consecutively, most employers issue one-year (renewable) contracts in order to be able to terminate the contract quickly when deemed necessary. Most contracts stipulate that workers face deportation if they participate in strike action—in Singapore this is defined as a situation where "two or more persons stop working without employer's agreement." In Japan, a workers' "promise letter," drawn up by an Osaka garment factory association (the Japanese government requires companies to hire foreign workers through their associations, and associations are designated as the "primary sponsors"), explains the trainees' agreement to meet the costs of their own return if they:

1. participate in assembly, strike, and collective complaining in any circumstance;

2. work for other organizations or people, regardless of whether the work is paid or unpaid;
3. terminate the contract unilaterally or leave the company;
4. repeatedly sleep in a different room other than [that] designated without permission;
5. report [internal disputes] to any Japanese organization or individual, or entrust other parties to handle the disputes.[7]

But employment contracts are not seen as powerful enough to guarantee compulsory return, and this often necessitates the physical removal of bodies. In Japan this task is taken up by the primary sponsors—the respective employers' associations. Tano Takashi is the full-time chief executive of an association of scaffolding companies in Kobe. The first thing he said to me, when he arrived for dinner at a Chinese restaurant in Osaka at my invitation for an interview, was that the job was "life shortening." His wife, through whom I secured the interview, said that she wanted him to meet me because she thought it would be good for his health to have someone with whom to talk these things through. Sending trainees back home before their contracts expired was an important part of his work. Tano emphasized that he had to move very fast to "put the worker in the airplane before he or she woke up from the shock." One particularly difficult *battle*—Tano used exactly the same word as Tanimura—arose when the association decided to send more than thirty workers, hired by different member companies, back to China before the termination of their contracts after five or six workers had absconded. The association was concerned that more would follow suit and immediately mobilized more than sixty men who formed different teams that stormed into the workers' dormitories across Osaka at 6 a.m. sharp. Most workers were shocked, some fought back strongly, but nevertheless they were dragged into cars and sent off to the airport. In such difficult circumstances, Tano said, he and his fellow members must rely on their "will and determination" to win the battle.

In Singapore, since the 1980s, the recurrent need for the physical removal, and sometimes the tracking down, of workers after their work permits are canceled has given rise to a new business: repatriation services. There were probably six such companies in Singapore that specialized in repatriating migrant workers in 2007,[8] all small, staffed with "tough guys," and registered as transport companies to circumvent the complex regulations that applied to operating private security companies. The price for secure repatriation is fairly standardized. In 2007 companies charged

USD 300 for the capture of an absconded worker when information on the worker's whereabouts was available, and USD 350–700 when there was no information. Companies house workers for USD 100–150 each per night and escort them to the airport for USD 300 each. When being housed prior to repatriation, workers are not allowed to step out of the door or get near to the windows because once their permits have been canceled, they have nothing to lose and can be particularly "unruly," as a deputy manager of one of the largest repatriation companies put it. Such companies also provide "offshore solutions" — to escort workers all the way home — for which prices are negotiated on a case-by-case basis.

The most important actors in enforcing compulsory return and indeed in regulating, if not policing, the entire migration process are recruitment agents, particularly those based in China, who operate transnationally. Employers in all three receiving countries are required to recruit Chinese workers through a number of designated nationally based recruitment agencies, which in the case of Japan and South Korea only deal with designated sending companies in China. All three receiving countries also blacklist designated sending companies if a certain number of their workers abscond or overstay. Under government pressure to keep migrant workers in line, recruitment agents in the receiving countries also outsource the cost of this responsibility. For each worker overstaying, an Osaka-based enterprises' association, for example, imposes a compensation of USD 50,000 on its designated counterpart in China. For the same purpose, recruitment agents in Singapore require a security bond of SGD 5,000 (USD 4,000) per worker from their counterparts in China, refundable only after the worker's timely return to China.

Bearing the onus of such punitive costs, agents in China habitually employ all manner of safeguards in their recruitment selections. For example, agents conduct detailed interviews with would-be migrants and reject anyone who has relatives or friends overseas, or who betrays some knowledge of the destination country, or any other reason that suggests that they could be emboldened to step out of the cage of legality. Most agents ban related candidates (for example brothers) from going to Japan together. Golden Stage Ltd., a recruitment agent in rural Hebei province in north China, pays village heads nearly USD 100 for detailed information on each candidate they recruit. In one instance, a woman chosen for a job in Japan was immediately dumped after the village head reported that she was in the throes of a divorce. Jin Wan, the general manager of Golden Stage, declared

FIGURE 4.1. Two Chinese migrants in Singapore waiting to be repatriated the next day. After having paid more than USD 5,000 to recruitment agents and having been in Singapore for only two months, they were both dismissed by their employers due to a dispute over salary. Their forced return hence entailed a huge financial loss for them. (Courtesy of the author [2007])

with some satisfaction: "The woman may be mentally and psychologically unstable when divorcing, and may create problems overseas!"

Since the early 1990s, sending agents have exacted sureties from migrants—about USD 3,500 for going to Japan and USD 5,000 for South Korea in 2006—for their timely return and guarantee of not having violated any state law or rules in the workplace. Migrants' own property certificates are often surrendered as an additional surety. But even these measures are not regarded as sufficient deterrents and, beginning in the late 1990s, it became compulsory for would-be migrants to name one or two civil servants as guarantors who would be held financially accountable to the agent for any wrongdoings overseas. Civil servants are usually the most influential figures in extended family or friend circles, and pressure from them is more powerful than the threat of financial loss in ensuring compliant behavior. Some agents also require migrants to take a vow never to break laws and contracts: this ritual of *xuanshi* in China is almost exclusively associated with joining the Communist Party or its youth league, where one faces the hammer and sickle flag, right fist raised, and loudly recites the vow of readiness to sacrifice everything for the liberation of the world proletariat.

Apart from predeparture preventive measures, agents in China are also proactive in repatriating migrants. The manager of a state-owned recruitment company in Shenyang in northeast China told me: "We need to make preemptive strikes [*xianfa zhiren*]. If we observe that someone may create problems, we will bring the worker back to China before the contract runs out." Thus, Tanimura's collaborator in China, a state-owned labor recruitment company, had dispatched staff all the way to Kobe to escort workers home in 2005 and 2007 after the Japanese government had tightened regulations for foreign trainees. The Chinese company, like Tanimura, was worried that the Japanese human cage might not be effective enough in preventing workers from escaping at the airport.

Of course the system of compulsory return serves the agents' commercial interest: "How can we make money if they all stay on overseas and foreign companies don't need new people?" asked a manager of a large labor sending company in China. Recruiters whom I interviewed in China often justified compulsory return by citing the principle of reciprocity. As one informant put it, "you qu you hui, zai qu bunan" (you go and you come back, more people can go), a modification of the proverbial wisdom that is held up as a universal moral principle, "you jie you huan, zai jie bunan" (you borrow and you repay, you can borrow again).

Refusal to Return!

Following the groundbreaking work by E. P. Thompson (1971, 1975, 76–136) and James Scott (1976, 1985, 1990), and informed by Michel Foucault, recent research on power and resistance has moved away from antagonistic binary frameworks to focus on how economic exploitation and political oppressions necessarily take place in a social milieu imbued with customs, symbols, and traditions. The processes of mediation often open new spaces for everyday actions of resistance, negotiation, and appropriation, particularly for the traditionally disadvantaged. For similar reasons, Sherry Ortner (1995) criticizes the "ethnographic refusal" in studies on resistance to recognize complex political and cultural dynamics in the resisters' own world. Yet international rupture and transnational policing create a special subject by reducing migrants to almost empty lives with minimal social networks and resources of their own world. The power and policing over the purchase of their labor is indeed crude, and the control over their lives is nearly total.

Are there possible strategies to avoid forced return? Among the minority who managed to fight back, three strategies of resistance can be discerned: to cry out, to clash, and to run away. To cry out entails seeking support from civil society or taking employers or agents to court. For example, in 2002 a group of Chinese workers in Chiba, Japan, brought their employer to court immediately before their return to demand compensation for salary deductions, and also because their sending company in China had failed to refund the security bonds of trainees who had returned on schedule. This group of workers intentionally set out to attract international attention and hedge against further losses upon their return to China (Zha 2002, 146). They were crying out transnationally. But such actions are rare because most migrant workers have limited access to the larger society beyond their workplaces.

The clash strategy is when workers use their bodies as weapons to confront or overcome the coercion of forced return. This was the experience of Tan Mei, a twenty-five-year-old woman from Shandong, east China, who worked in Japan between 2002 and 2004. After a year of working she discovered that her employer had been deducting a sum from her salary and transferring it monthly to the sending agent in China in violation of government rules. When questioned about this, her employer called the Chinese company and, on the spot, it was decided that Tan should be fired and deported. Two days later, the director of the employers' association led two men to Tan's dormitory room to take her away. Tan ran to the workshop and clung to a machine, but, after a struggle in which she was injured, she was eventually carted off to Kansai International Airport. At the airport Tan cried out for help in a female toilet—the only safe space she could find—and a flight attendant called the airport police. The police told Tan that she had to return to China since she had no legal grounds to stay on in Japan because the employer had fired her and escorted her to the immigration checkpoint. Tan refused to go through the channel, the flight took off and the police returned her to the employers' association team but, screaming, Tan made a run for it and the three men finally gave up and abandoned her in the airport. Illegal but now free, Tan contacted a local Chinese newspaper and, subsequently, an NGO and a trade union. She was finally reimbursed the deducted wages owed to her and returned to China voluntarily.[9]

Tan's strategy of clash is reminiscent of that of the suicide bomber analyzed by Michael Hardt and Antonio Negri (2004, 54); the strategy represents the "ontological limit" to the new hi-tech biopower aimed at a death-free state of permanent war. While states attempt to minimize (and legitimize) casualties in military operations, suicide bombers blow themselves up to call into question the very legitimation of violence itself. Similarly, in the case of international labor migration, states attempt to control temporary migrants through complicated rules and regulations rather than mete out physical punishments (now seen as ineffective and backward), while migrants turn their bodies into weapons of resistance against officials, employers, and, most importantly, the logic governing the current temporary labor regime. Peter Lee, the manager of a repatriation company in Singapore, told me that they would not repatriate pregnant women, but instead charged USD 400 per night, four times the average, to house female workers because women were considered too "troublesome and dangerous." When I asked what he meant by dangerous, his company staffers playing mahjong in the office piped up: "Women are insidious [*yinxian*], and "they can hurt themselves and then finger you for injuring them." In general, female migrant workers are more likely than men to succeed in refusing return, simply because the female body is regarded as more vulnerable and thus can be used more effectively to destabilize the so-called civilized mode of governance.

The most common strategy in refusing return is to run away—to go underground. Running away and escaping is obviously different from the strategy of exit or voting with your feet within a sanctioned system. Albert Hirschman's (1970) analysis of exit was concerned with how lapses in the market economy can be corrected at the right time so that the system as a whole sustains itself, but the migrants' strategy of running away aims to escape from and disrupt the dominant system itself as the tight controls render changes from within unworkable. Absconding workers manage to survive underground because, being illegal and therefore freed from tight social encapsulation, they are able to develop social networks and resources. In Japan, for example, there are numerous labor agents in industrial cities (such as Hamamatsu and Toyota City) that find jobs for both legal and illegal migrants. The working conditions can be highly exploitative, but the workers are free to change jobs. In Singapore, despite the small size of the city-state and the very tight government control, illegal migrants still manage to carve out spaces of survival. Huang Ji, originally a trader from China and now a permanent resident, knows a few migrant workers from Fujian province who have overstayed but get by (in the majority-Chinese Singapore) "because they have been around for so long, people see them as local." But refusing to return leads to the eventual difficulty of voluntary return (as an illegal) and is not a solution in itself. Huang Ji said,

> The problem is that they can't go home. Not to mention that the Singapore authorities will punish them [when apprehended at the airport], they have no face to go home. People at home are doing better than you. This is an awkward situation of Chinese migrants. If you are doing well and your country stays behind, it is okay; but what if your country is improving so fast and you stay behind and are illegal? You can't go home.[10]

Discussion

Government-initiated and -enforced return is not a new method of managing flows of temporary labor migrants. The guest-workers program crucial for postwar European reconstruction, particularly in Germany and France, was predicated on the idea that the workers would eventually return, which European governments enforced during the economic recession in the early 1970s (King 1986, 3). France introduced the *aide-au-retour* program, which offered cash to foreign workers who planned to return (Lawless 1986, 218; Rogers 1997, 152). W. R. Bohning (1979) estimates that 1.5 million migrant workers returned home from Western Europe in the mid-1970s. Forty years later, Spain and Japan offered similar incentive packages during the 2008 economic crisis (for the Japanese case, see Sasaki, this volume). Nor is it new in academic literature to use return migration as a lens to examine international labor relations. Bohning (1979, especially 404), for example, points out that return migration served as a mechanism whereby rich and powerful countries shifted burdens in economic downturn to the poor states. Samir Amin (1974) argues that in the absence of structural change, return migration perpetuates rather than ameliorates the economic dependence on work migration in sending places. Moreover, Claude Meillassoux's seminal work (1981) confirms that return transfers the costs of social reproduction, such as everyday caregiving for the young, old, and infirm, to peripheralized migrant places of origin. In Meillassoux's model, return serves as a critical link in the international articulation of the capitalist mode of production in the core (Europe) and in the precapitalist mode of reproduction at the periphery (Africa), thus enabling capital accumulation based on international exploitation. Such articulation of modes of (re)production is partially responsible for the partition of life and the selective subjectification of migrants as discussed in the introduction (Xiang, this volume).

While all these insights remain highly relevant, contemporary conditions differ from historical precedents in various respects and require a more nuanced theorization. First, in the current regime of labor migration in East Asia, compulsory return is no longer a reactive, post hoc solution, but is a primary concern that overshadows entire migration programs. Compulsory return is not only about how a migration project ends; it also determines how the migration journey starts. Second, compulsory return aims not only at maximizing capital accumulation but also at ensuring social control and the disciplining of individual migrant bodies. It is thus necessary for regulations to penetrate the fabric of everyday migrant life. This in turn uncovers a third characteristic, namely the societalization of compulsory return programs. That is, states either directly delegate authority to, or indirectly work with, a wide range of institutions in enforcing return. Multiple actors are closely involved in forming a system of transnational surveillance that exceeds the capacity of state agencies. These conditions, which I captured with the notion "transnational encapsulation," suggest that we are facing a somewhat different and much more complicated institutional infrastructure governing labor mobility in East Asia. The main issue is not whether temporary migrants workers should or should not return (very few migrants regard it as their entitlement to stay indefinitely in the receiving country); what is more important is how compulsory return is enmeshed with other arrangements, including recruitment, contract agreement, wage payments, and living conditions, and how forced return is used as a threat to impose unacceptable controls and varying degrees of exploitation.

Notes

1. Interview with Tanimura Shinji in his Kobe factory, Japan, April 3, 2006. Interviewed in Japanese and English, translated by Mika Toyota. All the names of the migrants, employers, and recruiters in the chapter are pseudonyms.

2. In cases of turnkey projects whereby Chinese companies hire workers in China and dispatch them overseas, especially to countries in Africa, the Caribbean, and Southeast Asia, to carry out the projects, the workers have to return once the projects

are completed. But since project-tied migrations take place collectively and the workers are directly hired by Chinese companies, return is much easier to enforce.

3. South Korea changed its trainee system in 2003 and then again in 2007; in Japan there have been debates about whether the system should be reformed since 2008. But they have not significantly changed the recruitment practices in China.

4. In order to encourage employers to act swiftly in cases where a migrant worker absconds, the Singapore government refunds the employer half of the security bond if the employer provides proof that reasonable efforts have been made to locate the worker, such as a missing persons report from the police.

5. See various reports by Cong Zhongxiao in *Guanxi huawen shibao* (Kansai Chinese Times) from May to August 2004 (for instance, Cong 2004). This event attracted so much attention that Sina.com, the largest portal in China as well as in the world, created a special website dedicated to this "peeping incident." See http://news.sina .com.cn/temp/z/watchgirl/index.shtml (accessed May 19, 2012).

6. Interview with Hayazaki Naomi, May 30, 2007, Osaka. Hayazaki, as the representative of the NGO Rights of Immigrants Network in Kansai (RINK) in Osaka, was the central resource person supporting the workers. Interviewed in Japanese and English, translated by Mika Toyota.

7. I obtained the Chinese version of the agreement from Rights of Immigrants Network in Kansai (RINK), an Osaka-based NGO. The document was signed by workers but not by the employers' associations or individual employers. It is unclear whether such agreements existed in Japanese.

8. Interview with a founding manager of one of the oldest repatriation companies in Singapore that specializes in migrant workers, August 18, 2007, Singapore. Interview with Mr. Jolovan Wham, August 12, 2007, Singapore. Wham is an NGO activist for migrant workers' rights in Singapore.

9. Interview with Sakai Kysosuke, May 28, 2007, Osaka, in English. Sakai, an officer at Rengo Osaka, a trade union that provides special support for migrant workers, oversaw the case of Tan Mei throughout and documented the development meticulously.

10. This phenomenon seems more common in large cities in countries with more liberal immigration policies such as New York and London. My brief fieldwork in Chinatowns in the two cities suggests that migrants with professional backgrounds may feel more constrained by the dilemma of return.

▾ CHAPTER FIVE ◄ ◄ ◄ ◄ ◄ ◄ ◄ ◄ ◄ ◄ ◄ ◄
▾
▾ **Cambodians Go "Home"**
▾ *Forced Returns and Redisplacement*
▾ *Thirty Years after the American War in Indochina*
▾ SYLVIA R. COWAN ▲
            ▲
            ▲
            ▲

Between June 2002 and late 2011, more than 310 permanent residents in the United States with Cambodian citizenship were repatriated to Cambodia after having served prison sentences, for mostly minor offenses (U.S. Department of Homeland Security 2011).[1] The majority of these returnees were male, were under forty, and had left Cambodia as young children with their families in the mid-1970s or the early 1980s (first with the evacuation of U.S. troops from Indochina immediately after the fall of both the U.S.-backed Cambodian and South Vietnamese regimes, and later after the overthrow of the Khmer Rouge).[2] After spending years in refugee camps in Thailand and sometimes also in the Philippines, the returnees were resettled in the United States, mostly in low-income inner-city neighborhoods dominated by other marginalized minorities, where a number of them became involved in street gangs.

The deportation of such "undesirable" noncitizens has been explicitly justified by the United States as being in the interests of public safety and homeland security, and implicitly rationalized by the notion of a natural return to the deportees' homeland. But, for most of these former refugees,

Cambodia is at best a vague childhood memory; in fact, for one in seven of those born in refugee camps and repatriated before 2007, Cambodia was a completely imaginary place where they had never before set foot (Stokes 2007, 57). The forced returns, then, certainly do not put people back "in place" but instead engender their redisplacement. While these expulsions provide U.S. politicians a seemingly quick fix to inner-city problems—even though they are complex, entrenched, and even trace to previous U.S. foreign policies—for the returnees the expulsions mean permanent separation from families, including their own young children. For the Cambodians, this repeats the cycle of traumatic family separations and breakdowns that many had already once suffered under Pol Pot's Khmer Rouge regime. This practice of deportation continues, as a large number of Cambodians in the United States remain queued up on the "deportable" list after serving prison sentences (Stokes 2007, 57).[3]

The stories of forced returnees expose deeply rooted paradoxes in America's self-professed claim to provide refuge to persons fleeing violent and oppressive conditions. Historically, American society has been inured to fear internal, sometimes invisible, enemies: paranoia about communism, and, currently, anxieties about so-called terrorism. These ideological specters and the interests they serve not only have justified America's right to resort to aggressive external interventions but also have simultaneously shaped U.S. immigration policies, particularly those pertaining to exclusions and deportation.

The paradox is clear: a global reach in policing has invited or materialized those same threats to American interests and has left behind an unraveling trail of political and economic fragility. Militarized intervention in Vietnam was in part sustained by a deep fear about a worldwide spread of communism. The intervention also involved illegal bombardments of eastern Cambodia, which directly resulted in large-scale internal and external displacements of Cambodian populations (along with Vietnamese and Lao). Economic challenges resulted from years of war. The ongoing deportations of some of those who arrived as refugees (another external solution of sorts) are again supported by America's unresolved fear of its internal "aliens." This interplay of fear and violent external interventions has defining implications for homeland security and contemporary global (dis)order. Deportation, in this case, serves as a means to redefine the relationship between displaced individuals and the nation-states of both America and Cambodia.

The issue of forced returns of former Cambodian child refugees has engaged me since 2000, when I began to research the Cambodian community that settled in Lowell, Massachusetts (my current home), which has the second-largest concentration of Cambodians in the United States (see Pho, Gerson, and Cowan 2008).[4] This chapter uses various documentary media sources and the results of my interviews and observations. It includes interviews obtained during my visits to Cambodia in 2006 and 2008.[5] This material provides a collective story of Cambodians who were involuntarily displaced from their birthplaces during successive phases of the American war in Southeast Asia and the ensuing civil wars, relocated as refugees in the United States, and have been forced to return. It is thus a history of multiple displacements.

In telling their collective story, I begin by framing their experiences historically in the context of how deportation—the forced removal of Others—has played a key (although often invisible) role in the making of the American homeland. Continuing from this larger context, I trace their multiple displacements, with the initial displacement ensuing from U.S. military actions across Indochina. The aftermath resulted in their displacements to refugee camps and then refugee settlement in the United States. This process of multiple displacements does not end with sudden expulsion back to Cambodia, but, as the final section describes, the process continues as those who were returned are once again socially displaced, or they inhabit spaces of exclusion from mainstream Cambodian society. I conclude by revisiting the multiple displacements through these people's life histories, and the likelihood of such collective experiences being repeated through the global reach of American policies and politics.

Systemic Exclusions and Summary Deportations in "the Nation of Immigrants"

The recent deportations of Cambodians, like the deportations of other legal nationals residing in the United States, were triggered more than a decade ago by changes in laws and the attacks on September 11, 2001. Just one month after September 11, amid elevated fear about so-called outsiders, the U.S. Patriot Act signed into law provisions for enhanced powers of officials to detain and deport immigrants perceived as threats to national security (section 411).[6] In March 2002, the U.S government and the Cambodian government signed a repatriation agreement for Cambodia to accept back Cambodian citizens who had served their sentences for crimes committed in the United States (Deeherd 2003).[7] The agreement allowed for the deportation of no more than ten people per month, and the United States provided USD 100 toward processing each deportee in Cambodia but no funding for their resettlement (Paddock 2003).

These deportations were part of a pattern of U.S. government actions that emphasized regulatory and legal systems as a central means of maintaining social order. We can observe a history of expulsion that had been progressively strengthened since the beginning of the last century. The numbers of the deported in the first half of the 1990s averaged 41,007 annually, which jumped to 135,510 between 1996 and 1999, before escalating to a 280,960 average in the years from 2000 to 2011 (U.S. Department of Homeland Security 2011, 102).

Deportation therefore has a long history in the United States, in direct contrast with the nationally stated ideals of America as a haven of freedom that has always been welcoming to those who resemble mainstream citizens. These ideals are written in the U.S. Constitution, engraved on the Statue of Liberty, and taught to American schoolchildren. David Haines (2010) questions the idea of America as a "safe haven" and notes the country's practice over time of both providing and refusing refuge. Some events in U.S. history illustrate this pattern. Indigenous communities that originally lived in the territory that has become the United States were decimated. The country's economy in its early years relied on the oppression of trafficked slaves from Africa. These are examples of aggressive and racialized policies of discrimination and fear that entered into the U.S. history of inclusions and exclusions and deportation. Recent changes in immigration legislation, such as those targeting racially profiled "terrorists" and "aliens," are similarly embedded in U.S. foreign policy and nationalistic attitudes (Kanstroom 2007).

From the country's earliest formation, the ideal of America as an asylum adhered to the notion that the new nation must exclude those "whose moral or social characteristics would introduce in America the decadence and corruption of Europe" (Marilyn Baseler, quoted in Kanstroom 2007, 30). Even while opening the country to refugees to be morally just, the question of how self-reliant the new entrants would be, as well as how they would fit in, has been a major concern. The idea of expulsion has been integral to this need to distinguish "them" from "us." In the 1790s, when the immigrant American society was fairly open to those who were similar to dominant power groups, the criteria for exclusion or expulsion were based on religion, ideology, economic conditions, health, and morality (Kanstroom 2007, 30–33). The Alien Act of 1798 empowered the president to deport all noncitizens deemed "dangerous." Carl Bon Tempo (2008, 75) notes the "feverish efforts to reassure Americans" in the 1950s that Hungarian refugees were "like them" and would be "good Americans." The present-day system for deportation took shape in the early twentieth century, with the centralization of immigration controls and the passing of various deportation laws (Kanstroom 2007, 161).

Three underlying concerns can be discerned in the extension of deportation programs since the late nineteenth century. First is the concern about race, for which the 1891 Immigration Act systematized a function of separating desirable and undesirable immigrants "by physical and moral qualities" (Kanstroom 2007, 115). Race was paramount in the treatment of Chinese migrants in the late 1800s; race was "perhaps the critical factor in the development of the modern deportation system" (Kanstroom 2007, 98). Racial exclusion became a central part of twentieth-century immigration, naturalization, and deportation law, and was increasingly manifest in the deportation of Others.

Second, during the First World War, as political loyalty to the state became a major concern, and especially in the wake of Russia's Bolshevik Revolution, U.S. deportations extended to political dissidents and labor organizers (Kanstroom 2007, 139). In the Cold War paranoia about communism, politicized fear had an even more pronounced influence on immigration and deportation policies. McCarran's Internal Security Act of 1950 required members of the U.S. Communist Party to be officially registered and authorized; the retroactive deportation ousted Communists or members of other groups considered to be dangerous to public safety; and, in 1952, the McCarran-Walter Act outlined politically based criteria for deportation and laid the groundwork for contemporary immigration law.[8] These strengthened exclusion laws maintained the quota systems of the 1920s that were based on national origin and eliminated statutes of limitation. More pertinent, these laws permitted deportation without hearings or judicial review.

Third, deportation had also been driven by concerns about employment opportunities. For example, the active recruitment of Mexicans as farm laborers (known as *braceros* under this program) between 1917 and 1921 gave currency to the trope that foreigners would steal too many jobs and resulted in over 92,000 Mexicans being deported during the period 1921–

29.[9] As Daniel Kanstroom (2007, 224) notes, "The remarkably symmetrical relationship between labor recruitment and the deportation system is illustrated by the fact that, up to 1964, the number of *braceros*, nearly 5 million, was almost exactly the same as the number of deportees." This symbiosis between employers and state interests and the expulsions of labor migrants bear remarkable resemblance to the pattern of labor flows in the contemporary world (see Lindquist, this volume; Xiang, this volume).

Since the passing of the 1980 Refugee Act, the situation has become more complicated. On one hand, there is the extension of civil rights and granting of political asylum to tens of thousands of otherwise deportable noncitizens (Kanstroom 2007, 226). Under the 1986 Immigration Reform and Control Act, some three million undocumented migrants were granted amnesty. On the other hand, deportation laws have become more rigid and harsher. Events such as the bombings of the World Trade Center in New York in February 1993 and the Murrah Federal Building in Oklahoma City in April 1995 have heightened and reinforced the reality of terrorism at home (R. Martin 1999). Immigration controls were tightened and deportations were accelerated.

In 1996 two laws—the Antiterrorism and Effective Death Penalty Act and the Illegal Immigration Reform and Immigrant Responsibility Act— introduced major changes to U.S. immigration policy. Deportation was made mandatory for all permanent residents who were sentenced to at least a year (or whose infraction could have resulted in a one-year sentence, even if it was not applied) for "aggravated felonies," "moral turpitude," or use of controlled substances (U.S. Senate 1996). Deportations of noncitizens were expedited and became increasingly frequent, because more minor criminal offenses resulted in automatic deportation (e.g., beginning in 1998, driving while intoxicated). Furthermore, these legislations eliminated a judge's discretion to consider relief from deportation on a case-by-case basis for permanent residents. In the twenty years prior, judges had been able to consider factors such as the individual's prison experience, attitude, behavior, family support, rehabilitation, ties to family, and length of time as a resident in the United States (Hing 2005, 268). Significantly, in addition to immigrants not having the right to legal counsel in immigration courts (since these are civil rather than criminal charges), deportation laws were considered to have extraconstitutional status. Thus, many rights and protections afforded by the U.S. Constitution were rendered inapplicable to those deemed deportable (Kanstroom 2007, 228,

229). In short, noncitizens convicted of deportable offenses became vulnerable to retroactively applied deportation, and their convictions led to their permanent exile from the United States (Gania 2006).

Multiple Displacements: From Refugee
to "Product of the American System"

In June 2002, the first group of Cambodian deportees from the United States arrived in Phnom Penh International Airport, handcuffed and shackled. There they were held in the Cambodian detention center for fifteen days before being allowed to leave, and only after a relative or friend (mostly people whom they had never met) vouched for them. Those with no identifiable family sponsor were taken in by the Returnee Assistance Program (RAP). RAP was a privately funded and individual initiative founded purposely, only days before the Cambodian returnees' arrival, to respond to the situation. The founder, Bill Herod, was a longtime American resident of Phnom Penh (Stokes 2007, 57).

How did these returnees come to be uprooted in the first place? Cambodia, as well as Vietnam and Laos, was turned into a bloody battleground in the 1960s and 1970s when the United States attempted to quell the communist-inspired nationalist movements that had risen up against French colonial rule in Southeast Asia. Contrasting ideologies materialized in combat zones in what the United States called "the Vietnam War" and in what was known in Indochina as "the American War." In Cambodia the United States supported an anticommunist military coup (Chandler 1993), which ousted the royalist Sihanouk regime. In an effort to postpone the victory of the communist nationalists, the United States dropped more than one thousand tons of bombs over Cambodia in 1973 (Chandler 1993, 207). While estimates of war dead vary, around 1.7 million people are said to have been killed between 1965 and 1973, and many more people were displaced (White 2005).[10] Throughout the region numerous internally displaced refugees were created by these bombardments and indiscriminate use of defoliants (Hein 1995). The U.S. efforts to help those displaced were hardly sufficient and were sometimes misguided. Back in the United States, many citizens protested the government's handling of the war.

The bombing and material support by the United States in installing, then propping up, illegitimate regimes did not stop the eventual overthrow of these regimes by nationalist communist forces. In fact, it is generally acknowledged that U.S. actions in Cambodia helped prepare the ground for the mobilizations of the Beijing-backed Khmer Rouge headed by Pol Pot (Chandler 1993), who ruled under the name Democratic Kampuchea from April 1975 to early 1979. Having inherited a desperate food crisis after years of war, the Khmer Rouge sought to establish a "pure" society that favored the rural poor—denoted as "the people" in socialist rhetoric—by literally eradicating educated and urban elite and turning the whole country into an agricultural work camp (Hing 2005). Under this regime, men and women were housed separately and families were broken up. More than 1.5 million people were killed or died of starvation, propelling those who dared, or were able, to escape. When the regime was overthrown by Vietnamese troops in January 1979, multitudes fled across mountains that were heavily mined, crossing into Thailand where they remained vulnerable to Vietnamese attack under ambivalent Thai protection and eventually spent from one to nine years in sanctioned refugee camps along the border in Thailand or in the Philippines (Smith-Hefner 1998).

More than 145,000 of these Cambodian refugees were resettled in the United States between 1975 and 1999 (Hing 2005),[11] comprising a significant proportion of the approximately 206,000 people of Cambodian descent accounted for in the 2000 U.S. Census.[12] Many were farmers and were from rural areas.[13] They were mostly relocated to urban settings where they competed for scarce resources with other minority or disenfranchised groups (Ly 2010).

The largest communities of Cambodian refugees are located in Long Beach, California, and in Lowell, Massachusetts.[14] These cities share some attributes: both are ethnically diverse, have median family incomes at or below the national average, and have a younger population than the national average; a number of these youths have also become involved in disreputable street-gang activities.[15] Long Beach is home to at least ten entrenched Asian street gangs and is located in Los Angeles County, which has a long association with gang violence in the United States.[16] These inner-city spaces of exclusion and crime became home to many of the victims of America's international military interventions in Indochina and what followed.

For most refugee families from Cambodia, the harrowing journey across mined terrain to find domicile in a new country was only the beginning of a difficult transition. Many went from a predominantly agrarian way of life to a world of tough inner-city locales. For some parents and elders, already marked by the traumas of surviving the brutalities of the Khmer Rouge and the anxiety of years in limbo in refugee camps, the responsibility of raising and supporting a family in the midst of totally unfamiliar urban environments (with different language, customs, and employment skill sets) was overwhelming and literally drove many elders into deep depression and chronic illness (Lee, Lei, and Sue 2001; Nou 2008; Sack, Him, and Dickason 1999). Others who had been farmers in Cambodia aspired for white-collar jobs in government agencies and to become a member of the middle class (Smith-Hefner 2010). Yet on arrival in the United States, many Cambodians were too busy "just trying to stay alive" to think of the future, or grieve the past (Jonathan Lee 2010, 349). Furthermore, parents and elders were often bewildered by the particular American youth culture they encountered (Mallozzi 2004). Generation gaps often divided parents and children (Ly 2010). Traditional structures of support, such as Buddhist temples and monks, were displaced in the everyday lives of refugees in America. Even though "Khmer are all Buddhist" and that was a familiar identity, the wat's role in community life had become compartmentalized or marginalized among the demands of survival, work, and fast-paced life in the United States (Smith-Hefner 1998, 32).[17]

Taunted and ridiculed at school, these children struggled, often alone, to figure out their places among the diverse groups of the American inner-city underclass. Young Cambodian child refugees soon discovered that they were the newest kids at the bottom of the pile in crowded, downwardly mobile urban neighborhoods. Many parents had to work two or three minimum-wage jobs to support the family, leaving them hard pressed for time to supervise or counsel their children. George Ellis, an American psychologist who managed the Returnee Integration Support Program (RISP) in Phnom Penh, succinctly summed up the returnees' predicament as largely deriving from the failure to help refugee parents adjust to life in the United States some decades ago:

> These were peasants from rural areas. . . . The Khmer Rouge killed the urban elite and the educated class. They were undereducated, even by Cambodian standards. They distrusted government. They'd been traumatized by the Khmer Rouge. They'd spent years in refugee camps with a whole different set of problems. Suddenly they're in the United States. Most ended up in tough, poor, racially-conflicted neighborhoods, surrounded by whites, Blacks and Hispanics. They didn't speak English. There was no Buddhist infrastructure. In Cam-

bodia, if there's a problem, you can go to the monks. They had no monks, no leaders. (Carlson 2007)

Therefore, it was no surprise that some refugee children joined street gangs, which, Ellis said, at least "let them belong to something."

Aihwa Ong describes Cambodian gangs in inner cities in the United States as mostly modeled after the Cambodian family, nonviolent, and a way for young males to seek camaraderie on the streets, get some cash, and thus acquire self-respect—the "most obvious way to explore what it takes to become an American male" (2003, 237). Billy,[18] a returnee who grew up in Long Beach, told me: "Man, our parents were traumatized, didn't know what was happening with us kids. I was a good boy at home—washed the dishes, cleaned up—so they didn't know anything about gangs. We just got into gangs to protect ourselves. We were just kids, thrown in the inner city with Mexicans and blacks. We're the product of the American system" (personal communication, August 2008).

Like Billy, Karney described himself as a "good boy," who had helped distribute water and food in the refugee camps, always fair and kind. In the United States, he tried to obey his strict uncle, who assumed the role of his father, but, never feeling he could measure up, Karney sought comfort elsewhere:

> I started going to school . . . and was getting harassed by everybody. The Hispanics. The blacks and the whites. Then I had my bike taken. My silver necklace taken. I started meeting other Asian males around there so we started going in groups. Not just alone. That way we'd feel more protected. Which worked. So that . . . you know, slowly but surely, it turned into more serious stuff. We started retaliating. We started fighting in school. And by the time I was fourteen . . . seventh grade . . . you know . . . I started not going to school. Then I started having problems failing. I went to different schools and after school and stuff. So that's how things got started. [It] got worse. (personal communication, August 2008)

The group solidarity of gangs often led youths such as Karney to commit punishable offenses. Convictions were for a wide spectrum of offenses, from urinating on the grass (in Houston this was interpreted as a sex crime similar to exhibitionism) to drug trafficking, robbery, or money laundering (Ehrlich 2003; Stokes 2007, 57), as well as more major offenses like robbery, rape, manslaughter, and murder.[19] All of the returnees whom I spoke to were involved in gang activity in their neighborhoods, which eventually led to their convictions. All had anticipated returning to their families after serving their jail sentences and had little notion of what awaited them.

"No, Man. You're Going Home Home."

When Karney completed his prison sentence, he was picked up by the Immigration and Naturalization Service (INS) officials,[20] taken to a detention center, and held there for twelve months before he was transported to Cambodia in 2003. A clean-cut young man with deeply gazing eyes, Karney was in his mid-thirties and rebuilding his life in Cambodia when we met. He had been displaced from Cambodia when he was ten, in 1979, and had spent two years in various Thai border refugee camps; eventually he was settled in the United States as a permanent resident. After twenty-two years he was forcibly uprooted and had to leave behind his three kids. It came as a shock for him: "I had a card as a permanent resident. I thought it meant 'permanent'!" His daughter asked him on the telephone, "When are you coming home, Daddy? You said you were coming home when you got out of prison."

Billy felt luckier than most other returnees because at least he had a few weeks' notice:

> Lots of guys, you know, just get a knock on the door, and that's it. You got no chance to close your banking account, you got no chance of saying goodbye to friends, family, nobody. . . . You're gone. . . . I was laying on the couch, and the phone rang, and nobody was home. And I went to go pick up the phone, like, and my lawyer called and said, "I got bad news for you. . . . You know, your final order for deportation has come in." . . . I was like, "What does that mean?" and he said, "Well, you're going to be deported." I said, "Well, in what time?" and he said, "Well, we don't know that yet, but we will keep in contact with you." . . . I got twenty days. (personal communication, August 2008)

With or without time to mentally prepare, the whole process of dislocation after receiving the deportation order is very disorienting. Deportees are picked up from various locations in the United States, flown from one location to another, and detained until their numbers are deemed sufficient to repatriate them to Cambodia on the same flight. During this time their families do not know where they are, and even find it difficult to connect with them via the authorities.[21] Sareth, a returnee who had served twelve years in prison, described how he had been moved several times from one immigration facility to another for a whole year before being told he was being sent to Cambodia:

> I knew something was wrong, 'cause the INS officer, he [usually] sees me and comes to talk to me. [That day] when he sees me, he starts moving away, like, don't want to talk to me. . . . And they call me to come down the stairs, so I went downstairs, he was like, "Hey, you're going home, right?" I said, "Hey, which home?" He said, "Which home you want it to be?" I said, "My home back in [U.S. city] with my family." He said, "No, man. You're going *home* home." . . . That night they put me in a cell. He said, "You're on the move." So, eight o'clock in the morning, I was taken by the INS people. Put on a plane to New Jersey. . . . Then I went to Louisiana. I don't remember the name. So, stayed there for part of the day. Then they flew me to Texas. Yeah, went to Texas. Then they flew us back to Chicago. Pick up some more people. And went back to San Francisco and San Diego. There for almost a month, I think. And then to Arizona. Flew out of Arizona. To here [Cambodia]. (personal communication, August 2008)

The most difficult part of the whole deportation process is the sudden, forced breakup of a family. Karney talked about how difficult it was: "It's the worst when [returnees] had a wife and kids in the States, and can't ever go back there. That's a punishment too harsh. They served their time. Didn't kill anybody. It's too hard to keep them from their families. It's hard on them, hard on their families. The kids end up growing up with no dad. And they can't support them" (personal communication, February 2006). Another Cambodian returnee, when he learned he was to be deported, had his two-month-old daughter's name tattooed on his arm so it would be there forever. Just like life under the Khmer Rouge, once again children are taken from their parents, and parents separated from their children, except that this time it is happening in America. Other deportees suffer the same pains and have similar profiles.[22] They are being deported to some of the poorest countries that are still recovering from the damage of violent civil wars stoked by U.S. "counterinsurgency interventions," such as El Salvador, where the twelve-year civil war (1980–92) drove more than a million refugees into Southern California. Others are deported to Haiti. These too are predominantly young males, poorly educated and often with a history

FIGURE 5.1. "KK" (gang-style initials for "Crazy Crip"), the thirty-one-year-old deportee from Long Beach, California, speaks Khmer but cannot read or write the language. He set up the Tiny Toones break-dancing troupe for local children in Phnom Penh. The house of the Tiny Toones also serves as a drop-in center for at-risk youths, where English lessons are offered. (© 2008 Stuart Isett)

FIGURE 5.2. This twenty-seven-year-old deportee from Memphis is unemployed and sleeps most nights in a park by the Independence Monument in Phnom Penh. (© 2006 Stuart Isett)

of gang activities, who are returned as outcasts to homelands they left in early childhood (Montaigne 1999, 45).

"I Can't Just Be a Normal Cambodian"

For forced returnees, going "home" to Cambodia is ironically rendered as banishment. Few returnees feel as if they have "cultural citizenship" or a connection with society in Cambodia (Ommundsen, Leach, and Vandenberg 2010). Those who have some memory of Cambodia often have a frozen sense of what being "Cambodian" and Cambodian culture *should* be (Poethig 2006). Compared to their unfamiliarity with Cambodia, the wariness that Cambodian society has toward them is more troublesome. Boomer, a returnee in 2003 and cofounder of Straight Refugeez, a hip-hop enterprise, expressed this dilemma clearly: "I could never be adjusted to Cambodia. Adapted, yes, I'm adapting pretty fast, but adjusted, no. The society won't let me adjust. I can't just be a normal Cambodian. They always want to look at me as Cambodian-American. . . . When they see us, they always have to add that word into it" (quoted in Melamed, July 30, 2005). Differences in food preferences, language problems, the swaggering walk and appearance—baggy pants, tattoos, and basketball shoes typical of inner-city streets in the United States—immediately signal "foreigner" in Phnom Penh. Those who do not want to stand out wear long-sleeved shirts, even in the hot weather, to cover their tattoos and adopt more conformist dressing in public and for work. Again, Boomer echoed how most of my interviewees felt:

> I can't stay away from the returnees; I need to be in that commu-
> nity. I need to be in the same culture as somebody. . . . I miss the cul-
> ture. I miss the lifestyle. I miss hanging out. I miss giving the proper
> handshake. I miss the culture. . . . On work days you just want to
> think about work—once I'm over here [workplace], I'm on another
> level. Once I'm over there [with the other returnees] I'm back in the
> States. (Quoted in Melamed, July 30, 2005)

What further compounds the situation for returnees is that Cambodia itself has been struggling to recover from past traumas and to seek its own identity. The 1993 Constitutional Convention identified as a future task the determination of who the "People of Cambodia" really are (Poethig, 2006, 74). The ruling Kanakpak Pracheachun Kâmpuchéa (Cambodian People's Party, CPP), led by Hun Sen, extolled "cultural purity" based on stationary

Khmerness—referring to those who had stayed put and not fled Cambodia (Poethig 2006, 75)—as key to the rebuilding of the nation. This line of thinking seemed crafted to undermine the credibility of the opposition FUNCINPEC party,[23] which comprised many who had fled Cambodia as refugees but have returned with dual citizenships. These returnees, labeled *anikachun* (a term originally used to refer to resident aliens and now to foreign domiciled Cambodians who are dominant in business and politics) or *anikachun chochun* (a derogatory term), were portrayed as having "betrayed their patriotism" and were considered inassimilable (Poethig 2006, 75). This popular debate had heightened general public consciousness of who is "true" Khmer and who is not and clouded perceptions of the first group of forced returnees arriving in 2001; this group was labeled as American criminals who had no place in the local society.

Furthermore, the anticipation of the steadily increasing number of deportees from the United States prompted the head of the Cambodian League for the Promotion and Defense of Human Rights (LICADHO), a large national-level NGO, to worry about them "planting the seeds for long-term social disruption." She said, "We already have a lot of problems. If we have thousands and thousands of these young Cambodians come back, it's going to be a burden to our society . . . [if they begin] training the young to become like them and join gangs" (quoted in Hyland 2007, 3). Such concerns in Cambodia were not backed up by any evidence of gang activities, even six years after the first group of deportees landed. A similar situation, where deportees are presumed to be criminals and bring shame to relatives who shelter them temporarily, has been observed among the five thousand Haitians deported from the United States from 1996 to 2009 (Bracken 2009).

The difficulties that the returnees face are also exacerbated by the lack of any officially supported system of assistance put in place by the U.S. and Cambodian governments.[24] Nor has the moral responsibility of the U.S. government to provide reparations been broached. Socially displaced again at "home," many Cambodian returnees are trapped in a vicious cycle: the little assistance and support they receive make them vulnerable to drugs, alcohol, and fights, which in turn alienate them further from the local community. A few have ended up in prison, and one committed suicide. Bill Herod and George Ellis estimated that a third of the returnees were employed and living independently, and another third seemed settled in but were financially dependent on families in the United States, while the rest faced difficulties with drugs, alcohol abuse, fights, depression, and anger (Melamed 2005; Stokes 2007, 58).

But there are also positive stories of resilience and reintegration into society in a foreign country. Some returnees have found work in the tourist industry and the nonprofit sector using their English, web-design, or other Internet-related skills. Karney, for instance, remarried and had found new meaning in life by helping others:

> I even help people that are the same as I was. I give 'em food, a place to stay in my house. As long as they don't mess up. Although I'm struggling myself, . . . it's time for me to give back and sometimes even though I get tired and wonder, "Why am I doing this?" I'm helping a few people myself with a lot of things. I have to do it. It's a way of giving back to what I've taken from society. (personal communication, August 2008)

Another returnee who goes by the name of KK founded Cambodia's first break-dance troupe in an inner-city community where drug and alcohol abuse was prevalent among the youths. KK founded Tiny Toones as a way of sharing his love for break dancing, which he learned on the streets of Long Beach as a member of a street gang. Now he wants to contribute to society by influencing Cambodian youths to avoid drug abuse (see Mydans 2008). When I spoke with KK in 2008, after his dance troupe had just returned from performing as invited guests at the International AIDS Conference in Mexico City, he told me that Tiny Toones had expanded through small centers across Cambodia to involve approximately two thousand youngsters. They teach not only break dancing but also Khmer, English, and computer literacy (personal communication, August 2008).

Another group of returnees work for Korsang, a small nonprofit organization dedicated to fighting HIV and drug-related problems among the street population in Phnom Penh. They are committed to promoting harm-reduction efforts, risk education, and health-related services, as well as to serve each person with the "highest level of dignity, compassion, and respect"—what they themselves yearned for as boys on the streets of U.S. cities.[25] In some ways those helped by this nonprofit organization became family for many of the newer returnees: they share a similar status of marginality in Cambodia, and returnees can relate to their circumstances from personal experience.

Discussion

This chapter has outlined the multiple displacements in the lives of forcibly repatriated Cambodian residents in the United States. These multiple displacements are interrelated. The forced return of these former refugees to Cambodia relates historically to the displacements caused by U.S. military interventions in postcolonial civil strife in Indochina, these Cambodians' consequent displacement within the American host society, and social displacement and rifts faced after they are deported to Cambodia. The history of how one form of displacement led to another to a great extent reflects the changing global order of the latter half of the twentieth century. There is a discernible shift in U.S. governmental strategy: military actions are largely regarded as undesirable, and overtly racist riots such as those targeting Chinese immigrants in the nineteenth century are unacceptable. Instead, regulatory and legal systems have become preferred modes for maintaining social order. The violent displacement induced by the wars in Indochina was indiscriminate; by comparison the displacement by deportation is selective, targeted, conducted according to legal procedures, and becoming a routine practice. While wars and revolutions seek to overthrow sovereignties, deportation is a measure that is readily available to U.S. authorities within the current political order. It relies on and seeks to enhance sovereign power.

Transnational agreements, such as that between the United States and Cambodia, have been critical to facilitating deportation. A Memorandum of Understanding between the governments of the United States and Vietnam (January 22, 2008) enables the forced repatriation of Vietnamese permanent residents who entered the United States after July 12, 1995, if they violate any U.S. laws.[26] As this chapter demonstrates, the legal terms of the relations between individuals and nation-states can involve, and sometimes necessitate, disruptions and displacement. Although the Cambodian returnees (and also Vietnamese returnees) lived most of their lives in the United States and came to know nowhere else as home, the United States refuses to recognize their political citizenship; yet, in Cambodia, despite their status as full citizens, these Cambodian returnees have been effectively deprived of cultural citizenship. Selective partial subjectifications by different sovereignties place the returnees in a very awkward position.

Still, the shift from military intervention to legal regulation is not irreversible. Underlying both modes of rule and the consequent displacements is an American paradox that results in external interventions or solutions driven by domestic fear. The year 2003 may turn out to have been another turning point in U.S. immigration history. In that year the INS was split, and jurisdiction over immigration was transferred from the Department of Justice to the Department of Homeland Security, signaling intensified fears about aliens within U.S. borders.[27] In the same period, the United States invaded Iraq, which then president George W. Bush explicitly related to the fear of terrorism post–September 11: "Since America put out the fires of September the 11th, and mourned our dead, and went to war, history has taken a different turn. We have carried the fight to the enemy. We are rolling back the terrorist threat to civilization, not on the fringes of its influence, but at the heart of its power."[28] This Iraq war and continued U.S. military presence have already generated more than two million international refugees (Refugees International 2007), 64,174 of whom had entered the United States as of March 31, 2012.[29] Many of these are children, living in families faced with poverty and many other difficulties (Jonsson and Chick 2009). Are these children potential deportees? Is this cycle repeating itself? Without attention to the ramifications of current policies and practices regarding interventions and subsequent resettlements, and the revision of these, alas, the potential is all too high for similar scenarios to be repeated.

Notes

1. Deportations have continued to escalate. In October 2011 the U.S. government reported that it had deported a record number (just under 400,000) of undocumented immigrants for the third year in a row, of whom 188,000, or 48 percent, were convicted of crimes (Simanski and Sapp 2012, 1). This report does not acknowledge the number who were "permanent residents" and not illegal. In the ten years between April 1997 and August 2007 the U.S. deported 87,884 Legal Permanent Residents for criminal convictions (average rate of 8,700 per year) (International Human Rights Clinic et al. 2010, 4). The number deported to Cambodia and classified as criminal removals reached 316 between 2002 and 2011, with a three-times increase between 2010 and 2011, from 25 to 74 (U.S. Department of Homeland Security 2012, 106–112).

2. The term *returnees* was how my informants referred to themselves, and it is widely used by the media, government officials, and NGO activists alike—rather than the stigmatizing term *deportees*.

3. See the U.S. Immigration and Customs Enforcement, "Removal Statistics," http://www.ice.gov/removal-statistics/ (accessed December 30, 2012). Statistics for previous years found at http://www.dhs.gov/yearbook-immigration-statistics.

4. Although accurate numbers are difficult to obtain, according to the 2010 U.S. Census, 28,424 individuals in Massachusetts and 102,317 in California identified themselves as Cambodians (SEARAC 2011, 5).

5. Over this period, I interviewed thirty returnees, twenty-nine men and one woman. In addition to, sometimes multiple, interviews (averaging ninety minutes with a minimum of one hour and a maximum of five hours each), I also did participant observation in workplaces, organizations, and other social settings. My interviews and observations are supplemented by extensive documentary studies and media reports that situate personal experiences and emotions in the larger historical and structural context. The interviews were conducted in English, as the interviewees were fluent in English and for most it was their dominant language. They were conducted in Phnom Penh, Siem Reap, and Battambang.

6. The USA PATRIOT Act, named in full, refers to the Uniting and Strengthening America by Providing Appropriate Tools Required to Intercept and Obstruct Terrorism Act, signed by President George W. Bush on October 26, 2001.

7. The Cambodian government, now called a democracy under a constitutional monarchy, is controlled by the longtime prime minister Hun Sen and his Cambodian People's Party, who have oversight over all institutions and exert power over those who challenge their authority. Opposition parties have been made ineffective through contestable elections and government tactics, and while the monarchy still exists, it has little influence (Picken 2011).

8. U.S. Department of State, Office of the Historian, "The Immigration and Nationality Act of 1952 (The McCarran-Walter Act)," see http://history.state.gov/mile stones/1945–1952/ImmigrationAct (accessed December 30, 2012).

9. The crash of a plane in January 1948 that was carrying deported Mexicans, who lost their lives, brought public attention to deportation practices and civil and humane omissions. The folk singer Woody Guthrie's song "Deportees" remains a poignant reminder today of the human cost of deportation. Lyrics available at http://www .woodyguthric.org/Lyrics/Plane_Wreck_At_Los_Gatos.htm, accessed February 14, 2013.

10. See "Death Tolls for the Major Wars and Atrocities of the Twentieth Century." Available online at http://users.erols.com/mwhite28/warstat2.htm, accessed February 14, 2013.

11. An estimated 1,250,000 Southeast Asian refugees entered the United States between 1975 and 1994, the country's largest refugee group since the Second World War. See http://www.answers.com/topic/southeast-asian-american, accessed February 14, 2013. Of the over two million estimated Cambodians, Vietnamese, and Lao refugees from the war, many others went to France. Other countries that accepted refugees in smaller numbers from this war included Australia, Canada, the United Kingdom, New Zealand, Italy, and the Netherlands.

12. In the 2010 U.S. Census, Cambodians were grouped in the Asian category, along with any of the people whose origin was in the Far East, Southeast Asia (except Vietnam), or India. In the period between 2000 and 2010, the Asian population grew faster than any other major designated racial group; it increased by 43 percent.

13. Carol Mortland (2010) describes four waves of immigrants: the first (approximately 6,000 between 1975 and 1977) was mostly made up of the educated and middle class, with connections to American businesses; the second (approximately 10,000 in

1979) was primarily rural farmers; the third and largest (approximately 122,228 between 1980 and 1986 alone [according to Niedzwiecki and Duong 2004, quoted in
Mortland 2010, 77]) was also mostly rural people with limited educational resources
and urban occupational skills; and the fourth (9,579 between 1987 and 1993 [accord-
ing to Niedzwiecki and Duong 2004, quoted in Mortland 2010, 77]) was made up of
mostly family members rejoining earlier refugees.

14. SEARAC (Southeast Asian Resource Action Center). See "SEA Statistics," 2010,
http://www.searac.org/content/publications-and-materials, accessed February 14,
2013, PDF, and Cambodia Town, http://portfoliolab.org/portal/DesktopDefault.aspx
?pId=1635&TabId=1718&HtmlId=7952&MenuId=5367.

15. Based on the 2010 U.S. Census, the population of Long Beach (462,257) was 46.1
percent white, 40.8 percent Hispanic, 13.5 percent black, 12.9 percent Asian (some in-
dicated more than one race). The median age was 32.7 (younger than the U.S. median).
Median household income was USD 52,945. Somewhat less diverse, the population of
Lowell (106,519) was made up of 60.3 percent white, 20.2 percent Asian, 17.3 percent
Latino, 6.8 percent black (some indicated more than one race). The median age (32.6)
was younger than the U.S. median. Median household income level was USD 51,471.
See American Fact Finder: U.S. Census 2010: Cities, at http://factfinder2.census.gov
/faces/nav/jsf/pages/community_facts.xhtml (accessed February 14, 2013).

16. "Asian Gangs in Los Angeles County," Streetgangs.com, http://www.streetgangs
.com/asian/ (accessed December 31, 2012).

17. There had already been shifts in the role of Buddhism during wartime in Cambodia, and the Khmer Rouge attempted to supplant Buddhist beliefs with its political
ideology (Smith-Hefner 1998). Efforts to establish temples in the United States were
also fraught with disputes and struggles for power (Gerson 2008).

18. This is a pseudonym. All informant names have been changed to protect their
identities.

19. Deportees from the United States to many other countries have similar profiles
to those of the Cambodians. They are predominantly young, male, poorly educated,
and often have a history of gang activities. Deportation is said to have exported the
gang culture to countries such as Haiti, where gangs were previously not at all part of
the social life (Bracken 2009). Across Central America and the Caribbean, criminal
deportees numbered more than 56,000 in 1998. This created dire problems for many
countries that were just beginning to recover from years of political violence (Montaigne 1999, 45). In a report from September 2, 2009, the mayor of Juarez, Mexico, Jose
Reyes Ferriz, pointed to the return of criminal deportees as a source of great harm,
because they added "a deadly ingredient to an already volatile state of security." Citing
gang drug activity, Juarez noted that "in the past 45 days, 10 percent of those killed in
Juarez had been deported from the United States in the past two years." He acknowledged, however, that there were no statistics noting how many of these had criminal
records in the United States (CNN World 2009).

20. This U.S. agency was reorganized into the Department of Homeland Security
and the Immigration and Customs Enforcement (ICE) became the agency with oversight.

21. ICE now has posted on its website a "detainee locator" form for family members to fill out to locate a relative. See U.S. Immigration and Customs Enforcement at https://locator.ice.gov/odls/homePage.do (accessed February 14, 2013). U.S. Public Broadcasting System, Frontline, film *Lost in Detention*, provides an insider's view of detention centers in the United States in 2011. See http://www.pbs.org/wgbh/pages /frontline/lost-in-detention/ (accessed February 14, 2013).

22. According to the study of Jacqueline Hagan, Karl Eschbach, and Nestor Rodriguez (2008), one-third of the Salvadoran deportees had lived in the United States for more than ten years, and one-third had spouses and children, while Haitian deportees had lived in the United States for twenty years or more (Bracken 2009).

23. The acronym FUNCINPEC is from the French phrase "Front Uni National pour un Cambodge Indépendant, Neutre, Pacifique, et Coopératif" (National United Front for an Independent, Neutral, Peaceful, and Cooperative Cambodia).

24. Bill Herod's Returnee Assistance Program, founded with small donations to provide transitional housing, assistance with job searches, and psychological support services, evolved into RISP. Set up with U.S. Agency of International Development (USAID) funding, RISP employed returnees to show newer arrivals the ropes. But in August 2008, just three years later, I learned that its USAID funding had not been renewed. In Haiti, similarly, returnees were seemingly abandoned without support or funding for resettlement, except briefly when the International Organization for Migration program assisted deportees arriving between April 2007 and August 2008 (Bracken 2009). By comparison, El Salvador has the program Bienvenido a Casa (Welcome Home), which is supported by the International Organization for Migration and Catholic Relief Services, to help Salvadorans deported from the United States (some 10,684 from 1999 to 2004) (Hagan, Eschbach, and Rodriguez 2008, 68). Apart from helping find jobs and reintegrate, the program also provides resettlement funds, referrals to social service agencies, and counseling services to assist with trauma and stress. Most of the Salvadorans have been deported for immigration violations, using fraudulent documents, or petty crimes (Hagan, Eschbach, and Rodriquez 2008, 66; U.S. Department of Homeland Security 2006).

25. Korsang was founded in 2004. See http://www.korsangkhmer.org (accessed February 14, 2013).

26. After ten years of negotiations, Vietnam and the United States reached agreement on the deportation of Vietnamese citizens, and it was signed by United States Homeland Security Assistant Secretary for Immigration and Customs Enforcement Julie L. Myers and Deputy Foreign Minister for the Government of Vietnam Mr. Dao Viet Trung. See the *New York Times*, January 23, 2008, at http://www.nytimes.com /2008/01/23/us/23immig.html?_r=0 (accessed February 14, 2013).

27. ICE was established in 2003, after the Homeland Security Act of 2002. Prior to this, other agencies performed many of the functions of ICE: U.S. Customs Service (Treasury), Immigration and Naturalization Service (Justice), and Federal Protective Service. ICE describes its functions as follows: "U.S. Immigration and Customs Enforcement (ICE) is the largest investigative arm of the Department of Homeland Security (DHS), responsible for enforcing the nation's immigration and customs laws that

protect national security and public safety. With more than 20,000 employees world-wide, ICE is a key component of DHS's layered approach to protecting the nation" (see the "Leadership Offices" page on the ICE website, http://www.ice.gov/about/offices /leadership/ [accessed February 14, 2013]).

28. George W. Bush, text of speech on Iraq, September 7, 2003. Available online at http://www.commondreams.org/headlines03/0907-10.htm (accessed September 27, 2009).

29. See Iraqi Refugee Processing Fact Sheet, U.S. Immigration and Customs Ser-vices, at http://www.uscis.gov/portal/site/uscis/menuitem.5af9bb95919f35e66f6141765 43f6d1a/?vgnextchannel=68439c7755cb9010VgnVCM10000045f3d6a1RCRD&vgnext oid=df4c47c9de5ba110VgnVCM1000004718190aRCRD (accessed February 14, 2013).

Rescue, Return, in Place

Deportees, "Victims," and the Regulation of Indonesian Migration

JOHAN LINDQUIST

Three significant changes in the current infrastructure of migration be-tween Malaysia and Indonesia, in particular, and in Southeast Asia, more generally, provide a useful starting point for this chapter. First, there has been an enactment of a series of formal and informal agreements between national governments aimed at enforcing documented migration at the expense of undocumented migration (Hugo 2009, 42). In this context, I am especially concerned with the emergence of a bilateral deportation regime from Malaysia to Indonesia. Second, there has been a proliferation of countertrafficking programs that are mainly concerned with the forced entry of women and children into prostitution. Third, a growing num-ber of actors—most notably nongovernmental organizations (NGOs) and journalists—have become engaged in recording and publicizing human rights violations, particularly through moving images, thus transforming human trafficking, migrant deportations, and related forms of abuse into media spectacles.

These developments should be considered together as measures aimed at both regulating and protecting migrants. This perspective shifts attention away from a primary focus on migrant experience, which predominates recent anthropological literature on migration, to one on emerging infrastructures that regulate migrant mobility. While there is much work that helps us understand why unskilled migrants leave home, as well as what abuses and problems they face upon arrival, we know much less about the particular channels that facilitate and constrain migrant mobility between departure and destination (Lindquist 2010a). More specifically, the production of these channels should be considered not only in relation to the political economy but also with regard to the humanitarian interventions that have a growing impact on transnational migrant mobility. In this context, the conceptualization of the "migration industry" must be broadened to include not only the actors and institutions that move migrants but also mass media and NGOs that are engaged in interventions that respond to abuses against, or aim to protect, migrants (Hernandez-Leon 2005; see also Rudnyckyj 2004).

Following the theme of this book, my discussion is focused on the question of "return," or more specifically "returning home," which stands out as a critical component in the changes outlined above, namely bilateral agreements, countertrafficking programs, and media reporting in the context of the migration industry. The transnational circulation of migrants on bilaterally regulated temporary contracts is premised on the return home of the migrant, programs focused on the struggle against human trafficking aim to "reintegrate" victims through return, while documentary films and other forms of media reporting frequently conceptualize the return home as a necessary response or an adequate solution to violations against migrants. As such, the return home of the migrant is facilitated by or enforced through various forms of interventions. More generally, return remains taken for granted and unproblematic in all these contexts—particularly in relation to "home"—and this comes to have important effects on the regulation of transnational migration. In this process, *home* becomes an empty signifier that is implicitly understood as either a safe haven for the migrant or the place where he or she belongs, according to state administrative definitions.[1] The return home of the migrant can come to be embraced through various forms of interventions. From this perspective, states, NGOs, and mass media that support return should not be understood in opposition to one another, but rather as together shaping an emerging transnational regime of circular migration (Vertovec 2007).

The notion of return is of course not alien to migrants. The external interventions that impose or facilitate return may either be in conjunction or in conflict with migrants' own perceptions of return. Since the 1970s both domestic and international migration have increased steadily throughout Southeast Asia and Indonesia (Hugo 2004, 35–37). In Indonesia, migration should be understood through the cultural logic of *merantau*, which means "to go out into the world before returning home again." In other words, return is implicated in the very meaning of migration. While historically associated with particular ethnic groups such as the Minangkabau of West Sumatra, and often understood as a process of transformation or a rite of passage in which the boy leaves the village and returns as a man, merantau, in its contemporary form, has become nationalized, increasingly feminized, and closely intertwined with capitalist development. The return home of the migrant—in any sustainable sense—becomes possible primarily through economic success, which in turn creates independence from the insecurities of temporary wage labor that characterizes everyday life across Indonesia. However, for many migrants who face failure, *malu*, meaning shame or embarrassment, keeps them on the move, suggesting an unresolved moral tension in relation to return home as an unproblematic response to migrant abuse abroad (Lindquist 2009). In other words, the cultural idiom merantau not only stresses the successful completion of the migration project, often in economic terms, but is also based on a circular movement that by no means implies emplacement.

Since the colonial era, Malaysia has been a key destination for merantau, a process that has intensified during the last two decades, as Indonesia has become one of the main sending countries for unskilled migrant labor in Asia. Malaysia is one of the largest receiving countries, having been transformed into a "tiger economy" with an expanding middle class and a growing demand for migrant labor on palm-oil plantations, on construction sites, and as domestic servants. As many as two million Indonesians, many of them undocumented, labor in Peninsular Malaysia and Sarawak, mostly on a circulatory basis (Hernández-Coss et al. 2008, 19). Since the 1997 Asian economic crisis there has been a move from undocumented to documented migration, as Indonesia and Malaysia, as well as other governments throughout Asia and the Middle East, have become increasingly concerned with regulating migrant mobility (Silvey 2004). This introduces new forms of return that are organized, facilitated, enforced, monitored, and evaluated by various parties according to purposively designed procedures.

In the introduction to this book, Xiang Biao argues that throughout

Asia, return has come to function as a form of migrant emplacement that reinforces particular forms of sovereign power (see also Malkki 1995a). This concern with return in the context of the regulation of transnational migration in Asia is, Xiang claims, a response to several decades of intensifying globalization and regional integration. More specifically, return is associated with state attempts to reestablish sovereignty in the face of increasing flows of undocumented migrants—or in some cases anxieties with such flows. This is notable in Malaysia, where unease with Indonesian undocumented migration in the context of crime and unemployment is evident in public discourse and political practice, particularly since the 1997 crisis (Chin 2008).

While the relationship between state sovereignty and return appears obvious in regimes of government-organized migrant deportation, this is less evident in countertrafficking programs and in media reports of migrant abuses, which both take a universalist human rights discourse as their point of reference and thus appear to be located beyond the political. But deportation, countertrafficking, and media reporting have increasingly come to intersect precisely in the shared concern with migrant return. A focus on return thus allows us to conceptualize a particular kind of relationship between state sovereignty and universalist human rights concerns, and to further consider how they generate common effects in the context of the control and protection of unskilled migrant labor through a shared mode of intervention. Nevertheless, it is also important to reiterate that in practice return remains contested and should not strictly be understood in terms of emplacement. In fact, the logic of merantau and the governance of migrant mobility can come into conflict, because the demands of success keep migrants on the move.

In order to more carefully consider these effects, I compare three different overlapping phenomena, each corresponding to the three major developments. Specifically, these refer to an Indonesian government program that handles deportees from Malaysia; an award-winning Australian documentary film, *Inside the Child Sex Trade*, in which two Indonesian teenagers are rescued from a brothel and returned home; and a project on the repatriation of trafficking victims run by the Indonesian office of the International Organization for Migration in collaboration with local NGOS. Through these different case studies I highlight how different forms of interventions—both in the name of state sovereignty and of human rights—become components of and reinforce a new order of mobility.

Organizing Deportation

Prior to 2002, return as an organized form of intervention for transnational migrants was rarely an issue in Indonesia. In the 1990s and particularly after 1997, as Indonesian migration became an increasingly important political issue, the Malaysian government created detention camps for migrants and initiated a series of ad hoc and chaotic deportation campaigns. The problem of government staff shortages led to the expansion of a state-sponsored civil volunteer corps, the self-styled heroic RELA (an acronym for Ikatan Relawan Rakyat Malaysia, or Volunteers of the Malaysian People), which was offered minimal training and cash rewards by the Malaysian government for the detention of undocumented migrants (Chin 2008; Kaur 2006, 49). This form of regulation—widely criticized by international observers as lacking in long-term vision—intensified with the 2002 Malaysian immigration act, which transformed immigration violations by both migrants and employers into criminal offenses (Kaur 2006, 48–49).

After a period of amnesty, the Malaysian government initiated mass-deportation campaigns in 2002 that sent migrants through a number of Indonesian ports, including Batam (Riau Islands Province), Dumai (Riau Province), and Nunukan on the eastern coast of Borneo (East Kalimantan Province). The scale of these deportations, which numbered nearly 400,000 people, caught government authorities in Indonesia off guard. The chaos that ensued in Nunukan in particular—with widespread media images of deported migrants lacking even basic clothing—led to a major public outcry with demands that future deportation processes be handled more humanely on both sides of the border (Ford 2006).

Following in the wake of these events, there has been a gradual shift toward bilaterally planned deportations. As a result, the process of return is now carefully controlled at the multiple transit points and via various modes of transportation until the migrants arrive in their home villages, with the Indonesian government covering all costs. Every week more than five hundred migrants who have been arrested and detained in different parts of Peninsular Malaysia depart from Johor and arrive at the port of Tanjung Pinang on the island of Bintan in Riau Islands Province.[2]

These deportees are handled on the Indonesian side of the border by a number of government agencies led by the Agency for Social Affairs and Labor (Despos for short) which transport the deportees a few kilometers from the center of Tanjung Pinang to a holding center that is rented from a labor recruitment company that sends migrants to Malaysia. Deportees are detained for up to a week before being sent on to Jakarta and then further afield.

The groups of deportees awaiting return in the holding center in Tanjung Pinang at any given time share space with migrants who are waiting to enter Malaysia legally through the same labor-recruitment agency that owns the holding center. "It shouldn't be like that" (*seharusnya tidak begitu*), the government official in charge told me when I visited the center with a local NGO in 2006, meaning that the two different groups of migrants—one inside and the other outside the law—should not be located in the same space. This intersection is far from coincidental since in the current transnational labor migration regime, the sustainability of labor exports through legal channels relies on the enforcement of deportation. It is important to note that for most observers this does not signal a chaotic process. In fact, on a visit to the holding center in 2006, the UN's special rapporteur on the human rights of migrants, Jorge Bustamante, noted that migratory movements in Tanjung Pinang were conducted "in a very orderly fashion."[3]

From Tanjung Pinang migrants are sent by regular passenger ship to Jakarta's main port, Tanjung Priok, which has historically been an international hub for goods and people traveling to and from Malaysia, Singapore, and further abroad. Tanjung Priok is an infamous transit site that various forms of brokers have used as fertile ground for making money off migrants (see Jones 2000), much like the migrant terminal at the Soekarno-Hatta International Airport in Jakarta, which was established precisely to protect them (Silvey 2007). With the rise of low-cost air travel, however, shipping companies are handling far fewer passengers and local entrepreneurs at the port are facing hard times. As a result, Tanjung Priok has been transformed from a hub for spontaneous outflows to a strategic site for organized returns.

While the Indonesian government handles the actual transport, representatives from the Indonesian migrant labor union Sarekat Buruh Migran Indonesia (SBMI, Indonesian migrant worker union)—many of them former migrants themselves—participate as monitors when deportees arrive from Tanjung Pinang. In May 2007, I joined SBMI's staff as a ship with seven hundred deportees and several hundred regular passengers docked at Tanjung Priok. At the port for passenger ships, officials from Depsos were waiting to let us in through the gate. It was obvious that SBMI and Depsos were on good terms as they chatted and joked with each other. I never heard SBMI staff members say anything negative about the work that Depsos was doing and neither noticed nor heard of any conflicts between them.

While the regular passengers exited first through the main gate, the deportees came last and were directed through a separate entrance by an official using a loudspeaker system. Once inside the large waiting room, which had been officially inaugurated by Indonesia's president in August 2006 as a "ruang tamu TKI" (Indonesian migrant waiting room),[4] the migrants — most of whom were men — were led to sit in sections that were divided according to their respective home provinces. In one of the corners of the room there was a small makeshift health clinic, and banners on the wall read: "Coordinating Post for the Sending Home [pemulangan] of Migrant Workers Deported from Malaysia" and "We Will Facilitate Return to Your Area of Origin [daerah asal]." The majority of the migrants were from the islands of Java, Lombok, and Sumbawa, with a handful each from Aceh, Sulawesi, and the eastern parts of Indonesia. As the names of provinces were called one by one, migrants lined up in front of a desk with two officials, where they were photographed and asked for their addresses, ages, places of origin, and where they had been in Malaysia. This took several hours. As far as I can understand, the data collected were not used for any further purpose than data collection itself, and the fact that the migrants were deportees was not held against them.

There were at least half a dozen journalists on site, two groups from television and the rest from major newspapers, a typical turnout for the weekly event in the ongoing story about the travails of Indonesian migrants abroad. One woman from Indonesian TransTV asked me if I had spoken to a migrant, preferably a woman, who had been caned by Malaysian authorities and might be willing to be interviewed. There were only a handful of women and just two children in the entire group. One of the women was obviously mentally ill and wandered around barefoot, singing and acting out, as a staff member from SBMI told me that she had been forced into prostitution and was *depresi* (depressed). The television journalist asked if she could interview her, but members of the SBMI staff, who apparently were the migrants' gatekeeper, refused. Instead, the journalist made a call to an Indonesian staff member at the Counter Trafficking Unit at the International Organization for Migration (IOM) in Jakarta, since she felt that this should be considered a case of trafficking. But after some background explanation, the IOM staff said that they could not take the woman since it was unclear where she was from and that they would not know where to send her back. Although IOM states in its Victims of

Trafficking program that victims do not have to return home,[5] clearly this was the norm. Victims who had nowhere to go—nowhere to be "reintegrated"—were a problem for this program.

Once all the deportees had been registered, they were loaded onto buses that took them to a public bus station where they waited with officials from Depsos to be escorted to their various destinations later that same afternoon. Those headed to Mataram, the capital of Lombok, were confronted with a thirty-six-hour bus ride. The head of the bus station claimed that one of the most infamous labor brokers at the Tanjung Priok harbor had offered to pay him 100,000 rupiah (about USD 10) per migrant he handed over—certainly hoping to broker them back over the border to Malaysia, which he apparently had many times before. But the man at the bus station had refused. It was, he told me, his duty that all the migrants arrived home safely to the provincial government offices.

It is possible to identify an infrastructure in which government officials, labor-recruitment agencies, NGO activists, and journalists share a common concern with the regulation and protection of migrants. Here, regulation and protection are not opposed to one another—as they potentially could be—precisely because "return home" is the agreed upon endpoint. The work of journalists concerned with abuses abroad and the NGOs that monitor government officials both reinforce the ethics of return and the sovereign power of the Indonesian state. The desires of individual migrants become irrelevant in this process as protection and regulation converge in the expansion of pastoral forms of power.

The Spectacle of Rescue

At the center of the debate on the regulation of international migration in Asia and across the globe is the reported rise in human trafficking, as well as the ensuing demand for intervention. In this process, mass media have been critical—often in explicit collaboration with NGOs—in transforming trafficking into a public issue, while NGOs are increasingly using moving images (Lindquist 2010b).[6] In her documentary film from 2005, *Inside the Child Sex Trade* (originally made for the Australian current-affairs program *Dateline*), the television journalist Olivia Rousset travels to the Indonesian island of Batam—located just a forty-minute ferry ride away from Singapore and in close proximity to Tanjung Pinang, along the Indonesian border—to create a documentary film about the island's prostitution industry, and particularly the sexual exploitation of children.[7] Rousset, a white woman and the film's narrator, tells us that in Batam's brothels, "Islam's moral code is non-existent" and that young women there "are brought from distant villages and sold into sexual slavery for a few hundred dollars." She further claims that "of the estimated 15,000 trafficked sex workers here [in Batam], nearly half of them are thought to be children."

In the film we are introduced to Batam through the work of the local NGO Prai (an abbreviation of Perlindungan Anak Indonesia, which translates to "Protection of Indonesian Children"). Ramses, the man who runs Prai, leads Rousset to Diana and Lina, two fourteen- or fifteen-year-old girls from the island of Madura (located just off the east coast of Java) who have become prostitutes in Batam's largest quasi-legal brothel area. Together with staff from Prai, Rousset visits the brothel "undercover" with a hidden camera, because they are run by the "local mafia." She tells us that the girls have been brought to the brothel by a trafficker, who sold them for USD 400 each.

The central plot of the film is the ensuing attempt to get the two girls out of the brothel and return them to their families in their home villages. The camera follows the NGO workers as they use another prostitute in the brothel as a go-between, since neither Diana nor Lina are interested in talking to them. Meanwhile, Ramses is able to contact the girls' parents in Madura and their uncles (or at least one uncle; this is not entirely clear in the film) travel to Batam along with two "concerned politicians and a social worker." This, Rousset claims, is the "rescue team," and "the girls' future depends on the success of their mission." Together they drive to the brothel, but neither Lina nor Diana has been told about the plan.

When the group enters the brothel, the camera moves straight toward Lina. She looks shocked and falls silent before beginning to cry hysterically. Her uncle puts his arm around her and tells her to stop, while the camera remains in her face. In the end she does not turn away or resist but continues to weep. Meanwhile, in the background there is some negotiation with the brothel owner who claims that the girls were not coerced but came of their own free will. "No one is being sold here," the man says. Lina's uncle follows her to her room where he tells her just to bring what is necessary and to leave everything else behind. She tells him that she does not have any money, but he says that it does not matter. The narrator claims that the fact that she has no money to show makes her even more ashamed. Meanwhile, Diana runs out of the brothel to the back of the building, and a local Madurese businessman who has come along to help goes out to find her, as the camera follows. Like Lina, she begins to cry hysterically as the camera stays on her while she packs her bag. As they leave the brothel and get into the waiting car, Diana says goodbye to everyone, including the brothel owner who, as the narrator phrases it, "imprisoned her."

After some downtime with Prai, Diana and Lina return by plane to Madura together with Ramses and Rousset. In the minivan that takes them home along the rural roads, the girls have put on their *jilbab* (Muslim headscarves) and we find out that their real names are Saharta and Sutia. They are obviously excited and overjoyed to be back. The camera joins them as they arrive in their separate villages, where they are reunited with their families. In Diana's village, her family is clearly moved and happy that she is back. In Lina's village, a half hour further away, the reaction is more subdued as her grandmother greets her by telling her to enter the house and stop crying. The narrator reveals that Lina's mother is absent, as she has been working in Malaysia during the last decade, while her father is ill. As they sit down to talk, Ramses asks her father where he wants to send her to school. The father says that he cannot afford schooling and even if he could, Lina says that she wants to help harvest the tobacco crop.

In the final scene, Lina is surrounded by friends, all young women wearing jilbab. Prompted by the filmmaker, she offers advice to others who want to leave: "Don't go. I wouldn't let them go." But as the narrator points out, in a village where it is difficult to survive on farming alone, "there's little choice but to leave." Rousset then asks if there are children who have traveled abroad, and Lina responds, "Lots, to Malaysia and wherever," while another adds "Saudi" (Arabia). Lina ends by saying, "No one tells them to go. No one makes them. I wanted to go. I wanted to help my parents. But I didn't help them, I hurt them instead." But as she speaks she looks straight into the camera, offers a crooked smile, and winks mischievously, adding emphasis to her claim that she has a will of her own.

There are multiple perspectives from which to consider this film, from the initial identification of the girls to the shocking rescue, and finally to their return home. There is also much to be questioned regarding statistical claims, the role of Rousset in the making of the film, and the representation of prostitution in Batam. Instead of addressing these problems, I focus on the relationship between rescue and return in the film. In the narrative structure of *Inside the Child Sex Trade*, the rescue is not only the obvious climax, but also the point where an ethics of witnessing takes precedence over an ethics of consent. This form of witnessing thus creates a particular type of "victim" who demands intervention and protection (see Pandolfi 2008, 173). This becomes most obvious through the spectacle of Lina and

Diana's shock and distress. The rescue had come to overshadow return, which initially appeared to have been taken for granted by the filmmaker and the NGO as a relatively unproblematic process. The potential complications associated with return were not even raised until after the girls left the brothel, when the question of schooling surfaced. In Diana and Lina's actual return there was a more general lack of closure, if not in the filmmaker's own recognition that for young people in the village "there's little choice but to leave," then in Lina's smile and wink, which ran against the grain of the film's moralizing tone and suggested that she might just decide to leave again. Even before Lina's departure, her mother had been gone for almost a decade, her father was clearly ill, and her grandmother did not appear to offer much empathy or support. With no money for school and irregular and low-paying wages in the fields, marriage or migration appeared to be the only routes forward.[8] But in the end the filmmaker was not able to offer a significant response to this apparent dilemma, and the camera left Diana and Lina behind.

Institutionalizing Return in Victims of Trafficking Programs

While the formation of trafficking as a media spectacle has been critical to creating public interest on a global scale, countertrafficking programs are another important component of the current migration infrastructure that I am describing. As one NGO activist involved in monitoring the Malaysian deportation program in Tanjung Pinang put it: "Before 2003 I didn't know the meaning of *trafficking*, but then I saw a brochure from IOM and I just knew. Apparently these things didn't just happen in films."[9] It was in this defining moment that she turned her organization's activities away from a concern with children's rights and toward a focus on trafficking, thus adding to a process of institutionalization that followed from the United States Trafficking Victims Protection Act and the United Nations Protocol to Prevent, Suppress and Punish Trafficking in Persons, Especially Women and Children. Adopted in 2000 (Kempadoo 2005, xii–xiv; Warren 2007), both of these documents came to legitimize trafficking as a problem that demanded intervention, thus generating new transnational funding circuits.[10]

During the last decade the struggle against human trafficking has gained a global institutional form through governments, agencies, organizations, journalists, and academics who generate various forms of knowledge, projects, and modes of intervention. *Inside the Child Sex Trade* is one example of this. Despite being dispersed over an uneven global landscape and pursuing radically different political agendas—faith-based right-wing Christian organizations in the United States and left-leaning Indonesian NGOs, to name but two examples—almost all these individuals and organizations have been able to converge around the figure of the trafficking victim. Generally speaking, those concerned with human trafficking focus on how migrants are transformed into victims in the migratory process, either through explicit coercion or other forms of trickery. In this process, overwhelming attention has been paid to the forced trafficking into prostitution of young women and children, who have become the iconic subjects of modern forms of slavery. The primary response has been a widespread call to find and free these individuals. As such, rescue in its various forms is at the heart of countertrafficking discourse, with return—usually "home"—following from the primary intervention (see, e.g., Doezema 2010).

Inside the Child Sex Trade was shot during the same period that IOM Indonesia initiated their Victims of Trafficking program in October 2004—the great majority of whom were women who had been to Malaysia, more than half legally as domestic workers—the program has generally been considered a success, and even a "model for the world" according to the director of the U.S. State Department's countertrafficking program.[11] Although the timing of the film and the IOM program may appear coincidental—much like the intersections of deportation and labor export—these two events should arguably be understood as part of an emerging transnational logic concerning trafficking, and in extension the regulation of human mobility.

NGOs such as Prai are located at the margins of these circuits, and it is here that another critical link between the IOM program and *Inside the Child Sex Trade* emerges; both have depended on direct collaborations with NGOs that have access to victims. Within the IOM program, victims of trafficking were identified and largely supported by more than fifty partner NGOs across Indonesia. The program itself explicitly focused on three chronological stages: return, recovery, and reintegration. In the first stage, typically a local NGO would encounter a potential victim—on rare occasions via a government agency (an embassy abroad or the local police, for instance)—and would then contact IOM. A standardized IOM form with a series of questions for the migrant would then be filled out and faxed to the head office in Jakarta, where it would be considered by the head of the Counter Trafficking Unit.[12]

If the migrant was cleared as a "victim," money would be wired to the NGO or government agency, which would be used to escort the victim or victims to the closest designated recovery center, housed in police hospitals in three major cites: Jakarta, Makassar, and Surabaya. Although this process was not supposed to be gendered—and despite the fact that the majority of the victims were men—female victims were generally brought to the hospitals, in keeping with the logic of countertrafficking. There they were medically and psychologically evaluated and tested for sexually transmitted infections before being escorted to IOM partner NGOs in their home provinces. Once in place, victims were offered support, for schooling if underage or to start a small business if they were adults. This could include funds for buying cattle or a motorcycle to be used as a taxi, or for opening a small shop. On average, there was around five million rupiah, or about USD 500, available for reintegration per victim, equivalent to one year's salary for an unskilled laborer in many parts of the country. In this process, victims were monitored by the partner NGOs who made evaluation visits to schools, places of work, or homes.

NGOs in Batam were among the most successful in identifying victims of trafficking within the Indonesian IOM program, which had sometimes led to intense competition for victims. For instance, when I showed *Inside the Child Sex Trade* to a man from another NGO in Batam (where several of Prai's staff members had previously worked), he complained that his organization had been in touch with Diana and Lina long before Prai, and that they had also been planning to take them out of the brothel. With funding available from IOM, several NGOs developed programs on the *identifikasi dan repatriasi* (identification and repatriation) of trafficking victims, which fit well with already running programs dealing with child protection or HIV/AIDS prevention.[13] While IOM made it clear that it did not fund "rescue missions,"[14] prior to the development of its program, neither government agencies nor NGOs had previously considered supporting the return of migrants or even the exit of prostitutes from brothels because of a lack of funding. In other words, the IOM program initiated the possibility of new forms of intervention. In keeping with the structure of development aid in the neoliberal era, local NGOs appeared as links to local communities and facilitated the return and emplacement of migrants. It thus becomes evident that sovereignty should be conceptualized not only as formal political power but also as a spatial constellation that comes to involve societal forces centered on the state and restricted by national boundaries.

If the contemporary regulation of migration in Asia can be understood in relation to the reestablishment of state sovereignty, it is also possible to claim that the intensifying concern with trafficking is part of this process. This may appear contradictory, since countertrafficking is explicitly concerned with the protection of victims in the context of the global exploitation of human life and labor, rather than the reinforcement of sovereignty per se. But as Ishan Ashutosh and Alison Mountz (2011) show, IOM reinforces the central role and sovereignty of the nation-state through the regulation of migration flows, while Diana Wong (2005) describes how IOM was a critical actor in the integration of trafficking into the broader issue of "illegal" migration, as rising numbers of asylum seekers led to growing concerns about migration management within the European Union after the collapse of the Soviet Union. In this process, trafficking, organized crime, and illegal migration were increasingly conceptualized together. Indeed, the 2000 United Nations Counter-trafficking Protocol, which in an important sense formalized trafficking as a global problem, is a supplement to the Convention against Transnational Organized Crime. More specifically, however, countertrafficking and deportation programs both engage in a strictly controlled process of return in which migrants are literally escorted back to their home villages in the name of their own protection (*perlindungan*)—a process that offers a very limited range of choices and in a sense demobilizes migrants, thereby at least temporarily emplacing them and reinforcing state sovereignty.

The actual effects of these programs of return became clear as I shifted my attention to the island of Lombok, located just east of Bali, and one of the main Indonesian sending areas for unskilled migrants to Malaysia, particularly to the palm oil industry. Largely agricultural, irrigated rice cultivation dominates the island's economy, but other cash crops such as tobacco are common. On Lombok, Panca Karsa was the local NGO partner for the IOM Victims of Trafficking program; receiving and monitoring victims from Lombok and Sumbawa. By 2006, more than one hundred victims—most of them from villages in Central and East Lombok—had been handled by Panca Karsa.

In one of those villages, I joined staff from Panca Karsa on a "monitoring" visit to one of the success stories of IOM's program. We arrived without an appointment and the man we were looking for was away on an errand. His wife, who ran the small shop that he had opened with reintegration funds, assured us that he would be back soon, so we decided to wait. Sitting on a bench to the side of the building was a man who had just returned from Malaysia a month earlier, after two years abroad as an undocumented migrant. Like most other male migrants on Lombok, he had borrowed money at 100 percent interest in order to pay the labor brokers. On his first trip to Malaysia five years earlier, he had sold what little land he had and now after two trips he had only just been able pay off his debts.

When Adi, the "victim" from the IOM project, finally arrived, he had much more to say. He admitted right away that he had been very lucky to be identified as a victim and that this had allowed him to transform his life. Together with sixteen other men and women from Lombok, Adi had been picked by SBMI in the Tanjung Priok harbor after having been deported from Malaysia via Tanjung Pinang—again highlighting the occasional conjuncture between deportation and the Victims of Trafficking programs. While the men were sent to the SBMI office, the women were taken to the recovery hospital before being returned to Lombok. Within a few months of having entered Malaysia legally with a private recruitment agency, Adi fled without his passport from the palm oil plantation where he had been sent, because the wages were far lower than promised. Six months later he was apprehended by a RELA volunteer group on a different plantation and was moved among three holding centers in Malaysia before being deported to Tanjung Pinang in November 2005.

Adi and I talked a bit about why between 50,000 and 100,000 people—out of a population of three million—were leaving Lombok annually, mainly to Malaysia and Saudi Arabia. Most of the work in Lombok was day labor (*harian*) and a salary could never be guaranteed, while in Malaysia migrants could make more than one and a half million rupiah (approximately USD 150) per month, about five times the average salary in Adi's village. With school fees and other regular payments increasing since the economic crisis and the ensuing liberalization of the economy, however, a predictable wage had become a necessity, making migration the only reasonable alternative. But now, after receiving support from IOM, Adi had developed a modest shop and had expanded his business to selling cellular phone cards. He was satisfied and had no plans to return to Malaysia. For the other man—who was basically destitute and sat quietly next to him—there appeared no way forward within the realm of the village.

On our way back to Lombok's capital, Mataram, the Panca Karsa staff admitted that Adi was their most successful victim (*korban*); in fact shortly after receiving compensation, many of the earlier victims had sold the commodities—cows and motorcycles, in particular—that they had been able to buy with IOM funding and left for Malaysia again. In this process, reintegration inevitably came to mean recirculation, suggesting that the refusal of migrants to stay in place followed from the logic of merantau, or circular migration, which demanded economic capital in excess of that which was offered by IOM. In fact, IOM's funding was approximately the same amount that it cost to pay labor agents to work in Malaysia on a two-year contract, around five million rupiah, or USD 500.

Conclusion: From Reintegration to Recirculation

I have moved between three overlapping projects—a deportee program, a documentary film, and a countertrafficking program—and discerned a common structure or logic that connects various models of engaging with the plight of Indonesian migrants. In particular, I have shown that any explicit problematization of "return home" is lacking in each of these projects. This lack is significant precisely because it makes obvious that which is taken for granted, namely that there is a particular type of migrant experience associated with loss and trauma that is strikingly similar to what Liisa Malkki (1995a) has previously identified in relation to refugees. The institutionalization of this type of migrant experience governs return through protection, because migrant victims are assumed to share a common experience. As Mariella Pandolfi (2008, 170) articulates, labels such as "victim" and "trafficked woman" come to "activate procedures" rather than "fully relate the experiences of surviving traumatic events." This is made most evident through the IOM program that evaluates each of its victims according to a standardized trajectory, with psychological and sexual evaluations being at the heart of the process of recovery; this is then turned into a spectacle for mass consumption through the "rescue" in media products such as *Inside the Child Sex Trade*. Meanwhile, the Indonesian deportee program, which makes no distinctions between "trafficking victims" and "stranded migrant workers,"[15] continues to return migrants to their home villages, making evident the intersections between state power and humanitarian intervention. More broadly, beyond the distribution of capital that makes possible both deportation and countertrafficking programs, and the production of spectacles that spread the "rumor of trafficking" (Wong 2005), the effects of the deportation program and the Victims of Trafficking program on the lives of migrants appear to be quite similar.

The sustainability of return, however, is dependent on the very economic capital that the migrants lacked before they left in the first place. This helps us understand Lina's shame (*malu*), Lina's wink, why Adi is satisfied with his life, and even why many of those who were supported by IOM's countertrafficking program have left again. Within the cultural logic of merantau, as well as the turn to documented migration and countertrafficking initiatives, return is clearly inscribed. In the documentary film and the countertrafficking and deportation programs that I have discussed, *home* is an empty signifier that can be understood as either a safe haven in humanitarian terms or the place where the migrant belongs from the authorities' point of view. But for the migrants themselves, the *kampung* (meaning both home and village) is a singular place that embodies various forms of relationships, hierarchies, and meanings that cannot be understood a priori according to the general model of the migrant victim, which predominates in contemporary discourse. The return home of the migrant must be understood in relation to this life world, which demands some form of success that allows for a transition in the life cycle. In the contemporary context of Indonesia, return without the possibility of such transitions is rarely sustainable and thus in direct tension with the interventions of governments, NGOs, and journalists that I have described.

In closing, it is worth briefly considering a broader and more complicated historical and sociological problem: namely, why the different programs that I have described have come to intersect in such striking fashion, and in particular how the figure of the trafficked person has gained such significance in this process. There is clearly wide-ranging support for the expansion of temporary circular migration, generally understood as a win-win-win situation, as receiving countries are guaranteed labor, sending countries receive remittances, and migrants earn employment and steady wages (Vertovec 2007, 2). This is in part a response to processes of globalization and regional integration, described by Xiang in the introduction to this book, but also more specifically to growing concerns about undocumented migration. In this process, the trafficking victim has become a key figure and a problem on which NGOs, international organizations, and state agencies can focus their attention. As labor markets become more precarious, fragmented, and difficult to govern in the era of neoliberalism, the concern with trafficking allows various actors to patrol the unclear boundaries of these markets, ostensibly in the name of human rights. Phrased more strongly, the figure of the trafficking victim allows actors to avoid more complicated political issues such as labor rights and freedom of mobility that might threaten liberalism's uncompromising distinction between free and unfree labor.

Notes

1. For a review on the literature about the meaning of home, see Mallet 2004.

2. This figure remained relatively stable for several years. During the first six months of 2009, just over seventeen thousand migrants were deported through Tanjung Pinang. By early 2013, however, these numbers had dropped to between 500 and 1000 per month (data from the Agency for Social Affairs and Labor, Tanjung Pinang).

3. Report of the Special Rapporteur on the Human Rights of Migrants, Jorge Bustamente, on his mission to Indonesia, December 12–20, United Natons General Assembly, at http://www.acnur.org/biblioteca/pdf/4992.pdf?view=1 (accessed February 8, 2013).

4. TKI is an acronym for Tenaga Kerja Indonesia, or Indonesian Migrant Worker.

5. IOM Jakarta (n.d.), "Recovery Centres for Trafficked Victims," brochure in author's possession.

6. Feature films such as *Lilya 4-ever*, which deals with a fictional young woman from Russia who is lured into prostitution in Sweden; news reports; and a seemingly endless stream of documentaries that take the form of melodrama—Carol Vance (2005) has termed them melomentaries, i.e., melodramatic documentaries—have become critical instruments in raising consciousness about trafficking. As Meg McLagan (2003) has noted, with the rise of digital video since the 1990s, mediated forms of testimony have become increasingly critical in making human rights claims public, a process that is particularly evident in the relationship between countertrafficking campaigns and media reporting. This is part of a broader trend since the 1980s in which testimonials and other "truth-telling discourses" have become forms of evidence of human rights abuses among feminist activists in particular (Hesford and Kozol 2005, 8).

7. See the Journeyman Pictures website for details on the film: http://www.journeyman.tv/?lid=18621. For a transcript of the film, see http://www.journeyman.tv/?lid=18621&tmpl=transcript. For a ten-minute clip, see http://www.youtube.com/watch?v=szKqtiKmbC8 (all accessed August 1, 2011).

8. In the end, it was perhaps this recognition that led Rousset to buy the girls goats and cows—local forms of capital—that offered them other possibilities. This was not part of the film. Ramses, the head of Prai, told me this in Batam in August 2006.

9. Fieldnotes, my translation, Tanjung Pinang, August 12, 2006. See Ford and Lyons 2012 for a series of strikingly similar quotes from their research on countertrafficking in Tanjung Pinang.

10. In conjunction with the Trafficking Victims Protection Act, an annual report is published by the U.S. Department of State ("Trafficking in Persons Report"), which includes a global ranking of countries according to how they are dealing with trafficking. Tier 3 countries are the worst cases, tier 2 ones are borderline cases, and tier 1 nations are considered to be compliant with the U.S. government's countertrafficking recom-

mendations. Bottom-tier countries face the threat of losing all nonhumanitarian aid from the U.S. government. In the first annual report in July 2001, Indonesia was placed in the lowest tier (www.state.gov/g/tip/rls/tiprpt/2001/3930.htm). The immediate response by the Indonesian government was to create a National Trafficking Commission, which by July 11, 2003, raised its ranking to tier 2, a position it has retained since (www.state.gov/g/tip/rls/tiprpt/2003/21276.htm).

11. For instance, at the opening of the first "recovery center" in Jakarta, Ambassador John R. Miller, the director of the U.S. State Department's Office to Monitor and Combat Trafficking in Persons, claimed that "it is a model for Indonesia and maybe a model for the world. The challenge is how to spread such centers across the country." IOM Indonesia, "Recovery Centers for Trafficking Victims a 'Model for the World' Says Top U.S. State Department Official," press release, November 4, 2006, http://www.iom.or.id/news.jsp?lang=eng&code=102&dcode=4 (accessed February 20, 2009).

12. During my interview with Kristin Dadey, the head of IOM's countertrafficking program in Jakarta, in August 2006, an assistant came in with a pile of papers for her to sign. She turned to me and said, "This is what I do all day, sign trafficking forms."

13. For a further description of IOM's collaboration with NGOs in the Riau Islands, see Ford and Lyons 2012.

14. Interview with Kristin Dadey, Jakarta, August 2006.

15. According to a report from IOM, the Department of Social Affairs has stopped distinguishing between the categories "stranded migrant workers" and "trafficking victims" and laments that any attempt to create datasets on trafficking victims has failed (David 2007, 36).

> > > > > > > > > > > > CHAPTER SEVEN ∨
Return of the Global Indian ∨
Software Professionals and the Worlding of Bangalore ∨
∧ CAROL UPADHYA ∨
∧
∧
∧

The debate on transnational migration between and from Asian countries usually focuses on low-skilled and semiskilled migrants. Less attention has been paid to the substantial streams of high-skilled and professional migrants who move from countries such as India to the West in pursuit of higher education or better job opportunities, who occupy very different social positions in both the home and destination countries, and whose transnational experiences are also distinct. Yet their migration choices are also deeply inflected by state policies at both ends.

Indian information technology (IT) professionals are a key example of this type of migration. As a group of mobile, transnational knowledge workers circulating within the global information economy, IT professionals have become a highly visible segment of the Indian diaspora in the West. While the dominant trend for several decades has been the movement of highly educated professionals from India to the West, many of these high-tech migrants have recently been induced to return to India—in part due to its newfound image as an emerging economy following the economic liberalization program of the late 1990s. The city of Bangalore in particular, with its burgeoning software industry, is viewed as a place that offers economic opportunities and lifestyles similar to those available abroad. Data on this reverse flow are unreliable, but the Ministry of Overseas Indian Affairs has estimated the number of returnees at 10,000 to 20,000 a year since 2000, and a NASSCOM (the software industry association) report claims that 35,000 IT professionals returned to Bangalore alone between 2000 and 2004 (Varrell 2011, 305).[1] These figures represent only a small proportion of highly educated international migrants from India, but they point to a significant shift in the migration pattern of skilled professionals, from a "brain drain" to a "brain gain" (see Chacko 2007; Khadria 1999).

The sojourn abroad, and the subsequent return of IT professionals to work or invest in Bangalore's software industry, is linked to the reconstitution of the nation and citizenship as well as to transformations in the urban milieu. I describe an emerging "global Indian" form of citizenship and identity that has been largely promulgated by the Indian state in its efforts to encompass Overseas Indians (the official nomenclature) within the national community, but which also has provided transnational professionals with new strategies for claiming, creating, and negotiating citizenship. This neonationalist discourse converges with the patriotic narratives of Indians living abroad who desire to give back to the motherland and help to build the "new India" by returning to share their wealth, knowledge, and entrepreneurial skills. The themes of return and the "new India" are both marked by the idea of the "global", which in turn signifies modernity and progress. But they are by no means placeless projects.[2] In this chapter I also explore how this kind of neonationalism is played out on the ground through returnees' strategies of emplacement, especially in the case of Bangalore. Returnees, driven by a desire to help India take its rightful place in the world, bring with them new ideas about modernity and proper civic life through which they reenvision the city as a global place. These practices of place making have clear material outcomes for urban society, economy, and politics. They also neatly dovetail with the program of neoliberal urban redevelopment that has been promoted by political and economic elites in order to transform Bangalore into a so-called world-class city. I flesh out this argument through an examination of the narratives and practices of IT professionals living abroad and those who have returned to Bangalore. I also look at broader discourses that circulate within transnational social fields inhabited by Overseas Indians and those living in Bangalore, especially through cyberspace and the media.[3]

A few clarifications about the notion of "return" and the cohort of IT professional returnees interviewed in Bangalore are in order. In many cases, the return of software professionals to Bangalore is not a simple move back home but is just one journey within a larger pattern of circular or multinodal transnational mobilities. Most Indian software workers are deployed on temporary contracts ("bodyshopped") or are employed by Indian software services companies who send them abroad on short-term onsite assignments (see Upadhya and Vasavi 2008; Xiang 2007).[4] But many IT professionals and other highly educated migrants connected with the IT industry have migrated more or less permanently to Western countries, or hope to do so.[5] However, even for IT professionals who have obtained a permanent-residence permit or foreign citizenship, the plan to settle down abroad is usually contingent, and the dream of return always hovers in the background. Moreover, for some techno-managerial professionals, coming back to India is not really a process of return but is just another stage in a transnational career strategy. In the context of career-driven global mobility, the terms *migration* and *return migration* do not really capture the complexity of these movements. In this chapter I primarily draw on the narratives and experiences of those who have lived abroad for a number of years and have then chosen to return to India, leaving aside for the present purpose the larger number of circulatory techno-migrants who come and go at frequent intervals (Ong 2005b).

The majority of techno-migrants as well as returnees are lower-level routine programmers or middle-level managers. However, a significant subcategory consists of those who have risen to senior levels in large tech companies in the United States and elsewhere and have been deputed to head their Indian subsidiaries. According to one source, 95 percent of foreign-owned multinational software companies in Bangalore are headed by Indians who have lived and worked abroad—mostly in the United States (Kapur 2002; cited in Chacko 2007, 136). A top headhunter (recruitment agent) estimated that around 250 to 300 high-level executives of IT companies in Bangalore have come back from the United States. In addition, a number of returnees relocate to India in order to start their own IT companies, feeding into Bangalore's growing startup culture. These entrepreneurs often shuttle between Bangalore, Europe, East Asia, and the United States as they look after their business interests that straddle several borders (Upadhya 2004). This chapter focuses primarily on these higher- and middle-level professionals and entrepreneurs, who in the popular imagination are the archetypical "global Indians." They also epitomize the neonationalist ideological stance and emplacement strategies of returnees in Bangalore.

Return and Neonationalism

Most returnees in Bangalore appear to be IT professionals in the younger and middle-aged groups who come back to India to work in the software industry or start their own companies. AnnaLee Saxenian (2004, 176–77) notes that until the 1990s, few of the thirty thousand Indian professionals working in Silicon Valley returned to India, unlike in the case of Taiwan where the return migration of engineers played a key role in realizing the "Taiwan miracle." However, from around 2000 the pattern of Chinese "astronauts" (referring to Chinese families whose members shuttle between Greater China, North America, and other places; see Ley and Kobayashi 2005; Ong 1999) began to be replicated among transnational Indian IT entrepreneurs and professionals, suggesting that the earlier pattern of brain drain is being replaced by "brain circulation" (Saxenian 2004). By most accounts, this reverse brain drain has been stimulated by the rapid growth of the Indian economy following liberalization; the rise of the software industry, which opened up new employment opportunities for highly educated professionals; the wider availability of consumer goods and leisure industries that cater to the upwardly mobile middle classes, which made India more attractive to returnees by affording them lifestyles similar to those that they enjoyed in the West; and the more difficult economic and political environment in the United States after September 11 and the subsequent series of economic crises. In contrast to earlier decades, India is now viewed as a place where IT professionals can both advance their careers and be "at home." Kishore, a marketing professional employed by a large American computer chips manufacturer, who relocated to Bangalore in 2005 after living in the United States for ten years, said:

> I am not really keen on coming back to India just because it is my birthplace. But from what my friends and associates tell me, things are going to move out to India in a big way. I want to be here to catch all the action happening. Also, I feel I have saturated there. I get paid well. Yet, I feel I am not doing much there. It is time I moved out to a different place. Experience a new place and new people. I am ambitious and I want to have new challenges.

But these economic and technological developments are not the only driving forces behind the return flows. This chapter calls attention to the political, cultural, and moral dimensions of return migration.

Politically, strategies of return and practices of citizenship among migrant professionals have shaped, and been shaped by, India's policies toward Non-resident Indians (NRIs), or Indian citizens living abroad,[6] and Overseas Indians (the current official designation for a broad range of people of Indian origin who are citizens of foreign countries). Unlike several East and Southeast Asian countries (Ong 2005a), India has not actively or systematically encouraged the return of highly skilled migrants as a development strategy. Instead, the Indian government has viewed techno-professional NRIs as a brain bank that can be tapped for financial resources and perhaps expertise from a distance (Kapur 2003; Khadria 2001). NRIs were initially courted by the Indian government in the 1970s as a significant source of remittances, foreign exchange, and capital investment (Lessinger 1992), and NRIs were encouraged to invest in India through the provision of special legal and economic privileges, such as favorable interest rates.[7] More recently, the state's interest in cultivating Overseas Indians has expanded beyond narrow economic goals, especially under the coalition government led by the Bharatiya Janata Party (BJP, or "Indian People's Party"), a right-wing Hindu nationalist party that came to power in 1999. This government floated the concept of a "global India" encompassing people of Indian origin (even several generations removed) across the world, similar to the category of "Chinese living overseas" (Nonini and Ong 1997, 9). India was reimagined as a potentially powerful country that is culturally (rather than geographically) defined through a transnationalized version of *hindutva* (a right-wing and exclusionary political ideology that promotes "Hinduness" as the basis of Indian culture; see Rajagopal 2000). Shampa Biswas writes, "In calling on Indian-Americans to contribute to the Indian economy, the Indian state has hailed them as 'Indians,' reminding them of their (cultural) connections to India" (2005, 58). This culturally redefined idea of the nation, which enjoins material, political, and other kinds of contributions by "citizens" living abroad, has been embraced by many NRIs and RNRIs (returned NRIs) who inhabit transnational social fields such as the one constituted by the circulation of IT capital and labor (van der Veer 2005).

India's approach to "transnational governance" has undergone significant shifts since the 1990s (Dickinson and Bailey 2007, 758), representing alterations in the prevailing notions of nation and citizenship. For instance, the government promulgated several changes in citizenship laws in order to create an official "global Indian" category of quasi-citizenship. A long-standing demand of the NRI lobby has been that India should permit dual citizenship, which would accord legal recognition to their transnational existence and greater ease of transactions and movement. Overseas Indians argue that dual citizenship will enable them, as patriotic diasporic subjects, to participate more fully in India's development even while retaining the "safety" of a foreign passport (see Faist 2000, 209–10). To address this demand, the Persons of Indian Origin (PIO) scheme was announced in 2002, which granted special rights such as visa-free entry and property ownership to certain categories of "people of Indian origin" who have acquired foreign citizenship. In 2005 the government went a step further by introducing an additional category of "Overseas Citizenship of India" (OCI), which provides a sort of quasi-citizenship for Indian-origin foreign nationals (Anupama Roy 2006).[8] These state actions concretized the official construction of a global-Indian community and effectively deterritorialized Indian citizenship (Anupama Roy 2008).[9] They represent a form of cultural nationalism that at once narrowed the definition of the citizen to include only particular classes and communities of Indians and broadened the definition to encompass certain categories of noncitizens of Indian origin living abroad. Eligibility for OCI membership was initially limited to those who had emigrated after 1950 to particular regions and countries, namely North America, Europe, Australasia, Singapore, and Thailand. This ensured the inclusion of primarily middle-class, educated migrants who left India in pursuit of economic success, and the exclusion of descendants of indentured workers who were shipped overseas during the colonial period as well as more recent labor migrants to the Persian Gulf (Anupama Roy 2008, 242). The OCI scheme clearly targeted highly skilled migrants of the post-1970s generation (Varrel 2011)—especially those deemed to be professionally successful (Dickinson and Bailey 2007, 765–66)—which is in line with the class bias of Indian policy toward Overseas Indians that has aimed to construct a "neoliberal economic cosmopolitan community" (Edwards 2008, 453).[10] These policy shifts have produced what Aihwa Ong (2006, 121) terms "latitudinal citizenship," creating divisions within the diaspora based on transnational market relations (Vora 2011, 313–14).

The deterritorialization of the nation-state has been augmented by the intensifying "materiality" of diasporic relations (Werbner 2000). Most of the policies directed at NRIs since the 1980s have been oriented toward garnering their resources, and more recently toward promoting NRI investment, for example by setting up Special Economic Zones (SEZs) exclusively for them. The reconstitution of Indian citizenship as well as the discursive construction of the global Indian community reflect a political reconfiguration of sovereignty and citizenship and are also firmly rooted in India's neoliberal development agenda. These policies have provided a mechanism and incentive for Overseas Indians who hold foreign passports to engage in business activities or freely pursue their careers across borders, or to return to India while retaining foreign citizenship—a kind of "flexible citizenship" (Ong 1999) or "diasporic citizenship" (Siu 2005) that has been particularly advantageous for affluent NRIs living in North America and Europe.[11]

Negotiating Citizenship and Belonging

Mobile software professionals are located in a liminal political-legal position from which they try to negotiate between different forms of citizenship and residence within India as well as in the countries where they live and work. As a result, the legal categories that frame their global movements are invested with different symbolic meanings and are manipulated in line with their transnational life strategies.

For many NRIs, a foreign passport appears to be nothing more than a convenient document. Very often, a decision to apply for a U.S. (or other foreign) passport is linked to a definite plan to return, because it provides assurance that one can always go back to the United States if things do not work out in India. While return is often framed in terms of a nationalist desire to help "develop" the nation or a more self-centered ambition to "catch the rising tide," returnees keep their options open for themselves and their children by retaining their foreign passports or residence permits. Like the Chinese "astronauts," Indian IT professionals may return to India to pursue their careers or to reconnect with Indian culture, but plan to send their children (who usually have U.S. passports) back to the United States for their higher education. Kishore speaks about his plans for his four-year-old daughter: "I want Pooja to have an *Indian grounding*. That's probably one of the main reasons I want to come back. . . . She speaks of Halloween and Easter. I want her to know Holi and Diwali too. . . . At least till her graduation she should be here. Then she can go to the USA again for higher studies." Although this example suggests that highly skilled migrants have evolved a form of "flexible" or "graduated" citizenship (Ong

1999, 2000), most IT professionals living abroad still struggle with questions of citizenship, identity, and belonging.[12] Acquiring a foreign passport requires the formal revocation of Indian citizenship, which for many NRIS signifies renunciation of the mother country—a decision that is fraught with moral and political anguish. For this reason, several long-term residents of the Netherlands whom my research team and I interviewed in 2005 were eagerly waiting for dual citizenship to be legalized by India so that they could acquire Dutch passports without losing their Indian citizenship. The OCI category has partly resolved this dilemma: while it does not represent full citizenship it allows migrants to think of themselves as citizens of India and to enjoy most of the privileges of Indian citizenship, rendering the acquisition of a U.S. or European passport a mere formality. The availability of PIO and OCI cards has effectively transformed the notion of citizenship among transnational professionals into one that is in some ways flexible, yet is firmly rooted in a reconstituted Indian national and cultural identity.

Although the OCI and PIO policies were not formulated with the intention of attracting Overseas Indians back to India, an unintended consequence of these schemes has been the facilitation of such returns. Prior to 2003 many migrants were hesitant to return to India because of legal problems associated with foreign citizenship.[13] Now, a foreign passport coupled with an OCI card allows them to live on par with other Indians in most respects while still being able to easily travel to and from India. For many NRIS, acquiring a U.S. passport is the tipping point that enables them to realize the dream of return. What is usually regarded as the final step in the assimilation of immigrants—attainment of citizenship—ironically has become the mechanism that allows them to return to the home country.

The redefinition of citizenship among transnational IT professionals is linked more broadly to the reconstitution of Indian identity, and the reimagination of India itself, from the autarchic nationalism of the freedom struggle and the early post-Independence period to the more expansive global-Indian identity that has emerged since the 1980s. The graduated form of citizenship that these policies have introduced is the legal counterpart of the figure of the global Indian that has been made popular by the mainstream English media—a new class of worldly, techno-savvy, progressive, and entrepreneurial professionals whose return to India will transform the social, political, and economic landscape.

Return as Reciprocity: Building the New India

For many IT migrants, the act of return is the culmination of a long series of movements and flows—including remittances to families at home, investments in Resurgent India government bonds,[14] or support for charities and NGOs. Although return may be regarded in many cases as a strategy for consolidating their new class position or social status within India, returnees' calculations are not purely financial or practical. As noted above, returning to India is often represented as a form of reciprocity, a way to repay their debt to the nation by contributing to economic development and social renewal.[15] In particular, they see themselves as helping India to become a global economic power—a "new India" that has cast off its Nehruvian socialist legacy in favor of rapid economic growth and capital-led change.

This attitude was expressed by several software professionals working in Europe, who voiced a nationalist pride in the IT industry and India's newly prominent place in the global economy. For them, software is India's special contribution to the world, a global industry at the vanguard of the new economic growth curve that will garner respect for India and Indians. The aspirations of transnational Indians merge into India's post-liberalization development narrative, and a newly assertive nation beckons Overseas Indians to return and be a part of this great change. The head of the Belguim office of a major Indian IT company put it this way: "I had a vision—that the Indian IT industry must grow large enough to be taken notice of, and this is what has happened. This was in the mid-1990s. Then, a lot of young people wanted to become software engineers because they thought it was a ticket to the West. But my vision was to position India so that people would queue up to come to India. And this is what is happening now."

NRIS returning to set up their own IT businesses speak of building the nation through investment in the "knowledge industries." According to the founder of a high-end startup in Bangalore who had moved back from Silicon Valley, professionals with the "right skills and mindset" are now returning to India, and this influx of brainpower and entrepreneurial talent will transform not only the Indian IT industry but also India itself. Rajiv, another entrepreneur who moved to Bangalore in 2004 after nearly twenty years abroad, is an example of this trend. He had established a successful telecom company in the United States, which he sold before returning to India to start a new enterprise. Soon after his arrival in Bangalore in mid-

2005 his relatives threw a welcome party for him, where Rajiv gave a long speech (in English) about his decision:

> I am happy to be back. To my country. To my family. To my people. This country gave me a lot of opportunities, and I am what I am because of that. Now I'm here to give back some of what I took. It's my turn to serve my country. I believe that if everyone who has left our shores and gone abroad were to come back and do their bit for our country, we would go leaps and bounds ahead from where we are today.

NRI websites showcase the experiences of successful returnees like Rajiv, reinforcing the patriotism that is echoed in many returnees' narratives. In an article about Vani Kola, the founder of two successful tech companies in the United States, who returned to start a venture in Bangalore, the reporter notes: "Indians are going back. Many are younger folks who see an opportunity to become India's version of a [Vinod] Khosla or [Desh] Deshpande.[16] . . . They want to jump into the nation's booming, crazy, thrilling tech industry and take advantage of their knowledge of both India and the USA. Some hope to get rich. Others want to help their homeland. Most want to do both" (Maney 2006). At the same time, returnee entrepreneurs highlight the obstacles they face as businessmen—bureaucratic red tape and corruption, inefficiency and inadequacy of basic services, and poor infrastructure, especially in software boomtowns such as Bangalore. Their desire to "develop" the nation along the lines of Silicon Valley goes hand in hand with the urge to reinvent and reform the city, urban governance, the polity, and society at large.

Emplacement and the City

I have argued that the return of highly educated IT professionals to India is not only linked to an emerging global pattern of expert labor circulation. It also reflects a neonationalist discourse emanating from the Indian state (and from the diaspora itself) that embraces these professionals as global-Indian citizens and bearers of a new globalized modernity. The return of global Indians is spurred and legitimized by the narrative and dream of a powerful "new India" that is economically developed and globalized as well as culturally grounded. Now I explore the articulation of global aspirations through the "worlding" of Bangalore—a process that is driven in part by RNRIs and more broadly by the software industry. Returnees regard Bangalore as a place where they can live and work while still dwelling largely in the transnational social field that connects them with the West. While narratives about migration and return are usually framed in terms of the nation-state, other sites (both below and above the level of the nation) have emerged as key places where processes of globalization are being worked out—in particular the new "global cities" of the South. It is to these cities that return migrants mainly gravitate (Chacko 2007).[17]

Bangalore is seen by returnees as a "happening place," because of the presence of the software industry and also due to the city's purportedly cosmopolitan culture and the availability of sophisticated lifestyle services—a vibrant pub culture, good restaurants that offer a range of international cuisine, shopping malls with all the essential brand-name stores, elite international schools, and expensive gated communities and residential complexes. Bangalore has become, symbolically as well as materially, the place where the idea of the "global" gets linked to that of the "Indian," a process that unfolds in part through returnees' strategies of "emplacement" (Narayan 2002).

Making Place, Making Class

While returning transnational professionals speak of going "home," their actual return is not to their places of birth but to an imagined "new India" embodied in global cities like Bangalore. Their sense of belonging and identity is wrapped up in global imaginaries of success and advancement, and the urban places where they live need to be refurbished and invested with new meanings. Return sets in motion a process of reterritorialization, driven by social and economic aspirations and diasporic longings, by which this home is created and materialized. While mobile individuals may construct their homes almost anywhere (Nowicka 2007), the recreation of India, or of particular places within India, as home involves a particular set of practices and orientations that draw on not only their experiences abroad but also imaginaries of the new India that circulate within the postliberalization new middle class (see Fernandes 2006; Upadhya 2009). To realize the dream of return and to lay claim to India as their own place, returnees must reinvent and colonize the city, in part by reproducing a model of contemporary living they have learned abroad. The act of return involves practices of emplacement as RNRIS attempt to locate themselves within the existing urban social matrix—putting down roots through the purchase of property, acquiring the material trappings of a lifestyle that marks them as cosmopolitan Indians, and enacting their status as successful professionals through new social practices and the articulation of modern, enlightened values aimed at establishing their distance from the (negatively marked) "old India." In this way, the wave of return has fed into ongoing processes of urban reconstruction that is linked to the implantation of the global software industry in Bangalore, as well as to the formation of new subcultures and lifestyles in the city that stem from the fracturing and transformation of the middle class.

This dual process of class making and place making is most evident in Bangalore's high-end, self-contained, and heavily securitized luxury-apartment complexes that enclose within their high walls an array of recreational and domestic facilities on par with affluent housing complexes in the West. Real-estate developers in Bangalore explicitly cater to returnees by building exclusive gated communities that make it possible to "survive" in India through separation from the disorder and the environmental degradation of the rest of the city (see Bose 2007). These posh residential developments with names (almost always in English) such as Palm Meadows, Oakwood, and Serenity self-consciously evoke American suburbia or European-style luxury. Inhabited mainly by RNRIS, Western expats, and wealthy Indian business families, these enclaves, most situated in the periurban periphery of a rapidly expanding and increasingly chaotic "megacity," successfully simulate affluent Western lifestyles. While many returnees are acutely conscious of, and even apologetic about, the contradictions inherent in their lifestyles, many believe that by introducing "better" ways of living they are helping to realize the dream of the new India. For them, Bangalore—or at least the locations within the city where they live—represents India's future.

Returnees attempt to establish their class position by enacting a lifestyle that is distinct from that of the older, local upper-middle and middle classes—a cosmopolitan one that in practice looks outside for its standards and models while retaining allegiance to an abstract notion of Indian culture. Returnees' narratives point to a constant search for the material appurtenances of this lifestyle—elements that are appropriately trendy, tasteful, and exclusive—Indian contemporary in style but "not too Indian."[18] The efforts of the returnees Kishore and Asha to establish their household in Bangalore illustrate this quest. This couple, in their mid-thirties, planned their relocation from the United States meticulously, making several visits to Bangalore during 2005 to find the right house in the best location as well as the best school for their daughter. During this lengthy process that entailed many discussions with Bangalore-based friends and relatives and long tours around the city with real-estate agents, Kishore repeatedly said that he wanted to live in the most "happening" and "up-market" part of town. Their other requirements reflected the model of living they had become accustomed to in the United States: "I would like an independent house, but it should also have all the modern facilities like gym, club house, health room, swimming pool, huge gardens, you name it. . . . It should be a big house, with very high ceilings. And it should be close to these up-and-coming international schools." While driving around the city in search of apartments, they frequently made disparaging remarks about the design of the buildings and houses they saw, which they thought compared poorly with homes in the United States. Kishore constantly criticized "south Indian homes," which are not "up-to-date with style and design." They finally settled on an apartment in a new complex located in a "hip" and central part of the city. They were happy with the location and facilities, but Kishore was concerned about the image that their address would convey because of the street name: "I wonder why they can't name the road something else? Papanna Road sounds so silly; it doesn't have the same class as saying, 'Hey, I live on Lavelle Road, or Richmond Circle.' *Papanna* sounds like some old, shoddy place."[19]

While the software industry, with its more than 250,000 well-paid and well-traveled employees, has been a major factor behind the restructuring of class as well as urban space in Bangalore, the influence of returnees such as Kishore and Asha, who bring with them new aspirations and ideas about the "good life," also appears to be significant. Within these larger processes of class (re)formation, transnational professionals emplace themselves as bearers of cosmopolitanism, a global-Indian identity, and contemporary international lifestyles, values, and social practices within an urban landscape defined by very different sets of social coordinates and histories. Globalizing cities of the South such as Bangalore are transformed by their transnational economic linkages, and also because they become sites for crystallizing diasporic imaginations.

Remaking the City

In addition to their pursuit of transnational lifestyles, RNRIs are remaking the city through direct involvement in civic activism and governance reforms. Returnees negotiate their reentry into India and positioning in urban society not just as successful migrant subjects who have achieved a new social status but as carriers of a specific ideology, set of social values, and mode of living through which they seek to transform India. They return equipped with self-proclaimed enlightened, liberal, and forward-looking orientations and practices, which form a lens through which they judge India's disorder, rampant corruption, and *chalta hai* (easy-going) attitude. Many returnees desire to reform local society and government and to contribute to India's development through various forms of social work, philanthropy, and civic activism. Bangalore is envisioned not as a chaotic Third World megacity but as what India is (or should be) becoming—a modern, well-ordered metropolis run by an efficient and transparent government that is aided by enlightened civil society.

These acquired values have directly fed into the processes of neoliberal reform and urban redevelopment that have been under way in Bangalore since the late 1990s, in which the globally oriented professional and business classes, especially IT industry leaders, have played a major role (Upadhya 2009). To promote Bangalore's status as a world city, regional political and business elites in tandem with international development agencies and the national government engage in intensive programs of urban restructuring and infrastructure development. NRIs who return to Bangalore to take advantage of its booming economy see themselves as part of these larger transformations. Many RNRIs express a wish to "make change happen" by contributing to the remaking of the new city and a refurbished civil society.[20]

The influence of RNRIs on middle-class public life and city politics in Bangalore became quite visible during the 2000s. To illustrate this, I refer to two high-profile RNRIs who are active in Bangalore, but this kind of civic involvement is seen among many other less prominent returnees as well. The first example is Ramesh Ramanathan, who gave up a successful banking career in the United States to return to India and become involved in public service. In 2001 he founded a civic organization, Janaagraha Center for Citizenship and Democracy, to push municipal reforms and citizen-centric urban development in Bangalore, such as decentralized ward-based planning and budgeting. Janaagraha's slogan is "be the change you want to see." Subsequently, Ramanathan became a key figure in the reformulation of national urban-development policies, especially through the Jawaharlal Nehru National Urban Renewal Mission—a large central-government program that provides matching grants for infrastructure development and urban-governance reforms in selected cities (a program that has been heavily criticized by urban activists for its elitist bias).

Ramanathan was nominated as a "Young Global Leader" by the World Economic Forum in 2007.

The second example is Rajeev Chandrasekhar, convener of ABIDe (Agenda for Bangalore Infrastructure Development), a private-public task force that was appointed by the newly elected BJP-led state government in Karnataka in 2008 to revive the city and address pressing urban problems caused by rapid growth. The task force includes key bureaucrats and politicians as well as representatives of the private sector, especially prominent RNRIS (including Ramesh Ramanathan). Chandrasekhar is a successful entrepreneur who began his career with Intel in the United States and returned to India in 1991, subsequently founding BPL Mobile, one of the earliest private-sector telecom companies in India. Now a venture capitalist, he has been extensively involved in public activities, including being chairman of the Infrastructure Task Force of the Government of Karnataka (1999–2002) and a director of the new Bangalore International Airport. He is also a member of Parliament.

A major focus of such high-profile returnees is to develop urban infrastructure—widening roads, building flyovers and underpasses, working on the new international airport project, and so on—and to put in place the physical facilities needed to make Bangalore a so-called world-class city (mainly by facilitating mobility and traffic flow). These efforts in turn are expected to attract and retain foreign investment and the IT industry's client base. The urban reform agendas of Janaagraha and ABIDe support this vision of urban transformation and the administrative and urban-land-market reforms that are deemed necessary to push through large urban redevelopment and infrastructure projects, including redrawing the map of Bangalore itself to create the largest metropolitan region in the country. In general, RNRIS like Chandrasekhar and Ramanathan advocate neoliberal and technocratic approaches to urban planning and governance, with an emphasis on private investment, public-private partnerships, and the introduction of the latest (usually imported) technologies. These "social entrepreneurs" also work closely with the state, whose policies are being rethought in line with this essentially corporate vision of urban development.[21] As Thomas Blom Hansen and Finn Steppatut (2005, 30) put it, transnational subjects who have become "proper citizens" through their class, education, and sojourn abroad are recruited to aid in the "civilizing process" needed to make urban India livable as well as amenable to foreign capital.

Many ordinary RNRIS also espouse an urge to improve their environment by remodeling political and governmental processes. For instance, many of these RNRIS are active members of city-oriented websites and Internet-based interest groups that focus on urban problems such as environmental degradation, traffic congestion, and bureaucratic inefficiency.[22] Similarly, young U.S.-returned IT professionals who populate the many large upmarket apartment complexes around the outskirts of the city organize their housing societies (residents' bodies responsible for the maintenance of common facilities) along the lines of apartment complexes in the United States. A comment frequently heard in residents' meetings, when problems such as garbage clearance or careless use of facilities are being discussed, is: "This could not have happened in the U.S."[23] Returnees thus bring with them a model of respectable living and civic life. By promoting a more "civilized" mode of existence, they help to establish the difference between themselves and the so-called old middle class or traditional Indian society.

Conclusion

I have explored the phenomenon of return migration among Indian IT professionals by locating it at the intersection of several broad trends: (1) the emergence of a new image of "India shining" in the era of liberalization, which is partly linked to the success of the software-outsourcing industry; (2) the creation of a global-Indian identity that draws on a new form of cultural nationalism premised on moral obligations of reciprocity rather than citizenship rights and duties, and is buttressed by legal changes that have underwritten practices of graduated citizenship among high-tech migrants; and (3) the worlding of Bangalore by political and economic elites in tandem with RNRIS' strategies of emplacement and class distinction. This assemblage of disparate processes points to the forging of new global pathways (Werbner 1999) through which international capital, expert labor, transnational professionals, managers, entrepreneurs, and cosmopolitan images of progress traverse and reshape the urban landscape of cities like Bangalore. These processes are also closely interlinked—the deterritorialization of citizenship represented in the OCI card is matched by the deterritorialization of Bangalore in the imagination of IT elites and RNRIS, for whom the city is largely an extension of Silicon Valley. At the same time, the globalizing of Bangalore is a project of a state eager to propel India onto the world economic stage, just as the reinvention of citizenship has been driven by a similar political agenda.

This interplay of the global, national, and local simultaneously generates within it a number of contradictions that are manifest at several levels. These include the category of the "global Indian," who is legally a noncitizen yet a true Indian patriot, the affluent professional who comes back to serve the motherland yet lives a Californian lifestyle, and the schizophrenic city of Bangalore, whose worlding has created multiple fissures and dissensions. But these transformations also provide a resolution to the contradictions that they have thrown up. For example, the global-Indian identity allows returnees to think of themselves as participating in the advancement of the nation even while living and working in globalized enclaves largely cut off from the rest of the city.

Return is always to a home, and home is constituted by the migrant's imagination, memories, and aspirations. In this case the home that IT professionals imagine is a future India, one that retains certain elements of its "glorious past" and ancient culture but that will soon leave behind the chaos and poverty of the current moment. The return of successful NRIS to Bangalore has aided the symbolic projection of the city as a place where the new India is being forged. Return also sets in motion simultaneous processes of deterritorialization and reterritorialization—reverse migration by IT professionals, impelled by both global economic trends and neonationalist sentiments, reinforces the remaking of Bangalore into a place that is attractive to mobile global capital and transnational subjects. The resultant processes of spatial and economic reconfiguration embed the city in the global while simultaneously inscribing the expanded space of the nation—conceived as a moral, cultural, and economic community—within the space of the reimagined city. Bangalore represents the new India, conceived not only as an economic power but also as a new nation and collectivity of citizens—one that crosses borders in embracing Indians with diverse nationalities, histories, and places of residence but that also incorporates them into an increasingly homogeneous transnational cultural and class identity. Impelled by the neonationalist dream of reinventing India, migrants returning to India have become, through their strategies of class making and place making, central agents in the realization of that dream.

Notes

1. Presumably these numbers do not include the large number of temporary migrant workers who have not acquired permanent residence or citizenship of foreign countries, but only those who have returned after relatively long sojourns abroad.

2. The term *global* appears in many contexts in contemporary India, from media reports to the narratives of IT professionals and entrepreneurs. The category has become so ubiquitous in middle-class and state discourses that it approaches Ernesto Laclau's (2005) concept of an "empty signifier"—one that is so malleable or multivalent that any meaning or function can be attached to it, depending on context. In this chapter there is no space to unpack the multilayered and often conflicting meanings of the global in different social fields (from the corporate world to middle-class lifestyles), or even for this group of transnational subjects, but the narrative should provide some sense of the shifting content and strategic uses of this category. While I sometimes use quotation marks to indicate these features of this term, their absence does not mean that I use the term to refer to a concrete set of processes or characteristics. Of course, in India the term *global* often stands in for the *West* or even *America*, but in combination with the term *Indian* it also represents a reconstructed national, modern, or class identity, a cosmopolitan outlook and subjectivity that is not purely Western nor traditional Indian. Moreover, it is a category that is under construction, highly mediatized, and politically inflected.

3. This chapter draws on data collected for a study of Indian IT/ITES (information technology and IT-enabled services) workers in India and abroad that was carried out by A. R. Vasavi and me, along with a research team at the National Institute of Advanced Studies, Bangalore, between November 2003 and March 2006. The field research was conducted in Bangalore, India, and in the Netherlands, Belgium, and Germany during 2004 and 2005. The research project was funded by the Indo-Dutch Programme on Alternatives in Development and was conducted in collaboration with Peter van der Veer of the University of Utrecht (Upadhya 2006; Upadhya and Vasavi 2006). The material on which the chapter draws consists mainly of long unstructured interview transcripts, notes on informal interactions with IT professionals and observations in their workplaces and homes, and gleanings from news media and the Internet. The chapter also draws on my earlier work on IT entrepreneurs in Bangalore (Upadhya 2003, 2004), and subsequent research based mainly on secondary sources, media, and Internet research. The informants quoted here are all given pseudonyms.

4. This type of circular techno-migration has been facilitated by the H-1B visa scheme in the United States (which has the largest demand for software workers), which was introduced in the early 1990s to attract highly skilled temporary workers. Other countries, such as Australia, Germany, and the United Kingdom, have similar schemes that have facilitated the immigration of Indian IT professionals.

5. Temporary workers often view an assignment in a foreign country as the first step toward migration, and they may use the opportunity to search for regular employment and acquire permanent residence. Significant numbers of H-1B visa holders converted their status to permanent resident during the 1990s, swelling the number of Indian immigrants to the United States to more than two million (Chakravartty 2005, 61; Khadria 2001).

6. To qualify for the NRI designation—which carries certain financial and tax benefits—a person must live outside India for more than 183 days a year.

7. According to one source, since 1991 NRIs and people of Indian descent have ac-

counted for almost a quarter of India's direct foreign investment (Visweswaran and Mir 1999/2000, 104; quoted in Biswas 2005, 57). Although India is the top-most remittance-receiving country in the world (World Bank 2011, 13), state policies target investments by high-worth NRIS and tend to ignore the greater significance of remittance inflows from lower-skilled workers, especially from the Persian Gulf.

8. These changes in citizenship law were promulgated through the Citizenship (Amendment) Act 2003 and the Citizenship (Amendment) Ordinance 2005. An OCI card provides a few more privileges compared to the PIO status, but does not include the right to hold an Indian passport or political rights such as voting or holding office. Although many NRIS see OCI as a form of citizenship, India still does not allow true dual citizenship (i.e., it is illegal for citizens to hold passports of other countries). The NRI category applies to Indian citizens living abroad, while the PIO and OCI cards are like long-term visas for noncitizens of Indian origin.

9. The apparent expansion in the definition of citizenship embodied in the Citizenship (Amendment) Act 2003 has occluded a deeper ideological shift from the principle of *jus solis* (birthplace) to that of *jus sanguinis* (blood ties and descent) (Anupama Roy 2008, 223, 237). Under the new definition, the migrant, even when permanently absent and having acquired a foreign passport, remains "Indian" by culture, descent, and emotional attachment to the motherland (Anupama Roy 2008, 240). This shift is in line with global trends in which the sending countries of international migrants are "expanding extraterritorially by de-territorializing political membership" while receiving countries are "stepping up the pressure aimed at assimilating and securing the loyalties of their migrant populations" (Berking 2004, 110). In the case of India, these changes have been driven by a clear political agenda—the attempt to create a deterritorialized Indian nation or "global Indian family" that is implicitly understood as Hindu (Hansen and Stepputat 2005, 34).

10. In 2005 the new Congress Party–led government extended the right to apply for an OCI card to PIOs living in other countries, except for Pakistan and Bangladesh (Anupama Roy 2008, 244). But membership was still restricted to Overseas Indians who had migrated from India after January 26, 1950, thereby applying mainly to highly skilled migrants in western and Persian Gulf countries (Edwards 2008, 459). Kate Edwards (2008) argues that this shift in policy mirrored a wider change in popular perceptions of NRIS, from the negative image of "not required Indians" to the "national reserve of India." This transformation was closely linked to economic liberalization, which "involved in state projects in new ways some strategically selected communities of the wider Indian diaspora" (454).

11. In the remainder of the chapter I use the terms "NRI" and "Overseas Indian" in their common generic sense, and interchangeably, to refer to Indians living abroad regardless of whether they have taken foreign citizenship or PIO/OCI status, rather than in their narrow legal sense. Although rules about investment and taxation vary depending on one's citizenship status, the government has tried to woo all well-to-do Indians abroad across nationality and residence categories. As the following discussion shows, the distinctions between citizen and non-citizen, resident and non-resident, are in any case blurred.

12. For an illuminating example of how Indian businessmen in Dubai negotiate between various forms of citizenship and belonging—transnational, diasporic, economic, and cultural—see Neha Vora (2011).

13. Before the introduction of the PIO scheme, a foreign passport was a liability for those wishing to work or establish a business enterprise in India because one needed a special visa, a work permit that had to be renewed yearly, and other such clearances. In addition, economic activities were hampered by restrictions on real estate and business investment and steep rates of taxation, which have been considerably reduced following economic liberalization. Moreover, returnees who still held Indian passports would lose their rights to return to the host country. A key difference between the PIO and OCI cards is that with the latter, a noncitizen of Indian origin can apply for reinstatement of Indian citizenship after five years of residence in India (the normal rule is residence of ten years), adding another level of flexibility to citizenship rules that primarily benefit transnational professionals and entrepreneurs.

14. These bonds were floated in 1998 by the State Bank of India on behalf of the Government of India to attract investments by overseas Indians and foreign corporate bodies. They were issued in foreign currency including US dollars and British pounds, the purpose being to augment India's foreign exchange holdings and mitigate the balance of payments problem. The Resurgent India bond scheme raised $4.2 billion mainly from Overseas Indians, while another scheme in 2000 called India Millennium Deposits raised $5.5 billion (source: Shefali Anand, "Rupee's Likely Defender: Bond, India Bond," *The Wall Street Journal India*, February 3, 2013, http://blogs.wsj .com/indiarealtime/2012/05/28/rupees-likely-defender-bond-india-bond/, accessed February 3, 2013). Although these schemes are marketed as an opportunity to contribute to India's development, cynics note that NRIs invest in them mainly for their high financial returns.

15. Aurelie Varrel (2011, 306) suggests that the discourse of reciprocity is part of the mythology that has been built up around the figure of the NRI as a "necessarily successful but homesick professional" (as in the Bollywood movie *Swades*), and that the popular notion that returnees are driven by patriotic values is misleading. However, we should not discount the strength of ideological or cultural motivation. The particular form of Indian national identity that has been produced within the affluent diaspora in the West, together with the efforts of the Indian state to woo NRIs as a key resource for development and to incorporate them into the body politic, have produced a compelling affective discourse and sense of national belonging among many migrants. This is indicated by the substantial flows of diaspora philanthropy and other kinds of NRI involvement in the "development" of their home villages and regions across India (Geithner, Johnson, and Chen 2004).

16. Vinod Khosla and Desh Deshpande are well-known and successful NRI tech entrepreneurs in the United States.

17. Recent scholarly work has focused attention on the worlding of metropolises of the Global South that have emerged as key nodes in the movement of labor, capital, and expertise across the globe, often bypassing nation-state structures (Ananya Roy 2008; Robinson 2002). Such cities attract not only expat (foreign) professional

and technical experts who manage their new deterritorialized industries but also a new class of "national" transnational professionals and technocrats who return from sojourns in the developed world to their own countries to work or invest in these off-shore enclaves (Nonini and Ong 1997; Ong 2005a).

18. While dwelling in the West, many IT professionals conspicuously display their Indian-ness by decorating their homes with various "ethnic" objects acquired in India, but upon return they usually subscribe to international styles and fashion and tend to deplore everything that symbolizes the "traditional Indian" (unless it is a valuable antique object).

19. Pappana is a personal name in Kannada (the language of the state of Karnataka where Bangalore is located), and the street is probably named after a local notable of that name or a bungalow that used to be on that road.

20. The circulation of global capital and transnational professionals through the city are of course only part of the story of the worlding of Bangalore, which also includes government-funded urban redevelopment and infrastructure projects and the booming speculative real estate market. On the role of international and transnational Indian capital in urban redevelopment in Bangalore, see Goldman 2011. The tighter focus here on the return of transnational IT professionals draws attention to just one facet of the materialization of the "extraterritorial" within territories of the metropolis (Ananya Roy 2008, 827).

21. Another example of RNRI activism is R. K. Misra, the winner of the Lead India contest run by the Times of India media group in 2008. See Udupa 2011 for an account of this and other English media-led campaigns to reinvent Bangalore in accordance with so-called global standards.

22. See, for example, the website Citizen Matters, http://bangalore.citizenmatters .in/.

23. Sahana Udupa, personal communication, Bangalore, November 20, 2006.

CHAPTER EIGHT ‹ ‹ ‹ ‹ ‹ ‹ ‹ ‹ ‹ ‹ ‹ ‹ ‹
Ethnicizing, Capitalizing, and Nationalizing
South Korea and the Returning Korean Chinese
MELODY CHIA-WEN LU AND SHIN HYUNJOON ▴

Since the 1980s the Republic of Korea (henceforth ROK or South Korea) has transformed itself from a country of emigration to one of immigration, and from a monoethnic country to a multicultural society open to the world. In defining and redefining its relation to the world and the South Korean nationhood in this context, the South Korean state has also correspondingly made regulation over the Korean diaspora's mobility an issue for policy deliberation. In particular, the notions of return and homecoming have been strongly invoked in both government policies and civil-society actions regarding overseas Korean communities. For instance, the orchestrated family-reunion programs in the late 1980s, the "hometown-visit visa" introduced in the 1990s, and the Overseas Koreans Act in 1999 are all aimed at welcoming some diasporic groups "home" while discouraging others from returning. But on the other hand, the term *return* has not been explicitly used in policies. The government's active engagement in ethnic Koreans' homecoming *without* articulating the meanings of *return* precisely signifies the tensions between nationalism and globalization, and the contradictions between ethno-nationalism and civic nationalism. This chapter sets out to disentangle this very ambiguity.

The South Korean state simultaneously adopts three strategies to manage return migration to its shores in ways commensurable with its state-centric globalization agenda. The ethnicizing strategy highlights biologically determined ethnicity as an overriding principle in mobilizing resources and defining memberships. *Capitalizing* in this chapter indicates the rationality that stresses economic value as the paramount concern, for instance by differentiating groups according to their skill levels and potential contributions to economic competitiveness. *Nationalizing* implies the recognition of civic and social contractual relations between state and citizens internally, and of other nations' sovereignty externally. There are obviously various discrepancies between the three strategies, and tensions between them have shaped the interaction between the South Korean state and the returning diaspora. In the end the ethnicizing and capitalizing strategies seem to be accommodated into the nationalizing principle of structuration.

In order to disentangle the intertwinement of these three strategies, this chapter focuses on the case of the Korean Chinese (*Chaoxianzu* in Chinese and *Joseonjok* in Korean) — citizens of the People's Republic of China of Korean descent. Korean Chinese are the numerically largest overseas Korean population, and their relation with South Korea has probably been the most complex, as evidenced by the policy changes and public contestations related to their return at different stages. Following the historical vicissitudes, we organize the chapter chronologically. We start by reviewing how Korean Chinese, as a population and as a category, emerged from the century-long history of mobility. The self-identity of the Korean Chinese and their relation to China, South Korea, and other ethnic Koreans were conditioned by the Japanese colonial rule, communist revolutions, and the Cold War geopolitics in East Asia. As a result, their return to South Korea has always been a complex and ambiguous project from the beginning. We then discuss how the South Korean government encouraged the conditional return of ethnic Koreans in the 1980s as part of the Korean vision of globalization. This is followed by two sections that examine the logic behind the exclusion of the Korean Chinese by the 1999 Act on the Immigration and Legal Status of Overseas Koreans (henceforth, Overseas Koreans Act or OKA),[1] and the subsequent contestation and amendment in the early 2000s. We conclude with an analysis of how the new policies, though more inclusively based on ethnic ties, remain differentiating, because they are based on national residency and skill levels.

The Making of the Korean Chinese: A History of Mobility and Return

Korean Chinese occupy a unique position in the Korean diaspora due to the specific history of and the politics in East Asia. Korean Chinese today are descendants of Koreans who migrated to China from the middle of the nineteenth century when the Qing dynasty opened up Manchuria in northeast China for Korean immigration. The famine in the late 1860s further quickened outflows from the peninsula. The Japanese colonization of Korea in 1910 and the establishment of the Republic of China in 1911 attracted many Koreans to Manchuria to develop overseas bases of resistance against the Japanese. After the Japanese annexed the region and created the puppet Manchukuo government (1932–45), they brought in a large number of Koreans to serve in their colonial projects, including agricultural and infrastructural developments (Chen X. 2005).

After Japan's defeat at the end of the Second World War in 1945, some Koreans in Manchuria returned to the Korean peninsula, but a sizeable number chose to stay and eventually became citizens of the People's Republic of China (PRC). During the Korean War (1950–53), some Korean Chinese participated as soldiers of the People's Liberation Army against U.S.-supported South Korea (Choi 2001, 124; Jeon 2004). In 1954, ethnic Koreans (Chaoxianzu) were designated as one of the fifty-five ethnic minorities of the PRC, and in 1955 the Yanbian Korean Autonomous Prefecture was instituted in the border region between China and North Korea. As a result of the PRC's ethnic-minority policy, Korean Chinese today enjoy a relatively high degree of cultural autonomy in the PRC, especially in the Yanbian Korean Autonomous Prefecture. For instance, they are free to choose between schools where Korean is the first teaching medium and other Mandarin schools that offer bilingual education.[2] Within the Korean diaspora, the Korean Chinese are the only ones who receive formal education in Korean and are fluent in both Korean and Chinese, spoken as well as written.

Throughout the Cold War period the contacts between Korean Chinese and South Korea were very limited. While South Korea was portrayed in China as a reactionary capitalist *zougou* (running dog) state of U.S. imperialism, Korean Chinese were regarded as traitors of the Korean nation in South Korea. They were seen this way because they fled the fatherland

in times of hardship, collaborated with the Japanese imperial govern-
ment, and, above all, participated in the Korean War in support of North
Korea. Until the 1980s, Korean Chinese were thus seen as allies of North
Korea. That affinity is still reflected in the name Joseonjok, a translation
of the Chinese name Chaoxianzu, in that the term *Chaoxian* (associated
with North Korea) was chosen instead of *Hanguo* (associated with South
Korea). In the 1960s the Chinese government decided to standardize the
Korean-language education for Korean Chinese and adopted the Joseoneo
dialect used in North Korea instead of Hangugeo used in South Korea. As
a result, Joseonjok in South Korea speak North Korean–accented Korean,
which is easily recognizable in South Korea. As Park Jung-Sun and Paul Y.
Chang put it: "It is not simply a matter between an ethnic homeland and
its diaspora, but among two ethnic homelands and their diaspora groups
that are divided along ideological lines" (2005, 8).

The mid-1980s marked the beginning of direct contacts between
Joseonjok and South Korea, with family reunions arranged by the ROK
government and endorsed by the PRC. This early wave of cross-border
mobility was officially called "hometown visit" by the ROK government.
Since there was no direct flight between China and South Korea at that
time, the Korean Chinese had to travel to Hong Kong first before transit-
ing to a flight to Seoul. The Korean Chinese were treated as quasi-citizens
by the ROK government, partly due to its ethno-nationalist perception
and partly because of the absence of diplomatic relations between the two
countries. The Korean Chinese were not required to produce passports or
apply for visas for entering South Korea; instead they were issued travel
certificates or entry permits.[3] After diplomatic relations between PRC and
ROK were established in 1992, large numbers of Korean Chinese migrated
to South Korea in a short period of time, partly because of the introduction of direct transportation between the two countries. The normalization
of bilateral relations also meant that the Korean Chinese were regarded as
fully fledged PRC nationals and were required to travel to South Korea
with passports and visas. Most of the Korean Chinese visited on the short-
term visa (c type) for the purposes of a hometown visit. A small number
were recruited as workers under the official Industrial Technical Training
Program (ITTP) (see Xiang, chapter 4)

In order to be eligible for return with the hometown-visit visa, Korean
Chinese needed to establish that they were born in the Korean Peninsula
or had parents or siblings who were currently ROK nationals. Applicants
typically did so by producing household registrations and birth certifi-

FIGURE 8.1. The *Xinhua News* Propaganda Billboard, a notice board in Garibong, Seoul, is almost identical to the once-ubiquitous billboards of the Xinhua News Agency in China that were dedicated to disseminate government policies and display party slogans, but the *Xinhua News* in the photo is a privately run Chinese-language newspaper that caters to migrants in South Korea. Migrants' mimicry of the state in public representation is another aspect of how transnational mobility is nationalized. (Courtesy of Melody Chia-wen Lu [2009])

cates issued before 1948 in the Korean Peninsula, Manchuria, or Japan. Suspicious that some of these documents might be fabricated, the ROK government set an age limit stipulating that only those who were aged sixty or above were eligible to apply for the hometown-visit visa, assuming that they were more likely to be genuinely born in Korea. Exceptions were given to younger offspring of principal applicants who needed company during travel for health reasons. The age limit was also meant to prevent the abuse of the hometown-visit visa as a backdoor for labor migration. In reality, however, many older Korean Chinese and their accompanying sons stayed on in South Korea and worked without being properly documented. A small number of them were naturalized. They referred to themselves as "returned compatriots in South Korea."[4]

Precisely because of the wide and deep connections between Korean

FIGURE 8.2. Korean Chinese migrants in front of a day-job agency in Daerim, a district in Seoul with a large concentration of Korean Chinese. These Korean Chinese have low status as compared to educated returnees, but they are privileged as compared to nonethnic Korean migrants because only ethnic Koreans on H-2 visas can work in the informal labor market. Ethnic Koreans from other countries also formed their own communities in different parts of Seoul. (Courtesy of Melody Chia-wen Lu [2009])

Chinese and South Korea, the return flows soon reached levels beyond that envisioned by the South Korean government, and brought many other actors into the picture. Despite the migration control imposed by the PRC and ROK governments, these return flows became rather "disorderly" (*luan* in Chinese). As summed up by Ms. Jin, a Korean Chinese turned Korean citizen who worked in a state-owned enterprise in northeast China before migrating to South Korea in her early sixties in the late 1990s: "Joseonjok came in numbers and in so many ways. Simple overstayers used their original names; others were smuggled, using fake passports; and you have bogus household registrations with bogus parents, sham marriages, bogus tourists, bogus students[,] . . . anything you can imagine. Han Chinese also came in these ways."[5]

Commercial migration brokerage was sought to facilitate various types of mobility, regardless of whether the person was potentially a genuine returnee as defined by the South Korean government. The brokerage fee could amount to ten million Korean won (roughly USD 8,500), which put many migrating Korean Chinese in heavy debt. It would take at least three years of full-time work in South Korea to repay the debt. Many overstayed. According to the official statistics, as of 2002 it was estimated that there were 84,793 Korean Chinese residing in South Korea, 79,737 of whom did not have legal status (Seol and Skrentny 2009, 155).

In sum, the social group of Korean Chinese emerged from multilayered histories of imperialism, national and socialist revolutions, and wars. Korean Chinese never had a fixed identity, and in the early stages, they took return more as an economic opportunity than as a response to ideological and political concerns. This also explains the chaotic conditions in the 1990s. This situation changed after 1999 when the South Korean government attempted to define its relation to overseas Koreans and made return a politically charged and ideologically significant subject. In order to understand this change, we need to first examine the South Korean state's perception of return.

Return as Part of "Korean Globalization"

Overseas Koreans have been an important concern of the South Korean state and public for various reasons. It was a dominant ideology in South Korea since its existence that the nation (*minjok*) ought to be the single ethnic Korean community consisting of the north, the south, and the diaspora, and the community's divide was due to Koreans' subjugated position in the world. The nation must be reunited again. The eventual return of overseas ethnic Koreans was seen as critical for addressing injustices of the past, as well as for helping to establish a more open and inclusive society for the future.

During the Cold War period, Koreans in China and the states of the former Soviet Union (or the present Commonwealth of Independent States, or CIS) were strategic targets of the South Korean state's "political work," aimed at infiltrating them, cultivating their loyalty, and even turning them into intelligence agents. Starting from the late 1980s when the iron curtain was gradually lifted, they were embraced as part of the transnational (ethnic) Korean community (*hanminjok gongdongche*) and included in official statistics as Overseas Koreans.[6] However, there was no official definition of *Overseas Koreans* until the OKA was promulgated.

A turning point came on June 14, 1998. On his return flight from a state visit to the United States, the then newly elected president, Kim Dae Jung, instructed his aides to draft a law governing Overseas Koreans. While a primary objective of that trip was to decide the international interventions needed to resolve the financial crisis that hit South Korea hard in 1997, it was also a diplomatic visit to seek the support of the Overseas Korean community. As a result of the president's instruction, the OKA was passed on December 3, 1999. The OKA regarded overseas Koreans as members of the (South) Korean nation-state by granting them various residential and social rights that were compatible with those of ROK citizens, such as long-term residence, property ownership, participation in medical insurance, and financial transactions (Articles 10–16). Park and Chang (2005, 3) call these entitlements "quasi-citizenship."

It is not the offer of quasi-citizenship but the definition of Overseas Koreans that created controversy. The OKA defined Overseas Koreans as consisting of two groups. There were nationals of the ROK who obtained the right of permanent residence in a foreign country or were permanently residing in a foreign country. And there were "Koreans with a foreign nationality" (OKA, Article 2, Definitions), referring to those who had previously held the nationality of the ROK and their lineal descendants. This definition is at once unusually broad and unusually narrow. It is broad because ROK nationals who resided overseas were defined as Overseas Koreans, thus differentiated from citizens who were actually based in South Korea, even though they held ROK passports. The main concern was that Korean nationals overseas did not fulfill their civic duties, such as paying taxes and serving in the military, and thus should not automatically enjoy the same rights as local citizens do (see Kalick 2009). In this sense the act expressed a deep civic nationalism that regarded formal membership alone as insufficient for determining one's status and rights in relation to the nation-state, emphasizing as well actual services that were being rendered to the country.

The OKA definition is unusually narrow in the sense that, by limiting Overseas Koreans to those who possessed or had possessed ROK citizenship, it effectively excluded a large number of ethnic Koreans who had never had any formal political ties to the country. It categorically ruled out North Korea nationals. As the vast majority of the Korean Chinese left the Korean Peninsula before the establishment of the ROK in 1948 and never had ROK citizenship, they were by definition no longer Overseas Koreans despite their strong kinship ties with Korean nationals and the fact that many regarded Korea as their second home. This definition also excluded those in the CIS countries for the same reason. By comparison, Koreans in Western countries, most of whom migrated recently, fell into the category of Overseas Koreans. A large number of Koreans in Japan also left Korea before 1948, but were never granted Japanese citizenship and remained as Korean (either as ROK or DPRK) citizens. The act thus created a divide between Koreans residing in developed countries (primarily the United States, Japan, and countries in Europe) and those residing in developing countries, resulting in what Seol Dong-Hoon Seol and John D. Skrentny (2009) call "hierarchical nationhood." In other words, different Korean diasporic groups were treated differently, according to their nation of residence and citizenship (see Lee C. 2003).

Academic publications and public commentaries in South Korea and overseas suggested that the act adopted the particular definition of Overseas Koreans partially for the purpose of excluding the Korean Chinese and Koreans in the CIS (Jeanyoung Lee 2002a, 2002b; Park and Chang 2005). There are a number of possible reasons for this. The first and most straightforward explanation is that Korean Chinese constituted the largest number of Overseas Koreans who were likely to stay permanently, unlike Korean Americans and other Koreans residing in Western countries who were not likely to return to South Korea or acquire ROK citizenship. The sheer size of the Korean Chinese population, in other words, would pose a demographic and social challenge. Second, in the highly sensitive geopolitical context of Northeast Asia, the idea of building a global Korean ethnic nation could potentially cause anxiety among South Korea's neighbors. It was alleged that China was wary of separatist movements among major ethnic groups within its borders, and the Korean Chinese's blood and cultural (language) ties with the two Koreas were deemed a threat (Jeanyoung Lee 2002b; Park and Chang 2005).[7]

The last and probably the most important reason is that Korean Chinese do not fit well in South Korea's vision of globalization. When President Kim Young-Sam institutionalized the nation-state's relation with the diaspora, the purpose was no longer for readdressing historical injustice; it was to embrace globalization (*segyehwa* in Korean). As Shin Gi-Wook (2006) points out, Kim Young-Sam's segyehwa drive was in essence to reform South Korea's political and economic systems in order to face the challenges of the rapidly changing global economy. The primary goal was to increase and maintain the nation's competitiveness, and globalization was seen as an instrument to achieve this. South Korea's pursuit of globalization was, as such, marked with a clear nationalistic agenda. The intensification of ethnic identity, or the "thickening of ethnicity" (Comaroff and Comaroff 2009, 92), was but one of the key characteristics of Korea's globalization agenda. The building of a global ethnic community was not seen as a reaction to globalization; rather, globalization was a tool for redefining the nation in the transition from Cold War ideology to neoliberal governance (Shin 2006).

Overseas Koreans are presently identified as important actors in South Korea's globalization because they can contribute to the economic development of the nation, and, more importantly, their brains and professional experiences can facilitate Korea's modernization and competition in the world (Lee 2002a; Shin 2006). In this developmental vision of nation building and globalization, a good command of English and a Western education are essential and basic qualities of global competitiveness. Therefore, when the nation-state evokes ethnic unity and belonging among a global Korean community, it is the Korean Americans, and to a lesser extent Koreans in other developed countries, whom they have in mind. In contrast, Korean Chinese as a group of non-English speakers who did not receive Western educations were undesirable and deemed an obstacle in South Korea's globalization process. In addition, their North Korean accent evoked memories of a Cold War that South Korea had not resolved but was eager to leave behind. As such, the OKA was designed, in practice, as an Overseas Koreans classification act.

The Korean Chinese were not only excluded from the privileged group of Overseas Koreans but were also positively categorized as disadvantaged migrant laborers. Following other developmental states in East and Southeast Asia, South Korea devised labor migration policies that favored high-skilled migrants and talents while ensuring that unskilled laborers remained transient (Lu M. 2011). Korean Chinese became the largest foreign labor force in South Korea. They filled the so-called 3-D (dirty, dangerous, demeaning) jobs in the manufacturing sector as well as in the service and care sectors; apart from these jobs, they also worked as street vendors and agricultural laborers. Their language abilities and cultural knowledge made them favorable workers in these sectors, which suffered from severe labor shortages. The places where Korean Chinese communities were concentrated, especially Daerim and Garibong in the southwestern parts of metropolitan Seoul, were often portrayed as the hotspots of crime and illegal gambling (Lim 2010, 114). Despite their cultural-ethnic affinity and the desirability of their labor, Korean Chinese were regarded as migrant workers, needed but unwanted.

Contestation: Return as Rights

The discriminatory clause of the 1999 OKA enraged Korean Chinese in South Korea. What triggered discontent was not necessarily the text of the act itself; the daily experiences of social exclusion and differentiated treatment that Korean Chinese received after the enactment of the law were the direct driving forces. South Korea tightened migration controls with the aim of protecting its citizens' employment rights in Korea while at the same time strictly limiting the migrant workers' status to one of transience (Lee H. 2008). Regular crackdowns and repatriations were intensified after the financial crisis in 1997. By the early 2000s, yet more migration regulations were put in place, while governmental institutions dealing with immigration issues were expanded and strengthened, and methods of migration management became more sophisticated (Lee H. 2008). Notable examples included the Immigration Control Act of 2002 and the Employment Permit System of 2003 and 2007.[8] What was particularly hurtful for the Korean Chinese was how the term *return* used to justify the repatriation of some of them who overstayed their visas. Once they were invited to visit their homeland Korea as compatriots, but now they were migrant laborers to be returned to their homeland China (see Xiang, this volume).

The Korean Chinese experience of contesting the Korean state can be illustrated by Ms. Choi's experiences. Choi came to South Korea in 1992 in her mid-fifties and soon obtained ROK citizenship. She had been selling Chinese herbal medicines and later groceries imported from China on a street in central Seoul before she, and consequently her business, was evicted by the police in 2000, purportedly to make way for a street gentrification project. Yet local Korean street vendors were allowed to continue running their businesses on the same street. She was the only one singled out despite having acquired ROK nationality. She argued with the police but was told that it was only lawful for returned Korean Chinese to work in restaurants, not as street vendors.

She started looking for other Korean Chinese with similar experiences. In 2003 she joined a Korean Christian activist group and started to organize study groups among Joseonjok to discuss the bias of the OKA. They were convinced that the OKA was the cause of the acts of discrimination that they had experienced after 1999, and that legal battles and public protests were the only ways to demand justice.[9] In the words of another Korean Chinese activist, Ms. Jin:

> We demand dual identities. From the international perspective, Joseonjok are Chinese nationals, black and white clear. China is Joseonjok's homeland. But we share the same blood with Korea, be it North or South. We share the same language, culture, and customs. How can you say that we are not compatriots? It is wrong that the ROK government does not recognize its "race" [*burenzhong*, or seeds]. . . . Our demand is very simple. We just want to be treated equally as the others [other overseas Koreans].[10]

At the same time, another movement, led by Christian pastors, advocating for "the right to return and live in the hometown" (*gohyange dorawa sal gwonri*) of Korean Chinese, was also under way. This movement highlighted Korean Chinese as "returnees" to be distinguished from North Korean "defectors" and non-Korean "migrants" (Park Hyun Ok 2005). On August 23, 1999, a petition was filed with the ROK Constitutional Court, arguing that the OKA violated Articles 10 (right to human dignity and worth and to pursue happiness) and 11 (right to equality) of the Constitution. Choi, Jin, and fellow Korean Chinese activists started an eighty-four-day public strike on April 15, 2003, in central Seoul, while several civil society groups supported them by organizing street protests, lobbying politicians, and rallying public support. Eventually the Constitutional Court ruled that the OKA was discriminatory and unconstitutional.[11] The claims of Korean Chinese were both universalistic—against selective and differential subjectification—and particularistic, with an emphasis on their ethnicity.

The indignation, mobilization, and organized contestation made the Korean Chinese more attached to South Korea and more determined to settle there. In other words, it was the process of fighting (for the right of return) that made return real. The process of protesting transformed the lives of Choi and Jin. Despite her ROK citizenship, Choi was planning to go back to China in 2000. When asked why she eventually stayed on in South Korea and devoted her time as an unpaid volunteer for the social movement, she said: "Thanks to our upbringing in China, we learned Mao's philosophy. . . . It is deeply rooted in our mind that when we see injustice we have to do something about it. I am not special. I don't want any personal gains. I just could not let the unjust and unequal treatment toward Joseonjok continue."[12]

The effort of fighting for justice brought the migrants back to their ideological roots and bridged their present to their past in a deep way, through which they were reenergized as social and political actors. This enabled them to develop meaningful social engagement with the host society and to create a new home in South Korea.

The Ethnicity-Nation-Capital Matrix

The victory of the Korean Chinese in 2004 did not usher in a total embrace of the ethnicizing rationality. Policies after 2004 introduced a complex matrix in calibrating returning Overseas Koreans' rights in South Korea, which reconciled the emphasis on ethnic identity with national membership through the emphasis on human capital. Two changes are significant apart from the extension of the category of Overseas Koreans. First, while the definition of the Overseas Koreans' entitlement in the 1999 OKA was vaguely worded, various practical arrangements, on issues such as the procedures of visa application and renewal, are specified with greater detail after 2004. Second, instead of differentiating Overseas Koreans explicitly according to place of residence or nationality, the new policies adopted individual educational level as the key criterion. In theory all Overseas Koreans could obtain the "status of sojourn" (F-4 visa), but in practice those who worked in "simple labor activity" were granted the visiting-employment visa (H-2 visa, implemented in 2007).[13]

The F-4 and H-2 visas entail differentiated rights in many aspects. In terms of residency provisions, F-4 visa holders are permitted to stay in the country for up to three years, but in practice, with possible visa extensions, there is no limit to the duration of stay. H-2 visa holders, on the other hand, can stay a maximum of three years within a five-year period, and upon the expiry of the visa are required to return to their "homeland" to reapply for another H-2 visa. As for economic activities, there is no specific limitation for F-4 visa holders except for the "simple labour activity." H-2 visa holders by definition are unskilled laborers. In the integrated Employment Permit System, jobs in a total of thirty-six sectors are reserved for H-2 visa holders.[14] In terms of freedom of employment, laborers in both categories are free to change jobs and employers, a privilege that other nonethnic Korean foreign workers do not have. Furthermore, there is no age limit for F-4 visa applicants. For the H-2 visa, only those who are above twenty-five years of age are eligible to apply; those who are below fifty-four years of age can apply for renewal from their home country. H-2 visa holders are also not allowed to bring their children, while there is no limit preventing F-4 visa holders from bringing their family members.

Differentiation based on country of current residence still exists, and residence is used as a proxy for skill level. Koreans in the developed countries (primarily in the West and Japan) are in practice almost automatically entitled to F-4 visas regardless of education and skill levels and are granted de facto permanent residence and preferential social rights as citizens as specified in the 1999 OKA. Skilled Koreans in China and in the CIS are also entitled to F-4 visas, but they have to submit a full set of documents to prove their educational and skill levels. Most Koreans in China and the CIS have become preferred guest workers as compared to other foreign workers, and transient workers with limited prospects of settling as compared to Koreans from (or in) the West.

Such an ethnicity-nation-capital matrix thus constitutes the latest manifestation of the partial, selective, and unstable subjectification of returnees by the Korean state. This complication may be inevitable, because the relations between nation-states and the mobile subjects are fraught with multiple contradictions. On the one hand, ethno-nationalism serves as the ideological foundation of policies that facilitate Overseas Koreans' returns, yet ethno-nationalism in the current context is meant to serve an expansive and deterritorializing economic globalization, which unsettles the direction of return (for how return defines the directionality of movement, see Sasaki, this volume). As such the South Korean state never encouraged "real" return whereby overseas Koreans and their families physically settle down and become citizens of South Korea. On the contrary, it fears that a relatively large number of Korean Chinese would become permanent returnees, prompting the adoption of the 1999 OKA to restrict the definition of "Overseas Koreans." The notion of return has to remain ambiguous in order to accommodate the contradictions between ethno-nationalism, civic nationalism, and economic rationality. Furthermore, while ethno-nationalism has been combined with globalization objectives to constitute a deterritorialized ethnic community, the practical method employed by the South Korean state to achieve this has ironically been to nationalize Overseas Koreans. Different overseas communities were divided and treated differently according to their nation of residence. Korean Chinese were able to become more empowered and less disadvantaged in 2004 partly because China's position in the global hierarchy had significantly improved.

In spite of these multiple contradictions, the partial, selective, and unstable subjectification highlighted in this chapter has been feasible only because the nation-state remains the central organizational framework. Internally, the civic contractual relation of the nation has never been undermined, let alone replaced, by ethno-nationalism. Externally the newly developed connections between diasporas and Korea hardly challenge the established world system of nation-states. While the South Korean nation-state has redefined its relation to Overseas Koreans, it has also carefully weighed the relations of Overseas Koreans with their nations of residence and particularly the relations between South Korea and these nations. After all, the Korean way of globalization is about repositioning the nation in the world. Thus, lying at the heart of the South Korean state's engagements with the diaspora is its experimentation with multiple strategies of coping with globalization. The return notion is thus ambiguous, and the ambiguity is productive. The productive ambiguity illustrates how South Korea has refashioned itself in the current global era.

Notes

This research is supported by the Korea Research Foundation Grant Fund by the Korean Government (MEST) (KRF-2007–361-AM0005) and by the Korea Foundation Fellowship for Field Research in 2009 for the research project Technologies of Governmentality and Migration Policies in South Korea and Taiwan. The authors are grateful to Xiang Biao for his intellectual inputs. Melody Chia-Wen Lu wishes to thank Professor Lee Hye-Kyung and Dr. Ye Dong-Geun for their assistance in searching policy documents and conducting interviews.

1. The text of the Act is available on the website of The Refugee Law Reader: http://www.en.refugeelawreader.org/index.php?option=com_docman&task=doc_view&gid=1051&tmpl=component&format=raw&Itemid=&ml=5&mlt=system. Last accessed February 20, 2013.

2. Although both Korean-medium and Mandarin-medium schools in China adopt bilingual education, the Mandarin schools are better equipped with resources and therefore are preferred. Korean Chinese students who migrate to other parts of China outside the three provinces do not receive formal Korean education (Huang S. 2011, 191).

3. A similar quasi-citizen status is granted by the PRC government to citizens of Taiwan. Instead of issuing visas to Taiwanese citizens who visit the mainland, the PRC grants them Return Certificates for Taiwan Compatriots (Taiwan Tongbao Huixiangzheng.

4. As of 2008, there were an estimated 70,000 naturalized Joseonjok returnees in South Korea. They formed Guihan Tongbao Lianhe Zonghui (or Guihan Dongpo Yeonhap Chonghoe in Korean, Association of Returned Compatriots in South Korea).

Interview by Lu with leaders of the Association, in Chinese and Korean, October 22, 2009, Seoul.

5. Interview with Ms. Jin, a Joseonjok community leader in Seoul, September 2009; our translation. She was involved in the protest against the OKA between 2003 and 2006.

6. See Ministry of Foreign Affairs, ROK, "Jaeoedongpo Hyeonhuang" [The current state of Overseas Koreans], http://www.mofat.go.kr/webmodule/htsboard/template /read/korboardread.jsp?typeID=6&boardid=232&seqno=334627 (published June 20, 2012, accessed February 14, 2013). The population of Overseas Koreans in China and CIS countries only became visible after 1991. Before that there were no credible statistics on Koreans in these countries.

7. The PRC has openly opposed South Korea's move to include Korean Chinese in the OKA and refused visa applications by Korean lawmakers in an investigation mission regarding the revision of the OKA in 2004. See Lee Jeanyoung 2002b.

8. See Immigration Control Act, Ministry of Legislation, Republic of Korea, last amended 2002, http://unpan1.un.org/intradoc/groups/public/documents/apcity/un pan011498.pdf (accessed Janaury 13, 2009). For information about the Employment Permit System, Ministry of Employment and Labor, see http://www.eps.go.kr/ph /index.html (accessed January 7, 2013).

9. This assessment was not supported by other Joseonjok groups initially and there was only a small number of Joseonjok initiating the protest.

10. Interview with Ms. Jin, September 2009.

11. Constitutional Court of Korea, "Constitutional Court Ruling No. 13-2 KCCR 714, 99Hun-Ma494," in "Decisions of the Korean Constitutional Court (2001)," 1–15, http://www.ccourt.go.kr/home/english/download/decision_2001.pdf.

12. Group discussion with Joseonjok activists who participated in the 2003 strikes, September 21, 2009.

13. The preference for Korean Chinese was first institutionalized in the Employment Management Scheme in 2004, which was integrated into the Employment Permit System in 2007: "The 'simple labor activity' refers to work that requires simple and usual physical labor, and the employment field of simple labour workers pursuant to the Korean Standard Occupation Classification in the Enforcement Decree of the Immigration Control Act" (Article 27–2[1]). Apart from "simple labor activity," other exclusionary criteria are more abstract, such as committing acts that violate good morals and other aspects of social order, such as gambling, and are deemed necessary to restrict relevant employment in order to maintain public interest and domestic-employment order ("Enforcement Decree of the Immigration Control Act," InvestKorea.org, 2007, http://www.investkorea.org/InvestKoreaWar/data/bbs /20081006/fdi_law8.pdf [accessed Janaury 13, 2009]).

14. For a detailed description of regulations and sectors reserved for H-2 visa holders, see Lee Jeanyoung et al. 2008.

SYLVIA R. COWAN is a professor and the program director of the Intercultural Relations Program in the Graduate School of Arts and Social Sciences at Lesley University in Cambridge, Massachusetts. She is a co-editor (with Tuyet-Lan Pho and Jeffrey N. Gerson) of *Southeast Asian Refugees and Immigrants in the Mill City: Changing Families, Communities, Institutions — Thirty Years Afterward*. Apart from academic research, she has provided extensive advice to educators, executives, and professionals on intercultural understanding and conflict over the last twenty-five years.

JOHAN LINDQUIST is an associate professor of social anthropology at Stockholm University. He is the author of *The Anxieties of Mobility: Development and Migration in the Indonesian Borderlands* and articles in journals such as *Ethnos*, *Pacific Affairs*, and *Public Culture*. He is also the director and producer of the award-winning documentary film *B.A.T.A.M.* (www.der.org).

MELODY CHIA-WEN LU is an assistant professor in the Department of Sociology, University of Macau. Her recent publications include *Asian Cross-border Marriage Migration: Demographic Patterns and Social Issues* (co-edited with Wen-Shan Yang) and a number of journal articles and book chapters on gender, family, and comparative migration regimes in East and Southeast Asia.

KOJI SASAKI is a research fellow of the Japan Society for the Promotion of Science. He has published in Japanese, English, Portuguese, and French.

His recent publications include "Togo to saikisei: Burajiru Nikkei shakai no keisei to imin chishikijin" [Integration and reflexivity: The immigrant intellectuals and the formation of the Japanese community in Brazil], *Imin Kenkyu Nempo* [Japanese annual review of migration studies], no. 17 (2001): 23–42. He is now researching Japanese immigrant intellectuals in Brazil and the Japanese government's engagement with the community in Brazil.

SHIN HYUNJOON is a professor at the Institute for East Asian Studies at Sungkonghoe University, Korea. He is the author of several journal articles on cultural industry and pop music in Korea and East Asia and on Korean diaspora in Northeast and Central Asia. He is currently on the international advisory board of the journal *Popular Music* and the editorial board of Inter-Asia Cultural Studies.

MARIKO ASANO TAMANOI is a professor in the Department of Anthropology, University of California, Los Angeles. Her publications include *Memory Maps: The State and Manchuria in Postwar Japan, Crossed Histories: A New Approach to Manchuria in the Age of Empires*, and *Under the Shadow of Nationalism: Politics and Poetics of Rural Japanese Women*, as well as articles in *American Ethnologist, Journal of Asian Studies, Annual Review of Anthropology, Ethnology, Japan Focus, South Atlantic Quarterly, positions, Bulletin of Concerned Asian Scholars*, and *Comparative Studies in Society and History*.

MIKA TOYOTA is an associate professor at the College of Tourism, Rikkyo University, Japan. She is a co-editor of *Migration and Health in Asia* (2005, with Santosh Jatrana and Brenda S. A. Yeoh), editor of "International Marriage, Rights and the State in East and Southeast Asia," a special issue of *Citizenship Studies*; and editor of "Bringing the 'Left-Behind' Back into View in Asia," a special issue of *Population, Space and Place*. Her articles have appeared in *International Development Planning Review, Ethnic and Racial Studies*, and *Asian Population Studies*.

CAROL UPADHYA is a professor in the School of Social Sciences, National Institute of Advanced Studies (NIAS), Bangalore, India. She has published extensively on globalization, transnationalism, the middle class, and entrepreneurship in India, and is co-editor (with A. R. Vasavi) of *In an Outpost of the Global Economy: Work and Workers in India's Information*

Technology Industry. She is currently the co-director of Provincial Globalisation: The Impact of Reverse Transnational Flows in India's Regional Towns, a collaborative research program with the Amsterdam Institute of Social Science Research, and she anchors the NIAS Urban Research and Policy Program.

WANG CANGBAI is a senior lecturer in contemporary Chinese studies in the Department of Modern and Applied Languages, University of Westminster. He is the author of *Huozai biechu: Xianggang huaren koushu lishi* [Life Is Elsewhere: Stories of the Indonesian Chinese in Hong Kong] and *Population Policies and Development in China and India: Comparative Perspectives* (co-edited with Wong Siu-lun).

XIANG BIAO is a university lecturer in social anthropology at the Institute of Social and Cultural Anthropology and at the Centre on Migration, Policy and Society, University of Oxford. He is the author of *Transcending Boundaries, Global "Body Shopping"* and *The Intermediary Trap*.

BRENDA S. A. YEOH is a professor (provost's chair) in the Department of Geography, as well as dean of the Faculty of Arts and Social Sciences, National University of Singapore. Her publications include *Contesting Space: Power Relations and the Urban Built Environment in Colonial Singapore, Gender and Migration, Gender Politics in the Asia-Pacific Region* (with Peggy Teo and Shirlena Huang), *Migration and Health in Asia* (with Santosh Jatrana and Mika Toyota), and *Asian Women as Transnational Domestic Workers* (with Shirlena Huang and Noor Abdul Rahman).

Amin, Samir, ed. 1974. *Modern Migrations in Western Africa*. London: Oxford University Press.

Anderson, Benedict. 1991. *Imagined Communities: Reflections on the Origins and Spread of Nationalism*. London: Verso.

————. 1994. "Exodus." *Critical Inquiry* 20, no. 2: 314–27.

Ando, Kiyoshi. 1949. "Hojin shakai no genron shichoshi ron" [On the history of the publication and thought in the Japanese society in Brazil]. In *Imin 40-nenshi* [40-year history of immigration], ed. Rokuro Koyama, 301–22. São Paulo: Private Edition.

Appadurai, Arjun. 1993. "Patriotism and Its Futures." *Public Culture* 5 (3): 411–29.

————. 1996. *Modernity at Large: Cultural Dimensions of Modernity*. Minneapolis: University of Minnesota Press.

Asahi Shinbun Tokuhakisha-dan. 1972. *Guamu ni ikita nijūhachinen: Yokoi Shōichi san no kiroku* [The twenty-eight years of survival in Guam: The records of the life of Mr. Yokoi Shōichi]. Tokyo: Asahi Shinbun-sha.

Ashutosh, Ishan, and Alison Mountz. 2011. "Migration Management for the Benefit of Whom? Interrogating the Work of the International Organization for Migration." *Citizenship Studies* 15, no. 1: 21–38.

Baerwald, Hans H. 1983. "Diet." In *Kōdansha Encyclopedia of Japan*, vol. 2, 94–96. Tokyo: Kōdansha.

Bai Ren. 1983. "Guiqiao rencai wailiu zai Xianggang" [Outflow of returned overseas Chinese talents in Hong Kong]. *Dipingxian*, no. 30: 22–23.

Balachandran, G. 2012. *Globalizing Labour? Indian Seafarers and World Shipping, c. 1870–1950*. Oxford: Oxford University Press.

Barabantseva, Elena. 2011. *Overseas Chinese, Ethnic Minorities and Nationalism: De-centering China*. New York: Routledge.

Battistella, Graziano, and Maruja M. B. Asis. 2003. "Southeast Asia and the Specter of Unauthorized Migration." In *Unauthorized Migration in Southeast Asia*, ed.

Graziano Battistella and Maruja M. B. Asis, 1–10. Quezon City: Scalabrini Migration Center.

Beijing Huawen Jiaoyu Zhongxin, ed. 2000. *Zouguo Wushi Nian* [Special issue for the fiftieth anniversary of Beijing Hauqiao Preparatory School]. Beijing: The School.

Benkan Bianjibu. 1958. "Dali guanche shehuizhuyi qiaowu luxian" [To vigorously implement socialist *qiaowu* Course]. *Qiaowu Bao*, no. 9: 16.

———. 1959. "Guanyu huaqiao nongchang ruogan wenti de huida" [Clarifications of some concerns regarding the returned Overseas Chinese farms]. *Qiaowu Bao*, no. 9: 35.

———. 1962. "Yikao qunzhong, minzhu banchang, zhengqu genghao shoucheng" [Relying on the masses, managing the farm in a democratic way and aiming for greater harvests]. *Qiaowu Bao*, no. 1: 4.

———. 1966. "Relie huanying ni, zuguo de hao ernv" [Warm welcome to the motherland's great children]. *Qiaowu Bao*, no. 12: 30.

———. 1980. "Guiqiao, qiaojuan zhishifenzi daliang wailiu de zhuangkuang hen zhide zhongshi" [The outflows of intellectuals among *Guiqiao* and *Qiaojuan* deserved our serious attention]. *Qiaolian Dongtai* 12: 22.

Berking, Helmuth. 2004. "Dwelling in Displacement: On Diasporization and the Production of National Subjects." In *Worlds on the Move: Globalization, Migration, and Cultural Security*, ed. Jonathon Friedman and Shalini Randeria, 103–15. London: I. B. Tauris.

Biess, Frank. 2006. *Homecomings: Returning POWs and the Legacies of Defeat in Postwar Germany*. Princeton: Princeton University Press.

Biswas, Shampa. 2005. "Globalization and the Nation Beyond: The Indian-American Diaspora and the Rethinking of Territory, Citizenship and Democracy." *New Political Science* 27, no. 1: 43–67.

Bohning, W. R. 1979. "International Migration in Western Europe: Reflections on the Past Five Years." *International Labour Review* 118, no. 4: 251–77.

Bon Tempo, Carl J. 2008. *Americans at the Gate: The United States and Refugees during the Cold War*. Princeton: Princeton University Press.

Bose, Pablo S. 2007. "Dreaming of Diasporas: Urban Developments and Transnational Identities in Contemporary Kolkata." *TOPIA: Canadian Journal of Cultural Studies* 17 (Spring): 111–30.

Bracken, Amy. 2009, September 1. "No Mercy: Haitian Criminal Deportees." North American Congress on Latin America Report. https://nacla.org/node/6090.

Burajiru Jiho. 1920a, January 23. "Hakukoku ni ochitsuke" [Settle down in Brazil]. Editorial.

———. 1920b, June 9. "Kika to kokuseki" [Naturalization and nationality].

Carlson, Gene. 2007, February 12. "Cambodia: From LA gangs to Phnom Penh, Lack of Citizenship Turns World Upside Down." *Refugees International*. http://www.refintl.org/content/cambodia-la-gangs-phnom-penh-lack-citizenship-turns-world-upside-down.

Castles, Stephen. 2004. "Why Migration Policies Fail." *Ethnic and Racial Studies* 27, no. 2: 205–27.

————. 2006. "Guestworkers in Europe: A Resurrection?" *International Migration Review* 40, no. 4: 741–66.

Census and Statistics Department of Hong Kong Special Administrative Region. 2000. "Returnees to Hong Kong." In *Social Data Collected via the General Household Survey, Special Topics Report No. 25*, 47–46. Hong Kong: Social Analysis and Research Section, Census and Statistics Department, Government of Hong Kong Special Administrative Region.

Centro de Estudos Nipo-Brasileiros. 2002. *Relatório: Pesquisa de Comunidade Nikkei* [Report: Study of Nikkei community]. São Paulo: Centro de Estudos Nipo-Brasileiros.

Chacko, Elizabeth. 2007. "From Brain Drain to Brain Gain: Reverse Migration to Bangalore and Hyderabad, India's Globalizing High Tech Cities." *Geojournal* 138 (2–3): 131–40.

Chakravarty, Paula. 2005. "Weak Winners of Globalization: Indian H1-B Workers in the American Information Economy." *AAPI Nexus* 3, no. 2: 59–84.

Chandler, David. 1993. *A History of Cambodia*. 2nd ed. Boulder: Westview Press.

Chatterjee, Partha. 1986. *Nationalist Thought and the Colonial World: A Derivative Discourse?* London: Zed Books for the United Nations University.

Chen Guojun. 1960. "Zuguo shi wennuan de da jiating" [Motherland is a big warm family]. *Qiaowu Bao*, no. 1: 22.

Chen Kuan-Hsing. 2010. *Asia as Method: Toward Deimperialization*. Durham: Duke University Press.

Chen Xiangming. 2005. *As Borders Bend: Transnational Spaces on the Pacific Rim*. Lanham, Md.: Rowman & Littlefield.

Chin, Christine. 2008. "Diversification and Privatization: Securing Insecurities in the Receiving Country of Malaysia." *Asia Pacific Journal of Anthropology* 9, no. 4: 285–303.

CHINCA (China's International Contractors' Association). 2004, December. *Zhongguo duiwai laowu hezuo niandu baobao 2004* [Annual report on China's international labor collaboration]. Beijing: Zhongguo Duiwai Chengbao Gongchen Shanghui.

Choi Woogill. 2001. "The Korean Minority in China: The Change of Its Identity." *Development and Society* 30, no. 1: 119–41.

Chusho Kigyo-cho. 1987. *Showa 61-nendo-ban chusho kigyo hakusho* [White book on small and medium enterprises in Japan FY 1986]. Tokyo: Chusho Kigyo-cho.

CNN World. 2009, September 2. "Mayor: Deportations Harm Juarez, United States." http://www.studentnews.cnn.com/2009/WORLD/americas/09/02/mexico.juarez .deportations/index.html.

Comaroff, John L., and Jean Comaroff. 2009. *Ethnicity, Inc*. Chicago: University of Chicago Press.

Comissão de Elaboração da História dos 80 Anos da Imigração Japonesa no Brasil, Sociedade Brasileira de Cultura Japonesa. 1992. *Uma Epopéia Moderna* [A modern epic]. São Paulo: Editora HUCITEC.

Commission of the European Communities. 2007, May 16. "Communication from the Commission to the European Parliament, the Council, the European Eco-

nomic and Social Committee and the Committee of the Regions: On Circular
Migration and Mobility Partnerships between the European Union and Third
Countries." CELEX no. 52007DC0248 Brussels. http://eur-lex.europa.eu/LexUri
Serv/LexUriServ.do?uri=com:2007:0248:fin:en:html.

Cong Zhongxiao. 2004, June 1. "Riben dedao toukui zhongguo nv yanxiusheng
de laoban zhengshi jugong daoqian" [Japanese boss in Tokushima who peeped
female trainees formally bowed and apologized]. *Guanxi Huawen Shibao* (Osaka).
http://www.chinanews.com/news/2004year/2004-06-01/26/443386.shtml. Last
accessed February 4, 2013.

Coppel, Charles A. 1983. *Indonesian Chinese in Crisis*. Kuala Lumpur: Oxford University Press.

Cotia Sangyo Kumiai. 1956. "Showa 30-nendo Cotia Sangyo Kumiai Tandoku Seinen
Koyo Imin no dai 1-ji boshu yoko" [The Guideline for the primary recruitment
of Cotia Agricultural Cooperative's Youth Employment Emigration for FY 1956].
Gaimu-Sho Gaiko Shiryokan [Diplomatic Archives of the Ministry of Foreign
Affairs of Japan].

Das, Veena. 1995. *Critical Events: Moments in the Life of a Nation*. Delhi: University
of Oxford Press.

David, Fiona. 2007. "ASEAN and Trafficking in Persons: Using Data as a Tool to
Combat Trafficking in Persons." Report prepared for ASEAN and IOM.

Deeherd, C. 2003, January 14. "Home Isn't Sweet for Cambodians Deported from
the U.S." *Seattle Times*, A10.

de Genova, Nicholas. 2002. "Migrant 'Illegality' and Deportability in Everyday Life."
Annual Review of Anthropology 31: 419–47.

de Haas, Hein. 2006. "Migration, Remittances and Regional Development in Southern Morocco." *Geoforum* 37, no. 4: 565–80.

Deportation Nation. 2011. "Round-up: Immigration and Enforcement Systems
under Fire Amidst Record-Number Deportations." http://www.deportation
nation.org/2011/10/round-up-immigration-and-enforcement-systems-under
-fire-admist-record-number-deportations/.

Dickinson, Jen, and Adrian J. Bailey. 2007. "(Re)membering Diaspora: Uneven
Geographies of Indian Dual Citizenship." *Political Geography* 26, no. 7: 757–74.

Dikotter, Frank. 1990. "Group Definition and the Idea of Race in Modern China
(1793–1949)." *Ethnic and Racial Studies* 13, no. 3: 420–29.

Doezema, Jo. 2010. *Sex Slaves and Discourse Masters: The Construction of Trafficking*.
London: Zed.

Dower, John W. 1979. *Empire and Aftermath: Yoshida Shigeru and the Japanese
Experience, 1878–1954*. Cambridge: Council on East Asian Studies, Harvard University.

———. 1986. *War without Mercy: Race and Power in the Pacific War*. New York:
Pantheon.

———. 1999. *Embracing Defeat: Japan in the Wake of World War II*. New York:
W. W. Norton and Company.

Duara, Prasenjit. 1995. *Rescuing History from the Nation: Questioning Narratives of
Modern China*. Chicago: University of Chicago Press.

———. 1996. "De-constructing the Chinese Nation." In *Chinese Nationalism*, ed. Jonathan Unger, 31–55. Armonk, N.Y.: M. E. Sharpe.

———. 2008. "The Global and Regional Constitution of Nations: The View from East Asia." *Nations and Nationalism* 14, no. 2: 323–46.

———. 2009. *The Global and Regional in China's Nation-Formation*. London: Routledge.

———. 2010. "Asia Redux: Conceptualizing a Region for Our Times." *The Journal of Asian Studies* 69, no. 4: 963–83.

Dudden, Alexis. 2008. *Troubled Apologies among Japan, Korea, and the United States*. New York: Columbia University Press.

Edwards, Kate. 2008. "For a Geohistorical Cosmopolitanism: Postcolonial State Strategies, Cosmopolitan Communities, and the Production of the 'British,' 'Overseas,' 'Non-resident,' and 'Global' Indian." *Environment and Planning D: Society and Space* 26 (3): 444–63.

Ehrlich, Richard S. 2003, September 1. "American Felons Deported to Cambodia." *The Laissez Faire Electronic Times*. http://www.oocities.org/asia_correspondent /cambodia03amerfelonset.html. Last accessed February 21, 2013.

Evans, Peter. 1995. *Embedded Autonomy: States and Industrial Transformation*. Princeton: Princeton University Press.

Faist, Thomas. 2000. "Transnationalisation in International Migration: Implications for the Study of Citizenship and Culture." *Ethnic and Racial Studies* 23, no. 2: 189–222.

Fang Fang. 1961. "Fang Fang fu zhuren xiang quanguo zhengxie baogao qiaowu gongzuo" [Fang Fang, the deputy director of state commission of Chinese affairs, reporting Overseas Chinese affairs to the National Political Consultative Conference]. *Qiaowu Bao*, no. 6: 2–3.

Fang Xiongpu and Feng Ziping. 2001. *Hauqiao Huaren Baike Quanshu: Qiaoxiang Juan* [Encyclopedia of overseas Chinese: The volume of *qiaoxiang*]. Beijing: Zhongguo Huaqiao Chubanshe.

Fernandes, Leela. 2006. *India's New Middle Class; Democratic Politics in an Era of Economic Reform*. Minneapolis: University of Minnesota Press.

Field, Frank. 2008, September 8. "Balance the Ins and Outs." *The Guardian*. http:// www.guardian.co.uk/commentisfree/2008/sep/08/immigrationpolicy.eu. Last accessed February 4, 2013.

Fitzgerald, John. 1996. "The Nationless State: The Search for a Nation in Modern Chinese Nationalism." In *Chinese Nationalism*, ed. Jonathan Unger, 56–85. Armonk, N.Y.: M. E. Sharpe.

Fitzgerald, Stephen. 1972. *China and the Overseas Chinese: A Study of Peking's Changing Policy, 1949–1970*. Cambridge: Cambridge University Press.

Ford, Michele. 2006. "After Nunukan: Recent Developments in the Regulation of Labour Migration from Indonesia to Malaysia." In *Mobility, Labour Migration and Border Controls in Asia*, ed. Amarjit Kaur and Ian Metcalfe, 228–47. London: Palgrave Macmillan.

Ford, Michele, and Lenore Lyons. 2012. "Counter-trafficking and Migrant Labour Activism in Indonesia's Periphery." In *Labour Mobility and Human Trafficking in*

Southeast Asia: Critical Perspectives, ed. Michele Ford, Lenore Lyons, and Willem van Schendel, 75–94. New York: Routledge.

Fujita, Toshiro. 1921, May 13. "Zairyumin shokun ni tsugu" [An announcement to the expatriates in Brazil], *Burajiru Jiho*.

Gaimu-sho. 1941. *Burajiu ni okeru Nihonjin hattenshi jo-kan* [The history of the development of the Japanese in Brazil, vol. 1]. Tokyo: Gaimu-sho America-Kyoku.

———. 1953. *Burajiu ni okeru Nihonjin hattenshi ge-kan* [The history of the development of the Japanese in Brazil, vol. 2]. Tokyo: Gaimu-sho Obei-Kyoku Iminka.

Gania, Edwin T. 2006. *U.S. Immigration: Step by Step*. Naperville, Ill.: Sphinx Pub.

Gao Mingxuan. 1956. "Bixu zuohao dui guiguo huaqiao zhigong de anzhi gong-zuo" [Must fulfill the task of allocating returned Overseas Chinese to state units]. *Qiaowu Bao*, no. 3: 3–5.

Geithner, Peter F., Paula D. Johnson, and Lincoln C. Chen, eds. 2004. *Diaspora Philanthropy and Equitable Development in China and India*. Cambridge: Global Equity Initiative and Harvard University Press.

Gerson, Jeffrey N. 2008. "The Battle for Control of the Trairatanaram Cambodian Temple." In *Southeast Asian Refugees and Immigrants in the Mill City: Changing Families, Communities, Institutions—Thirty Years Afterward*, ed. Pho Tuyet-Lan, Jeffrey N. Gerson, and Sylvia R. Cowan, 153–72. Burlington: University of Vermont Press.

Ghosh, Bimal. 1998. *Huddled Masses and Uncertain Shores: Insights into Irregular Migration*. The Hague: Martinus Nijhoff.

Gibney, Matthew J., and Randall Hansen, eds. 2005. *Immigration and Asylum: From 1900 to the Present, Volume 3*. Santa Barbara, Calif.: ABC-CLIO.

"Give Ops Tegas a Chance." 2005, March 22. *Daily Express* (Sabah, Malaysia). http://www.dailyexpress.com.my/news.cfm?NewsID=33404. Last accessed December 27, 2008.

Gladney, Druc. 1998. *Making Majorities: Constituting the Nation in Japan, Korea, China, Malaysia, Fiji, Turkey, and the United States*. Stanford: Stanford University Press.

Global Commission of International Migration. 2005, October 5. "Migration in an Interconnected World: New Directions for Action. Report of the Global Commission on International Migration." http://www.unhcr.org/refworld/docid/435f81814.html.

Godley, Michael R. 1989. "The Sojourner: Returned Overseas Chinese in the People's Republic of China." *Pacific Affairs* 62, no. 3: 330–52.

Goldman, Michael. 2011. "Speculative Urbanism and the Making of the Next World City." *International Journal of Urban and Regional Research* 35, no. 3: 555–81.

Goss, Jon, and Bruce Lindquist. 1995. "Conceptualizing International Labour Migration: A Structuration Perspective." *International Migration Review* 29, no. 2: 317–51.

Guowuyuan Qiaoban ji Zhongyang Wenxian Yanjiushi, ed. 2000. *Deng Xiaoping lun qiaowu* [Deng Xiaoping's speeches on *qiaowu*]. Beijing: Zhongyang Wenxian Chubanshe.

Hagan, Jacqueline, Karl Eschbach, and Nestor Rodriguez. 2008. "U.S. Deportation Policy, Family Separation, and Circular Migration." *Immigration Migration Review* 42, no. 1: 64–88.

Haines, David W. 2010. *Safe Haven? A History of Refugees in America.* Sterling, Va.: Kumarian Press.

Handa, Tomoo. 1966. "Doho syakai no shisoshi no ichi danmen" [An aspect of the intellectual history of the society of the compatriots]. In *Ima nao tabiji ni ari: Aru imin no zuiso* [Still on my journey: Essays of an immigrant], 140–55. São Paulo: San Pauro Jinmon Kagaku Kenkyukai.

———. 1987. *O imigrante Japonês: História de sua vida no Brasil* [The Japanese immigrant: The history of his life in Brazil]. São Paulo: Centro de Estudos Nipo-Brasileiro.

Hansen, Thomas B., and Finn Stepputat. 2005. "Introduction." In *Sovereign Bodies: Citizens, Migrants, and States in the Postcolonial World,* ed. Thomas Blom Hansen and Finn Stepputat, 1–36. Princeton: Princeton University Press.

Hardt, Michael, and Antonio Negri. 2000. *Empire.* Cambridge: Harvard University Press.

———. 2004. *Multitude: War and Democracy in the Age of Empire.* New York: Penguin.

Hayashi, Eiichi. 2007. *Zanryū Nihonhei no shinjitsu* [The reality of the Japanese soldiers who had been left behind]. Tokyo: Sakuhin-sha.

———. 2009. *Tōbu Jawa no Nihonjin heishi* [The Japanese soldiers in the eastern Java]. Tokyo: Sakuhin-sha.

Hayashi, Fumiko. 1988. "Furōji" [Homeless children]. In *Bungei Shunjū ni miru Shōwa-shi,* vol. 2, ed. Bungei Shunjū-sha, 26–34. Tokyo: Bungei Shunjū-sha.

Hein, Jeremy. 1995. *From Vietnam, Laos, and Cambodia: A Refugee Experience in the United States.* New York: Twayne.

Hemingway, Ernest. 1996. "Soldier's Home." In *In Our Time,* 69–77. New York: Scribner.

Hernández-Coss, R., G. Brown, C. Buchori, I. Endo, E. Todoroki, T. Naovalitha, W. Noor, and C. Mar. 2008. "The Malaysia-Indonesia Remittance Corridor: Making Formal Transfers the Best Options for Women and Undocumented Migrants." Working Paper no. 149, the World Bank.

Hernandez-Leon, Ruben. 2005. "The Migration Industry in the Mexico-U.S. Migratory System." On-line Working Paper Series, California Center for Population Research, UC Los Angeles, http://escholarship.org/uc/item/3hg44330. Last accessed February 18, 2013.

Hesford, Wendy S., and Wendy Kozol. 2005. "Introduction." In *Just Advocacy: Women's Human Rights, Transnational Feminisms, and the Politics of Representation,* ed. W. S. Hesford and W. Kozol, 1–29. New Brunswick, N.J.: Rutgers University Press.

He Xiankai, ed. 1994. *Guoji laowu hezuo shiwu* [Practical issues in international labor cooperation]. Beijing: Beijing Gongye Daxue Chubanshe.

Higuchi, Naoto. 2005, November 30–December 2. "Brazilian Migration to Japan: Trends, Modalities, and Impact." Paper presented at the Expert Group Meeting on International Migration and Development in Latin America and the Caribbean,

Population Division, Department of Economic and Social Affairs, United Nations Secretariat, Mexico City.

Hing, Bill Ong. 2005. "Deporting Cambodian Refugees: Justice Denied?" *Crime and Delinquency* 51, no. 2: 265–90.

Hirschman, Albert O. 1970. *Exit, Voice, and Loyalty: Responses to Declines in Firms, Organizations, and States.* Cambridge: Harvard University Press.

Holst, Frederik. 2009, August 8. "Creating the Outside 'Other': The Role of Migrant Workers in Malaysia's Media Discourse." Paper presented at Sixth International Convention of Asia Scholars, Daejeon, South Korea.

Homu-sho Nyuukoku Kanrikyoku. 2008. *Heisei 20-nendo Shutsunyuu-koku Kanri* [Emigration and immigration control, FY 2007]. Tokyo: Homu-sho.

Hong, Sisi. 1989. "Huaqiao dui xinhai geming de juda gongxian" [The great contribution of Overseas Chinese to the 1911 revolution]. In Zheng Min and Liang Chuming, eds., *Huaqiao huaren shi yanjiu ji, di yi ji* [Selected works of the research on Overseas Chinese history, volume 1], 146–63. Beijing: Haiyang Chubanshe.

Hong Kong Transition Project. 2002, May. "The First Five Years: Floundering Government, Foundering Democracy?" Hong Kong Baptist University, Government and International Studies. http://hktp.hkbu.edu.hk/5years/5years.pdf. Last accessed February 4, 2013.

Huang Jing. 1999. "Guiqiao zai Zhongguo dalu de wenhua shiying (1949–1998): Dui Beijing Yinni guiqiao qunti de diaocha fenxi" [Cultural adaptation of returned Overseas Chinese in mainland China (1949–1998): A survey on returned Overseas Chinese from Indonesia in Beijing]. *Huaqiao Huaren Lishi Yanjiu*, no. 45: 45–54.

Huang Shentien. 2011. "Yanbian Chaoxianzu shuanyujaoyu xiankuan ji fenxi" [Conditions and analysis of bilingual education among Chaoxianzu in Yanbian]. *Jiaoyu Jiaoxue Luntan* [*Education Teaching Forum*] no. 5: 191–92.

Huang Xiaojian. 2005. *Guiguo huaqiao de lishi yu xianzhuang* [The history and present situation of the returned Overseas Chinese]. Hong Kong: Xianggang Shehui Kexue Chubanshe Youxian Gongsi.

Huang Xiaojian, Zhao Hongying, and Cong Yuefen. 1995. *Haiwai qiaobao yu kangri zhanzheng* [Overseas Chinese and the anti-Japanese war]. Beijing: Beijing Chubanshe.

Hugo, Graeme. 2004. "International Migration in Southeast Asia since World War II." In *International Migration in Southeast Asia*, ed. Aris Ananta and Evi Nurvidya Arifin, 28–70. Singapore: Institute of Southeast Asian Studies.

———. 2009. "Best Practices in Temporary Labour Migration for Development: A Perspective from Asia and the Pacific." *International Migration* 47, no. 5: 23–74.

Hyland, Anne. 2007, April 13. "The Outsiders." *The Wall Street Journal.* http://online.wsj.com/article/SB117639427943467835.html. Last accessed February 4, 2013.

Instituto Brasileiro de Geografia e Estatística. 2003. *Atlas do censo demográfico 2000* [Atlas of the demographic census of 2000]. Rio de Janeiro: Instituto Brasileiro de Geografia e Estatística.

International Human Rights Clinic, UC-Berkeley School of Law; Chief Justice Earl Warren Institute on Race, Ethnicity and Diversity, UC-Berkeley School of Law;

Immigration Law Clinic, UC-Davis School of Law. 2010. *In the Child's Best Interest? The Consequences of Losing a Lawful Immigrant Parent to Deportation.* Report available at http://www.law.berkeley.edu/files/Human_Rights_report.pdf. Last accessed February 20, 2013.

International Organization for Migration. 2002, May. "Assisted Voluntary Return Programmes in Europe." Geneva: International Organization for Migration.

———. 2004. *Return Migration: Policies and Practices in Europe.* Geneva: International Organization for Migration.

———. 2006. *World Migration 2005.*

Itō, Tadahiko. 1972. *Nihonjin sono sei to shi: Yokoi Shōichi kiseki no nijūhachinen* [The life and death of the Japanese: Yokoi Shōichi and the miracle of twenty-eight years]. Tokyo: Nichigei Shuppan.

Jeon Hyeon-su. 2004. "Jungguk Joseonjok-ui hangukjeonjaeng chamjeon yeongu" [A study on the participation in the Korean War of ethnic Koreans in China]. *Gukminyunri Yeongu* 57: 241–70.

Jiang Zemin. 2001. "Jiang Zemin zai qingzhu jiandang bashi zhounian dahui shang de jianghua" [Jiang Zemin's speech at the celebration conference for the 80th anniversary of the founding of CCP], *Renmin Ribao* [People's daily], July 2. http://www. people.com.cn/GB/shizheng/16/20010702/501591.html. Last accessed May 16, 2013.

Jones, Sidney. 2000. *Making Money off Migrants: The Indonesian Exodus to Malaysia.* Hong Kong: Asia 2000.

Jonsson, Patrik, and Kristen Chick. 2009, June 18."Many Iraqi Refugees in U.S. Now in Dire Straits." *Christian Science Monitor.* http://www.csmonitor.com/2009/0618 /p02s15-usfp.html. Accessed February 16, 2013.

Kaigai Nikkeijin Renraku Kyokai. 1960. *Kaigai Nikkeijin Taikai ni tsuite: Kaigai Nikkeijin Kyokai setsuritsu* [On the Convention of the Overseas Japanese and Their Descendants: Founding the Association of the Overseas Japanese and Their Descendants]. Tokyo: Kaigai Nikkeijin Renraku Kyokai.

Kalick, Konrad. 2009. "Ethnic Nationalism and Political Community: The Overseas Suffrage Debates in Japan and South Korea." *Asian Studies Review* 33 (2): 175–95.

Kanstroom, Daniel. 2007. *Deportation Nation: Outsiders in American History.* Cambridge: Harvard University Press.

Kapur, Devesh. 2002. "The Causes and Consequences of India's IT Boom." *India Review* 1 (2): 91–110.

———. 2003. "Indian Diaspora as a Strategic Asset." *Economic and Political Weekly* 38, no. 5: 445–48.

Kaur, Amarjit. 2006. "Order (and Disorder) at the Border: International Migration and Border Controls in Southeast Asia." In *Mobility, Labour Migration and Border Controls in Asia*, ed. Amarjit Kaur and Ian Metcalfe, 23–51. London: Palgrave Macmillan.

Kawabata, Sajiro. 1941, May 10. "Koei aru taikyaku imin taran" [We shall be the glorious retreat migrants]. *Seisyu Shimpo.*

Kawasaki, Masumi. 2003. *Kaettekita Taiwanjin Nihonhei* [The Japanese soldier of the Taiwanese descent who returned home]. Tokyo: Bungei Shunjū Shinsho.

Kempadoo, Kamala, ed. 2005. *Trafficking and Prostitution Reconsidered: New Perspectives on Migration, Sex Work, and Human Rights*. Boulder: Paradigm Publishers.

Khadria, Binod. 1999. *The Migration of Knowledge Workers: Second-Generation Effects of India's Brain Drain*. New Delhi: Sage.

————. 2001. "Shifting Paradigms of Globalization: The Twenty-First Century Transition towards Generics in Skilled Migration from India." *International Migration of the Highly Skilled* 39, no. 5: 45–72.

King, Russell, ed. 1986. *Return Migration and Regional Economic Problems*. London: Croom Helm.

————. 2000. "Generalization from the History of Return Migration." In *Return Migration: Journey of Hope or Despair?*, ed. Bhimal Ghosh, 7–56. Geneva: IOM/UN.

Kishimoto, Kyuyo. 1947. *Nambei no senya ni koritsu shite* [Standing alone in the South American battlefield]. São Paulo: Private Edition.

Kokusai Kyoryoku Jigyodan. 1987. *Kaigai ijuu toukei Showa 27-nendo-61-nendo* [Statistics of the overseas emigration FY 1951–86]. Tokyo: Kokusai Kyoryoku Jigyodan [Japan International Cooperation Agency].

Kosei-sho Daijin Kambo Kikakushitsu. 1956. "Kosei hakusho: Showa 31-nendo-ban" [White paper of the health and welfare: FY 1955]. Tokyo: Toyo Keizai Simpo Sha.

————. 1997. *Engo gojūnen-shi* [The fifty-year history of the state's assistance of the repatriates]. Tokyo: Gyōsei.

————. 2000a. *Hikiage engo no kiroku* [The records of the state's assistance of the repatriates]. Tokyo: Kuresu Shuppan.

————. 2000b. *Zoku hikiage engo no kiroku* [The sequel to the records of the state's assistance of the repatriates]. Tokyo: Kuresu Shuppan.

Koser, Khalid. 2000. "Return, Readmission and Reintegration: Changing Agendas, Policy Frameworks and Operational Programmes." In *Return Migration: Journey of Hope or Despair?*, ed. Bimal Ghosh, 57–99. Geneva: International IOM/UN.

Koser, Khalid, and Richard Black. 1999. "The End of the Refugee Cycle?" In *The End of the Refugee Cycle: Refugee Repatriation and Reconstruction*, ed. Richard Black and Khalid Koser, 2–17. New York: Berghahn.

Kosonju. 1941a, July 5. "Zaihaku Nihonjin no yukue" [The future of the Japanese in Brazil]. *Seisyu Shimpo*.

————. 1941b, July 9. "Zaihaku Nihonjin no yukue" [The future of the Japanese in Brazil]. *Seisyu Shimpo*.

————. 1941c, July 12. "Zaihaku Nihonjin no yukue" [The future of the Japanese in Brazil]. *Seisyu Shimpo*.

Krishna, V. V., and B. Khadria. 1997. "Phasing Scientific Migration in the Context of Brain Gain and Brain Drain in India." *Science, Technology and Society* 2, no. 2: 348–85.

Krugman, Paul. 2006, March 31. "The Road to Dubai." *New York Times*. http://query.nytimes.com/gst/fullpage.html?res=F60F12FC39540C728FDDAA0894 DE404482). Last accessed February 4, 2013.

Labrianidis, Lois, and Brikena Kazazi. 2006. "Albanian Return-Migrants from

Greece and Italy: Their Impact upon Spatial Disparities within Albania." *European Urban and Regional Studies* 13, no. 1: 59–74.

Laclau, Ernesto. 2005. *On Populist Reason*. London: Verso.

Lakzco, Frank. 2000. "Return Migration: Reshaping Policy Approaches." In *Return Migration: Journey of Hope or Despair?*, ed. Bimal Ghosh, 153–80. Geneva: IOM/UN.

Lawless, Richard. 1986. "Return Migration to Algeria: The Impact of State Intervention." In *Return Migration and Regional Economic Problems*, ed. Russell King, 213–42. London: Croom Helm.

Lee, J., A. Lei, and S. Sue. 2001. "The Current State of Mental Health Research on Asian Americans." In *Psychosocial Aspects of the Asian American Experience: Diversity within Diversity*, ed. Choi N. G., 159–78. Binghamton, N.Y.: Hayworth.

Lee, Jonathan H. X. 2010. "Cambodian American Ethics of Identity Formation." In *Cambodian American Experiences: Histories, Communities, Cultures, and Identities*, ed. Jonathan H. X. Lee, 343–53. Dubuque, Iowa: Kendall Hunt.

Lee Chulwoo. 2003. "'Us' and 'Them' in Korean Law: The Creation, Accommodation and Exclusion of Outsiders in South Korea." In *East Asian Law: Universal Norms and Local Cultures*, ed. Arthus Rosett, Lucie Cheng, and Margaret Y. K. Woo, 106–36. London: RoutledgeCurzon.

Lee Hye-kyung. 2008. "Hanguk iminjeongchaegui suryeomhyeonsang: Hwakdaewa poseobui banghyangeuro" [The shift of immigration policy toward expansion and inclusion in South Korea]. *Hanguksahoehak* 42, no. 2: 104–37.

Lee Jeanyoung. 2002a. "Hangukui jaeoedongpo jeongchaek" [The policy on overseas Koreans in ROK]. IOM Migration Research and Training Center Working Paper Series, No. 2010–11.

——. 2002b. "Hanjung oegyogwangyewa jaejung dongpo: Jaeoe dongpobeob heonbeob bulilchi gyeoljeongeul jungsimeuro" [ROK-PRC diplomatic relations and Korean Chinese: On the decision that OKA violated the constitution]. *Gukgajeollyak* 8, no. 4: 77–99.

Lee Jeanyoung, Hye-kyung Lee, and Hyun Mee Kim. 2008. "Bangmunchuieopje-e daehan siltae mit dongpo manjokdo josa" [Research on the real conditions of visiting employment system and the satisfaction from the ethnic Koreans from abroad]. Report, Ministry of Justice Korean Immigration Service, Republic of Korea.

Lesser, Jeffrey. 1999. *Negotiating National Identities: Immigrants, Minorities, and the Struggle for Ethnicity in Brazil*. Durham: Duke University Press.

Lessinger, Johanna. 1992. "Investing or Going Home? A Transnational Strategy among Indian Immigrants in the United States." In *Towards a Transnational Perspective on Migration: Race, Class, Ethnicity, and Nationalism Reconsidered*, vol. 645, ed. N. Glick Schiller, L. Basch, and C. Blanc-Szanton, 53–80. New York: New York Academy of Sciences.

Ley, David, and Audrey Kobayashi. 2005. "Back to Hong Kong: Return Migration or Transnational Sojourn?" *Global Networks* 5, no. 2: 111–28.

Liao Hui. 1989. "Zai guowuyuan qiaowu gongzuo shuiyi shang de gongzuo baogao"

[Working report to the Overseas Chinese Affairs Conference of the State Council]. *Qiaowu Gongzuo Yanjiu* 4: 7.

Li Cheng, ed. 2005. Bridging Minds across the Pacific: U.S.-China Educational Exchanges, 1978–2003. Lanham, MD: Lexington Books.

Li Minghuan. 2001. "Oumeng guojia yimin zhengce yu Zhongguo xinyimin" [Immigration policies of EU states and new Chinese immigrants]. *Xiamen Daxue Xuebao*, no. 4: 105–12.

———, ed. 2005. *Fujian qiaoxiang diaocha: Qiaoxiang rentong, qiaoxiang wangluo and qiaoxiang wenhua* [An investigation of homes of overseas Chinese in Fujian: Identity, network, and culture]. Xiamen: Xiamen Daxue Chubanshe.

Lim Sun-il. 2010. "Esnisiti byeonhyeongeul tonghan hanguk sahoe ijunodongja-ui munhwa byeonyong yeongu: hangukgyewa bihangukgye ijunodongja-ui sarye bigyo" [A study on the acculturation through ethnicity transformation of migrant workers in Korea: A comparative analysis of ethnic Korean and non-Korean groups]. PhD diss., Sungkonghoe University.

Lindquist, Johan. 2009. *The Anxieties of Mobility: Development and Migration in the Indonesian Borderlands*. Honolulu: University of Hawai'i Press.

———. 2010a. "Images and Evidence: Human Trafficking, Auditing, and the Production of Illicit Markets in Southeast Asia and Beyond." *Public Culture* 22, no. 2: 223–36.

———. 2010b. "Labour Recruitment, Circuits of Capital and Gendered Mobility: Reconceptualizing the Indonesian Migration Industry." *Pacific Affairs* 83, no. 1: 115–32.

Li Tao, ed. 2000. *Zhonghua liuxue jiaoyu shilu* [A history of Chinese going abroad for education]. Beijing: Gaodeng Jiaoyu Chubanshe.

Liu Hong. 2005. "New Migration and the Revival of Overseas Chinese Nationalism." *Journal of Contemporary China* 14, no. 43: 291–316.

Li Yu-ning. 1971. *The Introduction of Socialism into China*. New York: Columbia University Press.

Long, Lynellyn D., and Ellen Oxfeld, eds. 2004. *Coming Home? Refugees, Migrants and Those Who Stayed at Home*. Philadelphia: University of Pennsylvania Press.

Lu, Melody Chia-Wen. 2011. "Appearance and Techniques of Migration Control: Examining Labour Migration Regimes in East Asia." In *Constructing and Imagining Labour Migration: Perspectives of Control from Five Continents*, ed. Elspeth Guild and Sandra Mantu, 87–108. London: Ashgate.

Lu Haiyun and Quan Haosheng, eds. 2001. *Guiqiao qiaojuan gaishu* [A general account of *guiqiao* and *qiaojuan*]. Beijing: Huaqiao Chubanshe.

Lu Xinyuan. 1956. "Guanyu jiedai he anzhi guiguo huaqiao de gongzuo: Zai zhonghua quanguo qiaolian chengli dahui shang de baogao" [On the tasks of receiving and allocating returned Overseas Chinese: A report to the inaugural meeting of All-China Federation of Returned Overseas Chinese]. *Qiaowu Bao*, no. 2: 13, 17.

Ly, Kuong Chang. 2010. "Between Two Lives." In *Cambodian American Experiences: Histories, Communities, Cultures, and Identities*, ed. Jonathan H. X. Lee, 332–42. Dubuque, Iowa: Kendall Hunt.

Mabogunje, Akin L. 1970. "Systems Approach to a Theory of Rural-Urban Migration." *Geographical Analysis* 2, no. 1: 1–18.

Mackie, J. A. C., ed. 1976. *The Chinese in Indonesia: Five Essays.* Canberra: The Australian Institute of International Affairs.

Maeyama, Takashi. 1982. *Imin no Nihon kaiki undo* [The Japanese immigrant's revitalization movement]. Tokyo: Nippon Syuppan Hoso Kyokai.

Mahbubani, Kishore. 2008. *The New Asian Hemisphere: The Irresistible Shift of Global Power to the East.* New York: Public Affairs.

Mainichi Shinbun-sha Henshû-bu, ed. 1972. *Saigo no ippei: Guamu-to shuzaikisha-dan no zen kiroku* [The last soldier: The records by the expedition group to the island of Guam]. Tokyo: Mainichi Shinbun-sha.

Malkki, Liisa. 1995a. *Purity and Exile: Violence, Memory, and National Cosmology among Hutu Refugees in Tanzania.* Chicago: Chicago University Press.

——. 1995b. "Refugees and Exile: From 'Refugee Studies' to the National Order of Things." *Annual Review of Anthropology* 24: 495–523.

Mallett, Shelley. 2004. "Understanding Home: A Critical Review of the Literature." *The Sociological Review* 52, no. 1: 62–89.

Maney, Kevin. 2006, June 22. "Indian Entrepreneurs Increasingly Go Home to Join Tech-Industry Explosion." USATODAY.com. http://usatoday30.usatoday.com/money/industries/technology/maney/2006-08-22-indian-enterpreneurs_x.htm.

Mao Qixiong and Lin Xiaodong, eds. 1993. *Zhongguo qiaowu zhengce gaishu* [A brief account of the *qiaowu* policies of the PRC]. Beijing: Zhongguo Huaqiao Chubanshe.

Martin, Philip. 2008, September 14. "Another Miracle? Managing Labour Migration in Asia." Working paper, United Nations Economic and Social Commission for Asia and the Pacific Population Division, Department of Economic and Social Affairs, Bangkok.

——. 2009. "Migration in the Asia-Pacific Region: Trends, Factors, Impacts." Human Development Research Paper 32, United Nations Development Programme.

Martin, Philip, Manolo Abella, and Christiane Kuptsch. 2006. *Managing Labor Migration in the Twenty-First Century.* New Haven: Yale University Press.

Martin, Robert A. 1999. "The Joint Terrorism Task Force: A Concept That Works." Anti-defamation League. http://www.adl.org/learn/jttf/default.asp.

McLagan, Meg. 2003. "Human Rights, Testimony, and Transnational Publicity." *The Scholar and Feminist Online* 2, no. 1. www.barnard.edu/sfonline/ps/mclagan.htm.

Meissner, Werner. 2003. "Collective Identity and Nationalism in Europe and China." In *China Today: Economic Reforms, Social Cohesion and Collective Identities,* ed. Taciana Fisac and Leila Fernández-Stembridge, 197–221. London: RoutledgeCurzon.

Meillassoux, Claude. 1981. *Maidens, Meal, and Money: Capitalism and the Domestic Community.* Cambridge: Cambridge University Press.

Melamed, Samantha. 2005, July 30–31. "Stranger in Their Homeland: Cambodians Deported from the U.S. Build New Lives on Fragile Foundations." *Cambodia Daily.* http://www.cambodiadaily.com/selected-features/cambodians-deported

-from-the-us-build-new-lives-on-fragile-foundations-1018/. Last accessed February 14, 2013.

Ministério do Trabalho e Emprego. 2003. *Brasileiras e Brasileiros no Exterior* [Brazilians abroad]. Brasilia: Ministério do Trabalho e Emprego.

Miyao, Susumu. 2003. *Shindo Renmei: Imin kuhaku jidai to doho shakai no konran* [Shindo Renmei: The time of vacuum in migration and the confusions in the Japanese society in Brazil]. São Paulo: São Paulo Jinmon Kagaku Kenkyujo.

Montaigne, Fen. 1999. "Deporting America's Gang Culture." *Mother Jones* 24, no. 4: 44–51.

Mori, Koichi. 1995. "Burajiru kara no Nikkeijin Dekasegi no tokucho to suii" [The characteristics and trajectories of the Nikkeijin Dekasegi migration from Brazil]. In *Kyodo kenkyuu Dekasegi Nikkei Burajirujin jo-kan: Syuurou to seikatsu (ronbun hen)* [Collaborative research on Brazilian Nikkeijin Dekasegis: Vol. 1, work and life (Papers)], ed. Masako Watanabe, 491–546. Tokyo: Akashi Shoten.

Mortland, Carol A. 2010. "Cambodian Resettlement in America." In *Cambodian American Experiences: Histories, Communities, Cultures, and Identities*, ed. Jonathan H. X. Lee, 76–102. Dubuque, Iowa: Kendall Hunt.

Mydans, Seth. 2008, November 29. "US Deportees Bring Street Dance to Street Boys of Cambodia." *New York Times*. http://www.nytimes.com/2008/11/30/world/asia/30dancer.html?_r=1. Accessed February 9, 2013.

Naicang, Jingzi. 2010. *Guxiang yu taxiang: Guangdong guiqiao de duoyuan shequ he wenhua shiying* [Home and away: A plural-pattern complex community, cultural adaptation of the home-returned Overseas Chinese in Guangdong]. Beijing: Shehui Kexue Wenxian Chubanshe.

Narayan, Kiran. 2002. "Placing Lives through Stories: Second-Generation South Asian Americans." In *Everyday Life in South Asia*, ed. Diane P. Mines and Sarah Lamb, 425–39. Bloomington: Indiana University Press.

Ngai, Mae. 2004. *Impossible Subjects: Illegal Aliens and the Making of Modern America*. Princeton: Princeton University Press.

Niedzwiecki, Max, and T. C. Duong. 2004. *Southeast Asian American Statistical Profile*. Washington: Southeast Asia Resource Action Center (SEARAC). Available at http://www.searac.org/sites/default/files/seastatprofilemay04.pdf. Last accessed February 22, 2013.

Nijkamp, Peter, and Maurice Voskuilen. 1996. "International Migration: A Comprehensive Framework for a Survey of the Literature." *European Spatial Research and Policy* 3, no. 1: 5–28.

Nippak Shimbun. 1924, October 10. "Kikokusha wo kaerimite" [Commentary on those who return home]. Editorial.

Noda Mitsuharu. 1976. "Horyo no ki" [The diary of a POW]. In *Documento Shōwashi: Sengo-hen*, ed. Nakajima Kenzō, 138–42. Tokyo: Heibonsha.

Nolin, Catherine. 2006. *Transnational Ruptures: Gender and Forced Migration*. Aldershot; England: Ashgate.

Nonini, Donald M., and Aihwa Ong. 1997. "Introduction: Chinese Transnationalism as an Alternative Modernity." In *Underground Empires: The Cultural Politics of*

Modern Chinese Transnationalism, ed. Aihwa Ong and Donald M. Nonini, 3–33. London: Routledge.

Norman, Herbert E. 1943. *Soldier and Peasant in Japan: The Origins of Conscription.* New York: Institute of Pacific Relations.

Nou, Leckhena. 2008. "Exploring the Psychosocial Adjustment of Khmer Refugees in Massachusetts from an Insider's Perspective." In *Southeast Asian Refugees and Immigrants in the Mill City: Changing Families, Communities, Institutions — Thirty Years Afterward*, ed. Tuyet-Lan Pho, Jeffrey N. Gerson, and Sylvia R. Cowan, 173–91. Burlington: University of Vermont Press.

Nowicka, Magdalena. 2007. "Mobile Locations: Construction of Home in a Group of Mobile Transnational Professionals." *Global Networks* 7, no. 1: 69–86.

Nyíri, Pál, and Joana Breidenbach, eds. 2005. *China Inside Out: Contemporary Chinese Nationalism and Transnationalism.* Budapest: CEU Press.

O Estado de S. Paulo. 1955, March 17. "Incidente no consulado do Japão nesta capital" [Incident at the consulate of Japan in the city].

Ommundsen, Wenche, Michael Leach, and Andrew Vandenberg, eds. 2010. *Cultural Citizenship and the Challenges of Globalization.* New York: Hampton Press.

Ong, Aihwa. 1999. *Flexible Citizenship: The Cultural Logics of Transnationality.* Durham: Duke University Press.

———. 2000. "Graduated Sovereignty in Southeast Asia." *Theory, Culture, and Society* 17, no. 4: 55–75.

———. 2003. *Buddha Is Hiding: Refugees, Citizenship, the New America.* Berkeley: University of California Press.

———. 2004. "The Chinese Axis: Zoning Technologies and Variegated Sovereignty." *Journal of East Asian Studies* no. 4: 69–96.

———. 2005a. "Ecologies of Expertise: Assembling Flows, Managing Citizenship." In *Global Assemblages: Technology, Politics, and Ethics as Anthropological Problems*, ed. Aihwa Ong and Stephen J. Collier, 337–53. Oxford: Blackwell.

———. 2005b. "Splintering Cosmopolitanism: Asian Immigrants and Zones of Autonomy in the American West." In *Sovereign Bodies: Citizens, Migrants, and States in the Postcolonial World*, ed. Thomas Blom Hansen and Finn Stepputat, 257–75. Princeton: Princeton University Press.

———. 2006. *Neoliberalism as Exception: Mutations in Citizenship and Sovereignty.* Durham: Duke University Press.

Onoda Hiroo. 1974. *Tatakatta, ikita, Lubangu-tō sanjūnen* [I fought and I survived: The thirty years of my life on the island of Lubang]. Tokyo: Kōdansha.

———. 1982. *Waga Burajiru jinsei* [My life in Brazil]. Tokyo: Kōdansha.

———. 1995a. *Tatta hitori no sanjūnen sensō* [The war I fought alone for thirty years]. Tokyo: Tokyo Shinbun Shuppan-kyoku.

———. 1995b. *Waga kaisō no Lubangu-tō* [My memory of the island of Lubang]. Tokyo: Asahi Shinbun-sha.

Onoda Hiroo, and Kazuo Sakamaki. 1977. *Harukani sokoku o kataru* [Speaking of my fatherland from afar]. Tokyo: Jiji Tsūshin-sha.

Orr, James J. 2001. *The Victim as Hero: Ideologies of Peace and National Identity in Postwar Japan.* Honolulu: University of Hawai'i Press.

Ortner, Sherry B. 1995. "Resistance and the Problem of Ethnographic Refusal." *Comparative Studies in Society and History* 37, no. 1: 173–93.

Paddock, R. C. 2003, March 28. "Cambodia's Black Sheep Return to Fold." *Los Angeles Times*, A27.

Pandolfi, Mariella. 2008. "Laboratory of Intervention: The Humanitarian Governance of the Postcommunist Balkan Territories." In *Postcolonial Disorders*, ed. Mary-Jo DelVecchio Good, Sandra Teresa Hyde, Sarah Pinto, and Byron J. Good, 157–88. Berkeley: University of California Press.

Pang Lu (Deputy Chair of Sixth Executive Committee of Sino-Japan International Training Cooperation Organization and Secretary General of China's International Contractors' Association). 2006, October 16. "Zhongguo Zhong-Ri yanxiusheng xieli jigou di liu jie lishihui gongzuo baogao" [Working report of the Sixth Executive Committee of Sino-Japan International Training Cooperation Organization]. Report presented to the Seventh Executive Committee of Sino-Japan International Training Cooperation Organization, Beijing, October 16–17.

Park Hyun Ok. 2005. "Repetition, Comparability, and Indeterminable Nation: Korean Migrants in the 1920s and 1990s." *boundary 2* 32, no. 2: 227–51.

Park Jung-Sun, and Paul Y. Chang. 2005. "Contention in the Construction of a Global Korean Community: The Case of the Overseas Korean Act." *Journal of Korean Studies* 10, no. 1: 1–27.

Parrenas, Rhacel Salazar. 2001. *Servants of Globalization: Women, Migration and Domestic Work*. Stanford: Stanford University Press.

Paulista Shimbun-sha. 1977. *Paulista Shimbun ni miru Koronia Sanjunen no Ayumi* [The thirty-year path of the Colônia in Paulista Shimbun]. São Paulo: Paulista Shimbun Sha.

Peutz, Nathalie. 2006. "Embarking on an Anthropology of Removal." *Current Anthropology* 47, no. 2: 217–41.

Pho, Tuyet-Lan, Jeffrey N. Gerson, and Sylvia R. Cowan, eds. 2008. *Southeast Asian Refugees and Immigrants in the Mill City: Changing Families, Communities, Institutions—Thirty Years Afterward*. Burlington: University of Vermont Press.

Picken, Margo. 2011, January 13. "The Beleaguered Cambodians." *New York Review of Books*, 4.

Poethig, Kathryn. 2006. "Sitting between Two Chairs: Cambodia's Dual Citizenship Debate." In *Expressions of Cambodia: The Politics of Tradition, Identity, and Change*, ed. Leakthina Chau-Pech Ollier and Tim Winter, 73–85. London: Routledge.

Quanguo Renda Changweihui Bangongshi, ed. 1987. *Quanguo Renda jiqi changweihui dashiji, 1954–1987* [The annals of NPC and its standing committees, 1954–1987]. Beijing: Falu Chubanshe.

Quanguo Renda Neiwu Sifa Weiyuanhui Bangongshi, ed. 1992. *Quanguo Renda Daibiao Dahui Zhuanmen Weiyuanhui gongzuo shouce* [NPC's special committees' handbook]. Beijing: Zhongguo Minzhu Fazhi Chubanshe.

Rajagopal, Arvind. 2000. "Hindu Nationalism in the US: Changing Configurations of Political Practice." *Ethnic and Racial Studies* 23, no. 3: 467–96.

Ravenstein, Ernest. 1985. "The Laws of Migration." *Journal of the Statistical Society of London* 48, no. 2: 167–227.

———. 2007, March 29. "Meeting the Needs of Internally Displaced and Refugees in FY 2008." http://www.refugeesinternational.org/policy/testimony/meeting-needs-internally-displaced-and-refugees-fy-2008.

Ritter, Peter. 2007, June 17. "Timeline: Hong Kong, 1997–2007." *Time*. http://www.time.com/time/photogallery/0,29307,1630252,00.html. Last accessed February 4, 2013.

Robinson, Jennifer. 2002. "Global Cities and World Cities: A View from off the Map." *International Journal of Urban and Regional Research* 26, no. 3: 531–54.

Rodriguez, Robyn. 2010. *Migrants for Export: How the Philippine State Brokers Labor to the World*. Minneapolis: University of Minnesota Press.

Rogers, Rosemarie. 1997. "Migration Return Policies and Countries of Origin." In *Immigration Admissions: The Search for Workable Solutions in Germany and the United States*, ed. Kay Hailbronner, David A. Martin, and Hiroshi Motomura, 147–204. Providence: Berghahn Books.

Roy, Ananya. 2008. "The 21st Century Metropolis: New Geographies of Theory." *Regional Studies* 43, no. 6: 819–30.

Roy, Anupama. 2006. "Overseas Indian Citizen: A New 'Setubandhan'?" *Economic and Political Weekly* 41, no. 15: 1421–24.

———. 2008. "Between Encompassment and Closure: The 'Migrant' and the Citizen in India." *Contributions to Indian Sociology (N.S.)* 42, no. 2: 219–48.

Rudnyckyj, Daromir. 2004. "Technologies of Servitude: Governmentality and Indonesian Transnational Labor Migration." *Anthropological Quarterly* 77, no. 3: 407–34.

Ruhs, Martin, and Philip Martin. 2008. "Numbers vs. Rights: Trade-offs and Guest Worker Programs." *International Migration Review* 42, no. 1: 249–65.

Sack, William H., Shanrithy Him, and Dan Dickason. 1999. "Twelve-Year Follow-up Study of Khmer Youths Who Suffered Massive War Trauma as Children." *Journal of the American Academy of Child and Adolescent Psychiatry* 38, no. 9: 1173–79.

Sankei Shinbun-sha Henshû-bu, ed. 1972. *Rikugun gochō Yokoi Shōichi: Sono nijū-hachinen no Guamu-tō seikatsu* [The army corporal Yokoi Shōichi: His life on the island of Guam for twenty-eight years]. Tokyo: Mainichi Shinbun-sha.

Sansom, George B. 1943. "Foreword." In E. Herbert Norman, *Soldier and Peasant in Japan: The Origins of Conscription*, ix-xii. New York: International Secretariat, Institute of Pacific Relations.

São Paulo Shimbun-sha. 1960. *Koronia sengo jugonenshi* [The history of the Colônia in the fifteen years after the war]. São Paulo. São Paulo Shimbun-sha.

———. 1966. *Nambei no Nikkeijin* [Nikkeijin in South America]. São Paulo: São Paulo Shimbun-Sha.

Sassen, Saskia. 1996. *Losing Control: Sovereignty in an Age of Globalization*. New York: Columbia University Press.

Saxenian, AnnaLee. 2004. "The Bangalore Boom: From Brain Drain to Brain Circulation." In *The IT Experience in India: Bridging the Digital Divide*, ed. Kenneth Keniston and Deepak Kumar, 169–81. New Delhi: Sage Publications.

Scott, James C. 1976. *The Moral Economy of the Peasant: Rebellion and Subsistence in Southeast Asia*. New Haven: Yale University Press.

———. 1985. *Weapons of the Weak: Everyday Forms of Peasant Resistance*. New Haven: Yale University Press.

———. 1990. *Domination and the Arts of Resistance*. New Haven: Yale University Press.

SEARAC (Southeast Asia Resource Action Center). 2011. *Southeast Asian Americans at a Glance: Statistical Profile 2010*. Washington: SEARAC. Available at http://www.searac.org/sites/default/files/STATISTICAL%20PROFILE%202010.pdf. Last accessed February 20, 2013.

Selden, Kyōko Iriye. 1983. "Hayashi Fumiko." In Kōdansha, *Encyclopedia of Japan*, vol. 3, 116. Tokyo: Kōdansha.

Seol Dong-Hoon, and John D. Skrentny. 2009. "Ethnic Return Migration and Hierarchical Nationhood: Korean-Chinese Foreign Workers in South Korea." *Ethnicities* 9, no. 2: 147–74.

Shimamura, Takashi. 1972. *Hiroku kaseki no heitai: Yokoi moto gochō kyokugen no nijūhachinen* [The records of a fossilized soldier: The twenty-eight years of survival of corporal Yokoi]. Tokyo: Banchō Shobō.

Shin Gi-Wook. 2006. *Ethnic Nationalism in Korea: Genealogy, Politics, and Legacy*. Stanford: Stanford University Press.

Silvey, Rachel. 2004. "Transnational Domestication: State Power and Indonesian Migrant Women in Saudi Arabia." *Political Geography* 23 (3): 245–64.

———. 2007. "Unequal Borders: Indonesian Transnational Migrants at Immigration Control." *Geopolitics* 12 (2): 265–79.

Simanski, John, and Lesley M. Sapp. 2012. "Immigration Enforcement Actions: 2011." Washington: Office of Immigration Statistics, Homeland Security. Available at http://www.dhs.gov/sites/default/files/publications/immigration-statistics/enforcement_ar_2011.pdf. Last access February 20, 2013.

Simmel, Georg. 1997. "Bridge and Door." In *Simmel on Culture: Selected Writings*, ed. David Frisby and Mike Featherstone, 170–73. London: Sage Publications.

Siu, Lok C. D. 2005. *Memories of a Future Home: Diasporic Citizenship of Chinese in Panama*. Stanford: Stanford University Press.

Skinner, William G. 1963. "The Chinese Minority." In *Indonesia*, ed. R. T. McVey, 97–117. New Haven: Southeast Asia Studies, Yale University.

Skrentny, John, Stephanie Chan, Jon E. Fox, and Denis Kim. 2007. "Defining Nations in Asia and Europe: A Comparative Analysis of Ethnic Return Migration Policy." *International Migration Review* 41 (4): 793–825.

Smith-Hefner, Nancy J. 1998. *Khmer American: Identity and Moral Education in a Diasporic Community*. Berkeley: University of California Press.

———. 2010. "Khmer Cultural Values and Economic Behavior." In *Cambodian American Experiences: Histories, Communities, Cultures, and Identities*, ed. Jonathan H. X. Lee, 274–82. Dubuque, Iowa: Kendall Hunt.

Stafford, Charles. 2001. *Separation and Reunion in Modern China*. Cambridge: Cambridge University Press.

Star (Kuala Lumpur, Malaysia). 2005, March 4. "Illegal Immigrants: None Will Be Spared from Ops Tegas." http://thestar.com.my/story.asp?file=/2005/3/4/nation/10322842&sec=nation. Last accessed December 23, 2009.

Stokes, Bruce. 2007. "Between Two Nations." *National Journal* 39, no. 2: 56–58.

Sugihara, Kaoru. 2005. "Patterns of Chinese Emigration to Southeast Asia, 1869–1939." In *Japan, China, and the Growth of the Asian International Economy, 1850–1949*, ed. Kaoru Sugihara, 244–95. New York: Oxford University Press.

Suryadinata, Leo. 1978a. *The Chinese Minority in Indonesia: Seven Papers*. Singapore: Chopmen Enterprises.

———. 1978b. *Pribumi Indonesians, the Chinese Minority and China: A Study of Perceptions and Politics*. Kuala Lumpur: Heinemann Educational Books (Asia).

Tagliacozzo, Eric, and Wen-Chin Chang, eds. 2011. *Chinese Circulations: Capital, Commodities, and Networks in Southeast Asia*. Durham: Duke University Press.

Takahashi, Tetsurō, Kōtarō Kaneko, and Tokurō Inokuma. 2008. "Kō hansei wa heiwa no tame ni tatakatta" [In the second half of our lives, we fought for peace]. *Sekai* 782: 300–11.

Tamanoi, Mariko Asano. 2009. *Memory Maps: The State and Manchuria in Postwar Japan*. Honolulu: University of Hawai'i Press.

Tanaka Nobumasa, Tanaka Hiroshi, and Hata Nagami. 1995. *Izoku to sengo* [The bereaved families and postwar Japan]. Tokyo: Iwanami Shoten.

Thompson, E. P. 1971. "Moral Economy of the English Crowd in the Eighteenth Century." *Past and Present* 50 (1): 76–136.

———. 1975. *Whigs and Hunters: The Origin of the Black Act*. London: Allen Lane.

Townsend, James. 1996. "Chinese Nationalism." In *Chinese Nationalism*, ed. Jonathan Unger, 1–30. Armonk, N.Y.: M. E. Sharpe.

Trouillot, Michel-Rolph. 2001. "The Anthropology of the State: Close Encounters of a Deceptive Kind." *Current Anthropology* 42, no. 1: 125–38.

Tsuda, Takeyuki. 2003. *Strangers in the Ethnic Homeland: Japanese Brazilian Return Migration in Transnational Perspective*. New York: Columbia University Press.

Tsuda, Yolanda Alfaro. 2005, December 1–2. "Current Migration Issues in Japan." UNESCO-CIMS International Conference Proceeding, International Migrants in Northeast Asia, Seoul.

Udupa, Sahana. 2011. "Informing News: Information Revolution and the Transformation of News Media in Bangalore." PhD diss., National Institute of Advanced Studies, Bangalore.

Unger, Klaus. 1986. "Return Migration and Regional Characteristics: The Case of Greece." In *Return Migration and Regional Economic Problems*, ed. Russell King, 129–51. Beckenham, UK: Croom Helm.

Upadhya, Carol. 2003. "Entrepreneurship and Networks in Bangalore's Information Technology Industry: A Sociological Study." Research report submitted to Indian Institute of Information Technology, Bangalore.

———. 2004. "A New Transnational Class? Capital Flows, Business Networks and Entrepreneurs in the Indian Software Industry." *Economic and Political Weekly* 39, no. 48: 5141–51.

————. 2006. "The Global Indian Software Labor Force: IT Professionals in Europe." IDPAD Working Paper Series 2006, no. 1.

————. 2009. "Imagining India: Software and the Ideology of Liberalization." *South African Review of Sociology* 40, no. 1: 76–93.

Upadhya, Carol, and A. R. Vasavi. 2006. "Work, Culture, and Sociality in the Indian IT Industry: A Sociological Study." Final Report submitted to IDPAD, National Institute of Advanced Studies, Bangalore.

————, eds. 2008. *In an Outpost of the Global Economy: Work and Workers in India's Information Technology Industry*. New Delhi: Routledge.

U.S. Department of Homeland Security. 2007. *Yearbook of Immigration Statistics: 2006*. Washington, D.C.: U.S. Department of Homeland Security, Office of Immigration Statistics.

————. 2011. *Yearbook of Immigration Statistics: 2010*. Washington, D.C.: U.S. Department of Homeland Security, Office of Immigration Statistics.

————. 2012. *Yearbook of Immigration Statistics: 2011*. Washington, D.C.: U.S. Department of Homeland Security, Office of Immigration Statistics.

U.S. Senate. 1996. "Antiterrorism and Effective Death Penalty Act." (Bill 735) http://www.govtrack.us/congress/bill.xpd?bill=s104-735. Last accessed May 24, 2013.

Vance, Carol. 2005, November 12. "Juanita/Svetlana/Geeta Is Crying: Melodrama, Human Rights and Anti-trafficking Interventions." Lecture presented at Stockholm University.

van der Veer, Peter. 2005. "Virtual India: Indian IT Labour and the Nation-State." In *Sovereign Bodies: Citizens, Migrants, and States in the Postcolonial World*, ed. Thomas Blom Hansen and Finn Steppytat, 276–90. Princeton: Princeton University Press.

Varona, Rex. 1998. "A Year After: Surveying the Impact of the Asian Crisis on Migrant Workers." *Asian Migrant Yearbook 1998*. Hong Kong: Asian Migrant Center, http://home.pacific.net.hk/~amc/papers/crisisdoc4.htm. Accessed May 25, 2013.

Varrell, Aurelie. 2011. "Return Migration in the Light of the New Indian Diaspora Policy: Emerging Transnationalism." In *Dynamics of Indian Migration: Historical and Current Perspectives*, ed. S. Irudaya Rajan and Marie Percot, 301–17. New Delhi: Routledge.

Vertovec, Steven. 2007. "Circular Migration: The Way Forward in Global Policy?" International Migration Institute Working Paper, University of Oxford. http://www.imi.ox.ac.uk/pdfs/imi-working-papers/wp4-circular-migration-policy.pdf. Accessed May 25, 2013.

Visweswaran, Kamala, and Ali Mir. 1999/2000. "On the Politics of Community in South Asian-American Studies." *Amerasia Journal* 25, no. 3: 97–108.

Vora, Neha. 2011. "From Golden Frontier to Global City: Shifting Forms of Belonging, 'Freedom,' and Governance among Indian Businessmen in Dubai." *American Anthropologist* 113, no. 2: 306–18.

Wakatsuki, Yasuo, and Joji Suzuki. 1975. *Kaigai ijuu seisakushi ron* [On the history of the emigration policy]. Tokyo: Fukumura Syuppan.

Wako, Shungoro. 1938. *Bauru kannai no Nihonjin* [The Japanese in the jurisdiction of Baurú]. São Paulo: Fazenda Tietê.

Wang Cangbai. 2006. *Huozai biechu: Xianggang Yinni huaren koushu lishi* [Life is elsewhere: Stories of the Indonesian Chinese in Hong Kong]. Hong Kong: Centre of Asian Studies, University of Hong Kong.

Wang Cangbai and Wong Siu-Lun. 2007. "Home as a Circular Process: A Study of the Indonesian Chinese in Hong Kong." In *Beyond Chinatown: New Chinese Migration and the Global Expansion of China*, ed. Mette Thunø, 183–209. Denmark: Nordic Institute of Asian Study Press.

Wang Cangbai, Wong Siu-Lun, and Sun Wenbin. 2006. "Haigui: A New Area in China's Policy toward the Chinese Diaspora?" *Journal of Chinese Overseas* 2, no. 2: 294–309.

Wang Gungwu. 1981. "A Note on the Origins of Hua-ch'iao." In *Community and Nation: Essays on Southeast Asia and the Chinese*, 118–27. Singapore: Heinemann Educational Books.

———. 1985. "External China as a New Policy Area." *Pacific Affairs* 58, no. 1: 28–43.

———. 1992. "The Origin of Hua-Ch'iao." In *Community and Nation: China, Southeast Asia and Australia*, 1–10. St. Leonards: Allen & Unwin.

———. 1996. *The Revival of Chinese Nationalism*. Leiden, The Netherlands: International Institute for Asian Studies.

Warren, Kay. 2007. "The 2000 UN Human Trafficking Protocol: Rights, Enforcement, Vulnerabilities." In *The Practice of Human Rights: Tracking Law between the Global and the Local*, ed. Mark Goodale and Sally Engle Merry, 242–70. Cambridge: Cambridge University.

Werbner, Pnina. 1999. "Global Pathways: Working Class Cosmopolitans and the Creation of Transnational Ethnic Worlds." *Social Anthropology* 7, no. 1: 17–35.

———. 2000. "Introduction: The Materiality of Diaspora—between Aesthetics and 'Real' Politics." *Diaspora* 9, no. 1: 5–20.

Willmott, Donald E. 1961. *The National Status of the Chinese in Indonesia, 1900–1958*. Ithaca, N.Y.: Department of Far Eastern Studies, Cornell University.

Wong, Diana. 2005. "The Rumor of Trafficking: Border Controls, Illegal Migration, and the Sovereignty of the Nation-State. In *Illicit Flows and Criminal Things: States, Borders, and the Other Side of Globalization*, ed. Willem van Schendel and Itty Abraham, 69–100. Bloomington: Indiana University Press.

World Bank. 2011. *Migration and Remittances Factbook 2011*. 2nd ed. Washington, D.C.: World Bank. Available at http://data.worldbank.org/data-catalog/migration-and-remittances. Last accessed February 19, 2013.

Wu, David Y-H. 1991. "The Construction of Chinese and Non-Chinese Identities." *Daedalus* 120, no. 2: 159–79.

Wyman, Mark. 1996. *Round-Trip to America: The Immigrants Return to Europe, 1880–1930*. Ithaca, N.Y.: Cornell University Press.

Xiang Biao. 2007. *Global "Body Shopping": An Indian Labor System in the Information Technology Industry*. Princeton: Princeton University Press.

———. 2011. "A Ritual Economy of 'Talent': China and Overseas Chinese Professionals." *Journal of Ethnic and Migration Studies* 37, no. 5: 821–38.

Xiang Biao and Shen Wei. 2009. "International Student Migration and Social Stratification in China." *International Journal of Educational Development* 29, no. 5: 513–22.

Yamanaka, Keiko. 1996. "Return Migration of Japanese-Brazilians to Japan: The Nikkeijin as Ethnic Minority and Political Construct." *Diaspora* 5, no. 1: 65–98.

Yamazaki Toyoko. 2008a. "Sensō no unda futari zuma wa" [What happened to the two wives that war engendered?]. *Sekai* 778: 280–91.

———. 2008b. "Sensō no unda futari zuma wa, 2." *Sekai* 779: 315–23.

Yuzo, Mizoguchi. 1989. *Hobo tosibteno Chugoku* [China as method]. Tokyo: Tokyo Daigaku Shuppan-kai.

Zha Daojoing. 2002. "Chinese Migrant Workers in Japan: Policies, Institutions, and Civil Society." In *Globalising Chinese Migration: Trends in Europe and Asia*, ed. Pal Nyiri and Igor Saveliev, 129–57. London: Ashgate.

Zheng Yijun. 2005. *Guiqiao Peng Guanghan de wangshi jinsheng* [The memoir of *guiqiao* Peng Guanghan]. Hong Kong: Xianggang Shehui Kexue Chubanshe Youxian Gongsi.

Zhongguo Qiaolian, ed. 1996. *Zhongguo Qiaolian Sishi Nian: 1956–1996* [Fortieth anniversary of All-China Federation of Returned Overseas Chinese: 1956–1996]. Beijing: Zhongguo Huaqiao Chubanshe.

Zhonguo Renmin Zhengzhi Xieshang Huiyi Quanguo Weiyuan Hui Wenshi Ziliao Yanjiu Weiyuanhui, ed. 1994. *Zhongguo Renmin Zhengzhi Xieshang Huiyi dansheng jishi ji ziliao xuanbian: Wuxing hongqi cong zheli shengqi* [Records and documents of the birth of CPPCC: The five-star flag rising from here]. Beijing: Wenshi Ziliao Chubanshe.

Zhou Nanjing. 1999. *Huaqiao huaren baike quanshu: Jiaoyu keji juan* [Encyclopedia of Chinese overseas: Volume of education, science, and technology]. Beijing: Zhongguo Huaqiao Chubanshe.

Zhuang Guotu. 1989. *Zhongguo fengjian zhengfu de huaqiao zhengce* [Huaqiao policies of the feudal governments in China]. Xiamen: Xiamen Daxue Chubanshe.

Zweig, David, Chen Changgui, and Stanley Rosen. 2004. "Globalization and Transnational Human Capital: Overseas and Returnee Scholars to China." *The China Quarterly* 179: 735–57.

Soviet Union, 40, 43, 47–48, 56, 60, 135, 168
Spain, 97
Sun Yat-sen, 67, 70, 81n7, 82n12

Taiwan, 28, 30, 59n1, 62n27, 79, 144, 176
territoriality, 16; deterritorialization, 146, 156–57; extra-, 16; reterritorialization, 151, 157
terrorism, 101, 105, 117, 118n6
Thailand, 2, 46, 100, 107, 146
trade union, 95, 99n9
trafficking in persons, 2, 5, 11–12, 14, 19n21, 19n23, 137–38, 139n6, 139n10, 140n15, 123, 125, 129, 132–33, 135; countertrafficking programs, 122–23, 125, 128–29, 132–35, 137–38, 139n6, 139nn9–10, 140n12; victims of, 133–34, 136–38

United Kingdom, 2, 18n7, 118n11, 158
United States, 2, 5, 12, 18n7, 19n15, 19n22, 23, 32, 39–40, 43, 48, 56, 60n5, 61n13, 100–101, 103, 105–10, 113–14, 116–17, 118n11, 119n17, 119n19, 120n21, 120n24, 120n26, 132–33, 143–44, 147, 149–50, 152–56, 158nn4–5, 160n16, 169, 170; places in: Arizona, 111; California, 107,

111–12; Chicago, 111; Guam, 50, 54, 57; Hawai'i, 23, 44; Louisiana, 111; Los Angeles, 107, 119n16; Massachusetts, 102, 107, 117n4; New Jersey, 111; New York, 99n10, 105; Oklahoma, 105; Saipan, 43; San Diego, 111; San Francisco, 111; Silicon Valley, 144, 149–50, 156; Texas, 111; Washington, 1

Vietnam/Vietnamese, 69, 75, 100–101, 106–7, 116, 118nn11–12, 120n26

wars, 9, 40–41, 96, 102, 111, 118n10; anti-Japanese war (China), 63, 67; Asia-Pacific War, 41; Chinese Civil War, 40, 47; El Salvador civil war 111; Fifteen-Year War, 41; First World War, 39, 40, 60n3, 60n6, 104; Greater East Asia War, 41; Iraqi War, 117; Korean War, 30, 164–65; Opium Wars, 66–67; Pacific War, 41; Second World War, 9, 16, 22, 26, 28, 30–31, 40–41, 45, 118n11, 164; Vietnam War/American War, 69, 102, 106–7, 116, 119n17
woman, 13, 40, 46–47, 52, 56, 60n8, 61n10, 82n12, 83–84, 89, 92–93, 95–96, 107, 118n5, 122, 128, 130–33, 136 37, 139n6